The New Science of Skin and Scuba Diving

A Project of the Council for National Cooperation in Aquatics

The New Science of Skin and Scuba Diving

Sixth Edition

Editor: **ROBERT W. SMITH,**
Chairman, CNCA

Leisure Press
Champaign, Illinois

Library of Congress Cataloging-in-Publication Data

The new science of skin and scuba diving / editor, Robert W. Smith.
    p.   cm.
    ''A project of the Council for National Cooperation in Aquatics.''
    Reprint. 6th ed. Originally published: Piscataway, N.J. : New
Century Publishers, c1985.
    ISBN 0-88011-378-2
    1. Skin diving. 2. Scuba diving. I. Smith, Robert W.
II. Council for National Cooperation in Aquatics.
GV840.S78N48 1989
797.2'3--dc20   89-27032
                                      CIP

The New Science of Skin and Scuba Diving (Sixth Edition) was previously published by New Century Publishers, Inc., under ISBN 0-8329-0399-X. Leisure Press, a Division of Human Kinetics Publishers, Inc., has acquired the publication rights for this book.

ISBN: 0-88011-378-2

Printed in the United States of America

16 15 14 13

Leisure Press
A Division of Human Kinetics Publishers, Inc.
Box 5076, Champaign, IL 61825-5076
1-800-747-4457

Ten Commandments for Safe Diving

1. *Be fit.* Have a medical checkup. Be a good swimmer. Exercise regularly. Don't dive if you feel below par.

2. *Get good training.* Reading a book is not enough; enroll in a good course. Learn the facts and procedures of safe diving.

3. *Have good equipment.* Be careful about bargains and don't build it yourself. Keep your equipment in top condition; check it before every dive. Use only tested and approved equipment. Refrain from alteration or untrained adjustment of equipment.

4. *Never dive alone.* Always have a buddy with you underwater. Have a tender at the surface whenever possible.

5. *Know the diving area.* Avoid dangerous places and poor conditions. Take whatever special precautions the area requires.

6. *Use a boat, float, or both.* Fly the diver flag. Be able to reach safety fast. If motorboats are in the area, surface only close to your diver flag and with caution. Wear an inflatable vest suitable for the diving activity.

7. *Plan your dive.* Solve the problems in advance. Know decompression rules. Keep track of depth and time. Stick to your plans.

8. *Be ready for emergencies.* Have plans of action ready. Know lifesaving, first aid, and rescue breathing. Have first-aid equipment. Have a diver's I.D. card. Know the location of the nearest recompression chamber.

9. *Beware of breath-holding.* WITH SCUBA: breathe continuously throughout the dive; exhale all the way up on an emergency ascent. WITHOUT SCUBA: avoid excessive "overbreathing" before skin dives; don't overexert; don't push your limit on breath-holding.

10. *Get medical attention* if any abnormality develops during or after a dive. Don't waste time; don't try to "drown the problem." Wear your I.D. card after any dive that might cause bends.

E. H. LANPHIER, M.D.

Bernard E. Empleton — "The father of recreational diving instruction in the United States."

INTRODUCTION

Organized recreational scuba diving instruction in the United States and the *New Science of Skin and Scuba Diving* began together; and both have developed apace during the last quarter of a century. In the autumn of 1954, the Council for National Cooperation in Aquatics (CNCA), an organization of the major national agencies involved in aquatic activities, committed itself to the safety of a new and growing sport—skin and scuba diving. This effort was led by Bernard E. Empleton, a man with great vision. In cooperation with many interested diving experts, a prototype diving course was set up and run during the winter of 1954–55. From this course grew the text the *Science of Skin and Scuba Diving*. Now in its sixth edition and known as the *New Science of Skin and Scuba Diving*, this book has developed along with the sport and the technology of underwater education; and now holds the unique status of both a classic work and a modern work horse for contemporary scuba instruction. Over two million copies of this publication have found their way into the hands of aspiring divers. It has had worldwide circulation and has been published in Japanese and British Commonwealth editions.

This book represents the spirit of cooperation that is the cornerstone of the structure of CNCA. Based upon the original publication in 1957, the first national scuba certification course was developed by the YMCA, a founding member of CNCA. Additional national programs rapidly followed, creating new national aquatic agencies in themselves, such as NAUI and PADI, which in turn became CNCA agency members. Today the Council has over thirty-five sustaining national agency members, and also has recently expanded into a broad membership organization for all individuals with an interest in aquatics in any of its many forms.

CNCA wants to gratefully acknowledge the many individuals who created and sustained the *New Science of Skin and Scuba Diving* through six editions for almost thirty years. Some of those listed as Contributors helped produce the first edition, and some of their words remain in the sixth, as valid now as they were then. Others have contributed to later versions of the text, and some to many editions. Special note must go to James Young and Loyal Goff, who were there at the beginning and who remained as major contributions through the fourth edition. A particular tribute is due to Edward H. Lanphier, M.D., the mainstay of the physiological and medical wisdom in this publication through its present edition.

The guiding light of the *New Science of Skin and Scuba Diving*, and of much of recreational diving instruction in the United States today was Bernard E. Empleton. As Chairman of the CNCA Skin and Scuba Diving Committee in 1954, Bernie brought together and kept together the vast resources reflected in the list of contributors to this book. He remained the driving force behind this publication and other CNCA efforts in and on the water until his death in 1980. He was an incredible and marvelous man, and it is to his memory that this book is dedicated.

Robert W. Smith
Chairman, CNCA

Contributors

Gilbert Abbe
James Allen
Eric Anderson
Greg Apia
Virginia Bowerman
Ken Brock
William T. Burns
Diane Christian
Lowell Collier
Allen Corey
E. R. Cross
Charles Cundiff
Lloyd DeKay
Bernard E. Empleton
Harold T. Friermood
Robert Geeslin
Loyal Goff
James Griffen
Wallace Hagerhorst
Jon Hardy

Paul Heinmiller
Robert Hill
William Kessen
Joseph Kimber
George Knode
Edward H. Lanphier
Dustin Leer
Robert Lenhard
John Malony
Ralph Marusak
John McAniff
Paul Meng
Richard Morris
Juergen Mueller
Fred Schwankwsky
Phillip Sharkey
Robert Smith
James Wren
James Young
John Zumbado

CONTENTS

THE NATURE OF THE SPORT

You are about to embark on an experience that is truly an adventure in depth. It is not a pun to say that this experience may be pursued at several different levels, each one taking the adventurer further into the depths. As reflected in the title of this book, the two general experiences available to the sport diver are skin diving and scuba diving. The fundamental aspect of skin diving is snorkeling, where the individual views the wonders of the underwater world without ever entirely leaving the surface. Breath-hold diving takes the swimmer to greater depths without the use of an artificial breathing device, and, as in most sports, this form of skin diving can be practiced at either the basic or the more advanced level. Finally, scuba diving, the use of self-contained underwater breathing apparatus, enables a person to explore greater depths of the underwater world at a leisurely pace. The rapidly expanding technology in scuba diving now provides a wide range of opportunities for the sport diver, ranging from basic open-water diving through advanced use of scuba and a variety of special activities.

By simply knowing the terminology and differences between snorkeling, skin diving and scuba diving, and being aware of the different levels at which these activities may be practiced, you have already taken the first step toward intelligent progress into the underwater world.

ONE

GETTING READY

With or without scuba, diving and underwater swimming make unusual demands on the participant, both physically and psychologically. A person will run more than ordinary risks in this kind of activity if he or she has certain physical defects, is not in good general physical condition or tends toward emotional instability. Both the health and the fitness of an individual are important in getting ready to dive.

HEALTH

Physical Status

People who get into trouble in water always endanger their companions to some degree, at times very seriously. For the candidate diver's own good as well as for this reason, most organizations concerned with underwater activities set up some kind of physical standards and insist that each prospective participant be examined by a doctor. Many organizations also make an effort to size up whether the candidate is "in shape," either through special fitness tests or in the course of checking swimming ability. They also remain alert for evidence of psychological difficulties in the course of both testing and training.

From the doctor's standpoint, evaluating a person's fitness for diving, and deciding just where to draw the line on minor or questionable defects, is not always a simple matter. Most physicians have had little direct experience with diving problems, and even the best set of "specs" is bound to leave much to the doctor's judgment. There are also important matters which the doctor may have a hard time evaluating unless he or she has known the candidate for a long time. Episodes in a prospective diver's medical history and factors like psychiatric problems can easily remain undisclosed in a routine examination, and a doctor should not be blamed when such things slip by. The candidate, if willing to be honest, can help the doctor greatly and may be able to do a good part of the "sizing up" job himself. (In the process, the candidate may even spontaneously come to the conclusion that diving is not for him or her.)

Partly with such possibilities in mind, as well as to save the doctor's time, the suggested medical history and examination forms included in this chapter have a "do it yourself" section and include useful notes for the candidate as well as for the doctor.

Medical History and Examination Forms

To The Applicant:

You have undertaken an activity that makes considerable demands on your physical condition. Diving with certain defects amounts to asking for trouble— not only for you but for anybody who has to come to your aid if you get into difficulties in the water. For these reasons, the Council for National Cooperation in Aquatics insists that you have a doctor's OK on your fitness for diving.

You are asked to fill out the Medical History form mainly to save the doctor's time. Not all the questions have a direct bearing on your fitness for diving. Some have to do with medical problems that should be looked into whether they concern diving or not. All are questions the doctors would ask you if they had the time.

In many instances, your answers to the questions are more important in determining your fitness than what the doctor can see, hear or feel when examining you. Obviously, you must give accurate information, or the whole process becomes a waste of time. The forms will be kept in confidence. However, if you feel that any question amounts to an invasion of your privacy, you may omit the answer *provided you discuss the matter with the doctor* and he or she indicates that you have done so.

If the doctor concludes that diving would involve undue risk for you, remember that he or she is concerned only with your well-being and safety. Respect his advice.

MEDICAL HISTORY

Name: _____ Age: _____ yrs. Male _____ Female _____

Address: _____

Telephone: _____ Height: _____ inches Weight: _____ pounds
(If answers to the following questions require explanation, use the space labeled "Remarks," giving the number of the question.)

1. Have you had previous experience in diving? Yes _____ No _____ Have you done any flying? Yes _____ No _____ If so, did you often have trouble

equalizing pressure in your ears or sinuses? Yes ____ No ____ Can you go to the bottom of a swimming pool without having discomfort in ears or sinuses? Yes ____ No ____

2. Do you participate regularly in active sports? Yes ____ No ____ If so, specify what sport(s). If not, indicate what exercise you normally obtain.

_____

_____

3. Have you ever been rejected for service or employment for medical reasons? Yes ____ No ____ *(If "Yes," explain in "Remarks" or discuss with doctor.)*

4. When was your last physical examination? Month _____ Year_____

5. When was your last chest X ray? Month _____ Year _____

6. Have you ever had an electrocardiogram? Yes ____ No ____ An electroen-cephalogram (brain wave study)? Yes ____ No ____
(Check the blank if you have, or ever have had, any of the following. Explain under "Remarks," giving dates and other pertinent information; or discuss with the doctor.)

7. Frequent colds or sore throat _____

8. Hay fever or sinus trouble _____

9. Trouble breathing through nose (other than during colds) _____

10. Painful or running ear, mastoid trouble, broken eardrum _____

11. Asthma or shortness of breath after moderate exercise _____

12. Chest pain or persistent cough _____

13. Spells of fast, irregular or pounding heartbeat _____

14. High or low blood pressure _____

15. Any kind of "heart trouble" _____

16. Frequent upset stomach, heartburn or indigestion; peptic ulcer _____

17. Frequent diarrhea. Blood in stools _____

18. Belly or back ache lasting more than a day or two _____

19. Kidney or bladder disease; blood, sugar or albumin in urine _____

20. Syphilis or gonorrhea _____

21. Broken bone, serious sprain or strain, dislocated joint _____

22. Rheumatism, arthritis or other joint trouble _____

23. Severe or frequent headaches _____

24. Head injury causing unconsciousness _____

25. Dizzy spells, fainting spells or fits _____

26. Trouble sleeping, frequent nightmares or sleepwalking _____
27. Nervous breakdown or periods of marked depression _____
28. Dislike for closed-in spaces, large open places or high places _____
29. Any neurological condition _____
30. Train, sea or air sickness _____
31. Alcoholism, or any drug or narcotic habit (including regular use of sleeping pills, stimulants, etc.) _____
32. Recent gain or loss of weight or appetite _____
33. Jaundice or hepatitis _____
34. Tuberculosis _____
35. Diabetes _____
36. Rheumatic fever _____
37. Any serious accident, injury or illness not mentioned above *(Describe under "Remarks," giving dates.)* _____

REMARKS

_____

_____

_____

_____

I certify that I have not withheld any information and that the above is accurate to the best of my knowledge.

Signature _____

MEDICAL EXAMINATION OF DIVERS

To The Physician:

The bearer requests evaluation of his or her fitness for *diving with breathing apparatus*. He or she has completed a medical history form that should assist you. Besides assessment of this history, he or she requires a general physical examination. Attention to psychiatric status is also appropriate. Other procedures are at your discretion *(see below)*.

Please bear in mind that diving involves a number of unusual medical considerations. The main considerations can be summarized as follows:

1. Diving involves *heavy exertion*. (A diver must be in good general health, be free of cardiovascular and respiratory disease, and have good exercise tolerance.)
2. All body air spaces must *equalize pressure* readily. (Ear and sinus pathology may impair equalization or be aggravated by pressure. Obstructive *lung* disease may cause serious accidents on ascent.)
3. Even momentary *impairment of consciousness* underwater may result in death. (A diver must not be subject to syncope, epileptic episodes, diabetic problems, etc.)
4. Lack of *emotional stability* seriously endangers not only the diver but also his or her companions. (Evidence of neurotic trends, recklessness, accident-proneness, panicky behavior or questionable motivation for diving should be evaluated.)

Suggested Additional Procedures (at physician's discretion):
Routine: Chest film (if none within one year), urinalysis, wbc, hematocrit.
Divers over 40: Electrocardiogram with step test.
Questionable respiratory status: Lung volumes, timed vital capacity.
Inoculations:
Divers often enter polluted water and are subject to injuries requiring antitetanus treatment. It is strongly advised that all routine immunizations be kept up to date: tetanus, typhoid, diphtheria, smallpox, poliomyelitis.

(Please detach and return to examinee)

IMPRESSION

I have examined _____ and reached the following conclusion concerning his or her fitness for diving:
_____ Approval. (I find no defects that I consider incompatible with diving.)
_____ Conditional approval. (I do not consider diving in examinee's best interests but find no defects that present marked risk.)
_____ Disapproval. (Examinee has defects that I believe constitute unacceptable hazards to his or her health and safety in diving.)
The following conditions should be made known to any physician who treats this person for a diving accident (include medical conditions, drug allergies, etc.):

Signature: _____ M.D.

Address : _____

Date: _____

The following paragraphs, extracted from an article by Dr. E. H. Lanphier ("Medical Progress: Diving Medicine," *New England Journal of Medicine)* may assist you in evaluating the applicant:

One of the primary considerations is that diving involves *heavy exertion*. Even if a man does not intend to engage in spearfishing or other activities which are obviously demanding, he will sooner or later find himself in situations which tax his strength and endurance. Even the best breathing apparatus increases the work of breathing, and this adds to the problem of exertion under water. Lifting and carrying the heavy equipment on dry land is also hard work. The necessity for *freedom from cardiovascular and respiratory disease* is evident. Individuals who are sound but sedentary should be encouraged to improve their *exercise tolerance* gradually by other means before taking up diving. The influence of exertion on conditions such as diabetes should be considered carefully. It is not reasonable to apply a fixed age limit to sport divers, but *men over 40 deserve special scrutiny.*

An absolute physical requirement for diving is the *ability of the middle ear and sinuses to equalize pressure changes*. The Navy applies a standard "pressure test" in a recompression chamber to assess this ability since usual methods of examination have insufficient predictive value unless obvious pathology is present. However, even going to the bottom of a swimming pool will generally tell a man whether his Eustachian tubes and sinus ostia will transmit air readily or not. In the case of middle ear equalization, part of the problem is learning the technique of "popping your ears." Presence of *otitis* or *sinusitis* is a definite contraindication for diving, even in a man who can normally equalize pressure. A history of disorders of this sort suggests that diving is unwise; but as in the case of frequent colds or allergic rhinitis, prohibition of diving is not invariably justified. Here, much depends on the individual's common sense and ability to forego diving if he has trouble. A *perforated tympanic membrane* should rule out diving because of the near-certainty of water entering the middle ear. The use of ear plugs presents no solution to any of these problems and is, in fact, strongly contraindicated.

Any organic *neurological disorder,* or a history of *epileptic episodes* or *losses of consciousness* from any cause, makes diving highly inadvisable. A more difficult problem for the physician to evaluate and handle adroitly arises in the *psychiatric* area. The *motivation* and *general attitude* of some aspirants make safe diving unlikely from the outset; and those individuals who tend to panic in emergencies may well find occasion for doing so in diving. *Recklessness* or *emotional instability* in a diver is a serious liability for his companions as well as for himself.

FITNESS AND WATERMANSHIP

A person interested in skin and scuba diving should be able to do the following:

1. Tread water, feet only, 3 minutes.
2. Swim 300 yards without fins.
3. Tow an inert swimmer 40 yards without fins.
4. Stay afloat 15 minutes without accessories.
5. Swim underwater 15 yards without fins—without pushoff.

These requirements are not difficult, but they demand a degree of watermanship that would enable divers in difficulty to help themselves without the aid of special gear.

TWO

SNORKELING

Every year, thousands of people, many of whom will never descend beneath the surface of the water, enjoy coral reefs and other subaquatic environments through the sport of snorkeling. When properly supervised, this sport can be pursued with on-the-scene training by those with only fundamental swimming ability. At the same time, snorkeling skills are generally the first to be acquired by those who seek the greater challenges of skin diving and scuba diving. The mask, fins and snorkel used by the snorkeler are also basic equipment for the skin diver and the scuba diver, and, of course, many of the techniques are similar. The information in this chapter is fundamental to learning more advanced underwater activities.

SEEING

Face masks are designed to provide a constant layer of air between the eyes and a transparent lens. This basic piece of equipment should cover only the nose and eyes and permit pressure equalization of air contained in the mask with that of the surrounding water.

Designs are multiple and purposeful. Individual facial contours must be accommodated. Personal needs or desires will dictate size, volume and lens design. Associated functions may be provided for by incorporation of purge valves and nose-pinch devices.

The final choice should be governed by size, shape, comfort and positive seal. Size and shape are optional, although low volume and profile are preferable. Comfort and positive seal are imperative. Essential features are a soft, flexible, face-fitting skirt and an adjustable, head-fitting, well-anchored head strap. Not essential but desirable are a clearing (purge) valve and a design that permits blocking the nostrils. A mask of high-quality black rubber will outlast colored materials, and silicone masks are the most durable of all. The lens should be

9

made of tempered or safety glass and should indicate in print which it is. The frame holding the lens in the mask should be made of a noncorrosive material, and may be removable to permit replacement of the lens if necessary.

To check the fit of a mask, place it over your eyes and nose *without donning the head strap*. Observe the skirt contour to avoid placing the mask on upside down. The skirt edge should contact your face completely. Inhale slightly with the mask in place. If the desired seal is obtained, the mask will remain in place until you exhale. Try several types, keeping in mind adaptability, comfort and efficiency.

DIVING MASKS

A mask deserves good care. Avoid contact with oil or grease (suntan lotions, hair dressing and rubber-destroying cosmetics). Rinse or wash the mask after each use. Protect the lens from scratches or cracking. Check all parts, especially purge valves, before and after diving. Before wearing the mask in the water, it will be necessary to apply a fog preventative to the inside of the lens. Some of these antifogging substances are saliva, seaweed, tobacco, raw potato or one of the commercial preparations designed for the purpose. Application of other than the commercial preparations should be followed by rinsing with clear water until the lens is clear. In using the commercial preparations, follow the directions of the manufacturer. Liquid soap is a favorite of many divers.

BREATHING

This extension of the body's airway through the use of a snorkel is thought by many divers to be as essential as fins and mask. It permits normal breathing without interruption of the snorkeling diver's underwater viewing and eliminates raising or turning the head to get a quick breath when moving on the surface.

The snorkel is worn under the mask strap or attached to it by a rubber "keeper," which allows the snorkel to be raised or lowered for comfortable positioning of the mouthpiece. It also holds the tube vertically for maximum length

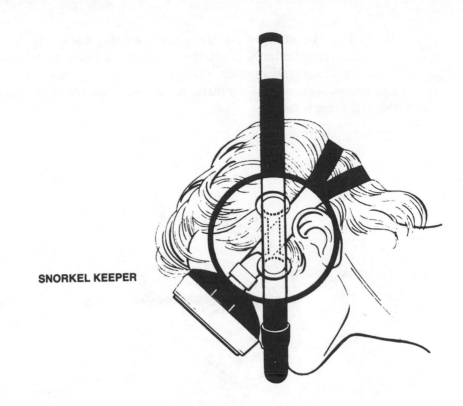

SNORKEL KEEPER

above water when swimming face down at the surface. Most divers wear the snorkel on the left side of the head to avoid confusion with the regulator mouthpiece and its hose, which leads in from the tank on the right side.

The smaller bore in most snorkels, as compared to the human air passages, plus the added distance air must travel both in and out, often makes initial use difficult. Practice will result in development of a deeper inhalation and heavier exhalation than in normal breathing. This will serve to provide desired volume when inhaling and prevent possible build-up of "dead air" in the tube. Snorkel fatigue may be further reduced by shifting to a type that has a more comfortable mouthpiece and/or a larger bore. A sufficiently large, smooth bore will reduce airflow turbulence and water retention. This will allow more efficient breathing and clearing than do smaller bore, "corrugated" bend snorkels. The large, smooth-bore item is standard equipment.

In order to clear water from the breathing tube, a snorkeler may wish to use the "puff" or "blast" method. Upon surfacing, exhale strongly to force water out of the tube. If the first puff does not clear the snorkel entirely, inhale cautiously and slowly and repeat the action with another quick, strong outward blast. Water remaining in a snorkel with a flexible bend can be exhausted by pinching the

11

upper part of the bend together. This narrows the size of the bore and helps in the clearing effect, particularly if the head is tilted back or to the side.

Drinking the small portion of water remaining in the snorkel is not advisable because water may be impure or salty. The snorkel should be thoroughly cleansed after each use.

PUFF CLEARING

MOVING

The now-familiar swim fin is the key to any diver's effective movement through the water. The evolution of this foot-area-increasing attachment from a board on the shoe to the many scientifically designed fins now available is an excellent example of the combined research and development that have helped man adapt to the underwater environment. Variations of total blade area, outline, curvature and stiffening govern flexibility and influence efficiency of thrust. Combined with a slipper, or foot pocket and heel strap, such designs provide positive control and comfort to the wearer. No single design is satisfactory for all divers, so the choice must be governed by individual needs. Most fins are available in graduated sizes to fit small through large feet (usually two shoe sizes are accommodated by each fin size). Since blade size is usually proportional to foot size, only a limited degree of personal preference in relative blade size is possible.

Fins will be more satisfactory if the individual considers that most diving activity will involve wearing neoprene boots or other foot covering. Fin size should be governed by foot size plus the boot.

FINS

Transition of the surface swimmer to the underwater swimmer or diver involves a change in leg strokes. The addition of many square inches of surface to the foot when fins are worn makes some conventional kicks inefficient.

Before experimenting with the following kicks, learn to don your fins properly. Wet your feet (with or without boots or socks), then wet the fins. Hold the ribs of the blade and push your foot firmly all the way into the pocket. Next, pull the heel strap or back of the slipper into position. If slipper-type fins are being used, turning the heel portion inside out will help. When the foot is in the pocket, gently pull the heel part back up into position.

In the flutter, scissors and dolphin kicks, only a small bend in the knee should be allowed. This will keep the upper and lower leg in a straight line, which will increase the power and efficiency of the kick. That in turn will reduce fatigue and increase relaxation as a slow, even tempo becomes natural to the swimmer. A good kicking action will also make it unnecessary to use the hands for swimming.

The flutter and the dolphin are the easiest and most efficient kicks to use with fins. Because the flutter kick is readily usable in the face-up, face-down and either left-or right-side swimming position without any change, it will be considered first.

Flutter kick. This is the leg stroke most commonly used in diving. With the legs kept as straight from hip to foot as is comfortable, and the toes pointed, an up and down, reciprocating motion will give the diver a strong, constant thrust forward with the aid of fins. Distance between the feet when the legs are fully open underwater should be approximately 24 inches. An easy, relaxed kick that saves energy is preferable and is more efficient than a rapid flutter. The faster the forward speed, the greater the water resistance and therefore the greater the amount of energy used.

The back should be arched to keep the body inclined slightly upward. Arms are trailed close along the sides to reduce drag, or one or both may be extended forward to protect the diver in conditions of reduced visibility. When swimming on or near the surface, the opening of the kick should be reduced to keep the fins underwater for maximum efficiency.

Scissors kick. Although this kick is not generally used as the primary leg stroke in diving, it serves as a variation and allows a kick-and-glide technique for

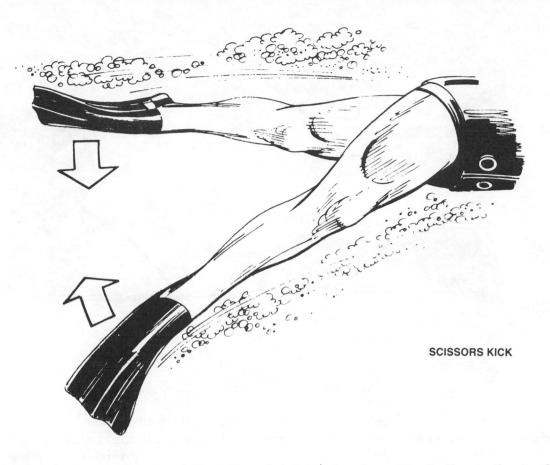

SCISSORS KICK

resting between thrusts while still maintaining headway. Basically similar to the flutter kick, the legs are opened about 24 inches and brought together strongly and stopped when they are parallel. This is a power stroke. A rest follows as the diver glides forward for several seconds. The legs are then reopened easily and thrust together again strongly, like a pair of scissors.

Frog kick. Like the scissors kick, the frog kick is not a first choice among divers, but it does allow a variation in the use of muscles and a rest after each stroke. The legs are opened slowly in froglike fashion and brought together to thrust the diver forward in a powerful stroke, followed by a relaxing glide. Before forward motion stops, the kick is repeated.

Dolphin kick. Simulating the undulating movements of the dolphin's body provides the diver with a strong leg kick. As illustrated, start with the knees slightly bent, toes pointed. Thrust downward by straightening the knees and bending slightly at the waist. The return, upward stroke is made with toes pointed, legs straight. About halfway up, the knees begin to bend, and at the peak of the stroke the knees are again in the starting position. Avoid extremes in

15

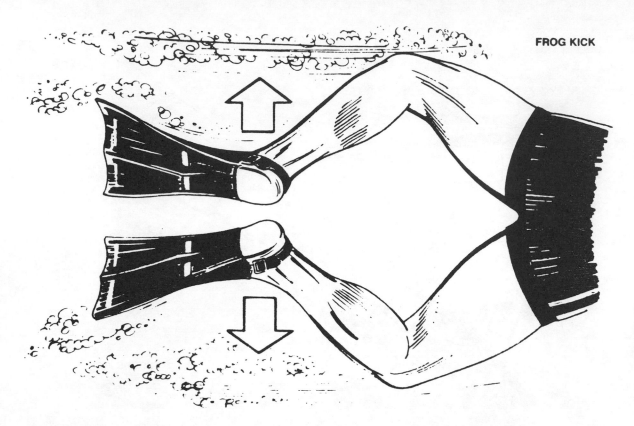

bending the waist or knees. Practice will develop a slight flip of the fins at the peak of upward and downward motions, which will give additional thrust. This is accomplished by ankle movement and will come with the improvement of timing.

FLOATING

A snorkeler not involved in breath-hold diving should have positive buoyancy; that is, he or she should float when relaxed on the surface and breathing normally.

A swimmer who is kept afloat naturally by the water and must use additional weight or physical force to sink below the surface is buoyed up because the water has greater density than his or her body does. In a sense, that swimmer's body is not dense enough, or heavy enough, to push an equal bulk or volume of water out of the way so that it can sink. Such a body, or other object, floats, and is said to have *positive buoyancy*. One that tends to stay at the same depth under water has *neutral* buoyancy. And one that tends to sink has *negative buoyancy*.

Whether something will sink or float in a liquid follows *Archimedes' Principle:*

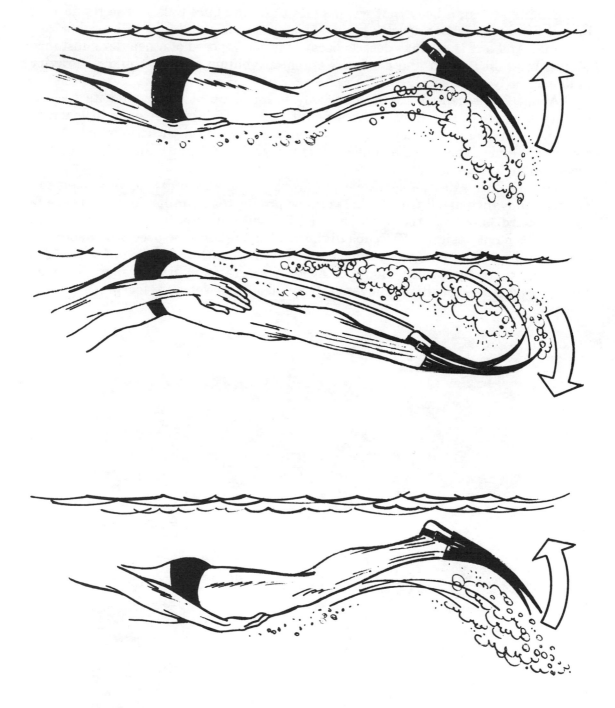

A body placed in a liquid is buoyed upward by a force equal to the weight of the liquid it displaces.

Simply stated, a body that weighs less than an equal bulk of the liquid it is in will float. One whose density is the same as that of the liquid will neither rise nor sink. And one that sinks does so because it is composed of a heavier substance than the liquid it is in and displaces an equal volume of that liquid as gravity pulls the body downward.

About 70 percent of the human body is made up of water, and its specific gravity is slightly less than 1. As a result, most people find it easy to learn to float and can spend long periods in the water safely and with little effort. A few swimmers and divers have a comparatively high body density and must scull or tread water to stay afloat.

For absolute safety, a snorkeler may wish to use a skin-diving vest to ensure positive buoyancy at all times. This is a low-profile vest, similar in appearance to the standard buoyancy compensator used by scuba divers but much smaller in volume. It is not designed for scuba diving and should only be used when snorkeling. It will provide emergency flotation either by mouth inflation or by use of a small CO_2 cartridge, which should be at least 16 grams in size. A snorkeler may also receive some positive buoyancy from use of a wet suit for protection or warmth.

SKIN DIVING VEST

KEEPING WARM

The primary reasons for wearing protective clothing are the prevention of body heat loss and protection against scrapes and other minor injuries. Choice of clothing type will depend on intended use, body area to be covered and individual need. Because heat loss in water, even as warm as 85°F, is much more rapid than in air, an exposure suit is one of the most valuable items among a diver's scuba gear.

For sport diving, the most commonly used type of protective clothing is the wet suit. It is snug fitting and made of neoprene, a synthetic rubber, and consists of small closed-cell gas bubbles that provide insulation against the outside water. Closely fitted to the individual diver's body shape, it allows only a small amount of water to enter, and this forms a thin film between suit and skin. This limits heat loss and makes donning and doffing of the synthetic rubber suit easier. It is this film of water between suit and diver that gives the suit its name.

A suit that does not fit snugly allows water to enter at the various openings and carry off heat as it flows over the body and into the spaces created by the lack of contact with the skin. A close, comfortable fit is the chief consideration when selecting an exposure suit. Various thicknesses of wet-suit material are available, and the one chosen should be a matter of personal body-temperature comfort and local water conditions where it is used.

More information on protective suits and their use is provided later in this book, in the chapters dealing with skin diving and scuba diving.

ENTRIES AND EXITS

There are several acceptable methods of entering the water while wearing skin- and scuba-diving equipment. At all times a primary concern should be the diver's own safety and that of any other diver already in the water. To avoid landing on someone else, look carefully around the entry point just before entering the water. Know where your diving buddy is and be certain that he or she knows you are entering. This check will also increase your own protection in case you should become disoriented following entry.

A diver should never enter the water without first determining that there are no obstructions in the entry path. In general, only three entry methods from a point above the surface should be followed, whether from boat, float, dock or ledge. They are the "giant stride," the back roll and the sitting entry.

Entry techniques are generally the same for skin divers and for scuba divers, as can be seen in the following illustrations. Scuba-diving students generally practice entries without the use of scuba tanks until they become proficient.

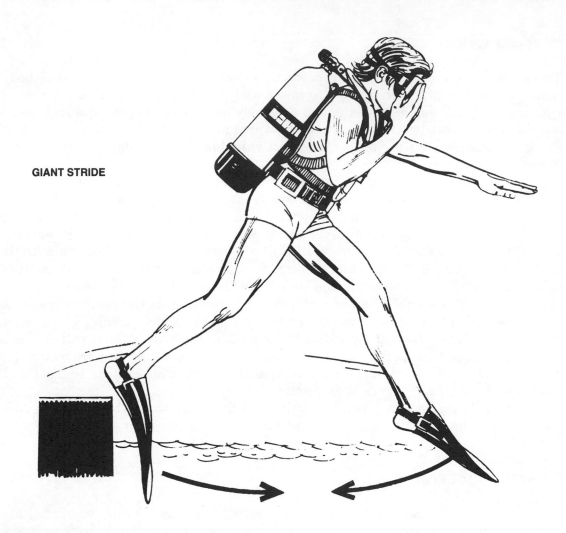

GIANT STRIDE

Giant Stride

Some divers prefer to step off a raised edge feet first with legs open as when walking, or to jump in with legs straight and closed. Both methods may allow you to sink to an undesirable depth before coming to a surface position. Therefore, to prevent possible underwater disorientation and striking bottom in shallow water, and to stay on or close to the surface, the "giant stride" is recommended. To use it, take a full stride into the water, legs wide apart, and, still holding the mask with one hand, raise the other arm to a horizontal position. As the legs enter the water, bring them together strongly and strike the surface with the extended arm. This will slow the entry and keep your head near the surface, especially when wearing fins.

Back Roll

From a crouched or sitting position, close to the surface, with back to the water, roll backward. Under ideal conditions this method of entry is acceptable, otherwise it can leave you disoriented and exposed to underwater obstructions. It is often used to avoid rocking a shallow boat or rubber raft. Keep a tight grip on the mask with one hand.

BACK ROLL

Sitting Entry

Entry from a sitting positon, or "seat drop," is the most desirable because it is done from a surface close to the water and allows complete control. From a sitting position on boat, pool deck or ledge, with feet in water and holding to edge, turn and lower the body gently into the water. This eliminates sharp impact, submersion of head and possible disorientation.

SITTING ENTRY

Entry From Shore

In entering the water from the shore, without fins, walk slowly and carefully forward to a depth at which you can begin to swim. On a sharp or tricky bottom, wearing fins, walk backward to swimming depth and begin swimming. Also walk backward when approaching light surf. A backward, shuffling movement allows better control of fins on the bottom and greater upright body control and balance against the surf.

Whether snorkeling, skin diving or scuba diving, the key to an effective exit from the water is to think about how to accomplish it *before you enter the water*. Always make sure that you can get out before you get in.

22

Exiting from the water on a ladder should be accomplished only after removing the swim fins. Swim fins should be retained either by holding them in your hand or by slipping the straps over your wrist until you are safely in the boat. This will provide you with ready access to your swim fins should they accidentally fall back into the water during exit. By the same token, a diver should retain his or her mask or snorkel in place while exiting the water, removing them only after he or she is securely ashore. This same principle holds true for the snorkeler while in the water. The face mask and snorkel should be kept in place to enable the snorkeler to see and breathe comfortably while in the water, even when on the surface.

Another useful form of exit from the water for the snorkeler or skin diver not weighted down by a scuba tank or weight belt is a "muscle up." This procedure is essentially a reverse of the sitting entry illustrated earlier. Thrusting the body out of the water until the weight is resting effectively on the arms is greatly expedited by vertical use of the flutter kick using a swimmer's fins.

THREE

SKIN DIVING

Skin diving includes all of the snorkeling skills and equipment discussed in the previous chapter. The information in this chapter includes what you need to know to hold your breath, however briefly, and to descend to shallow depths for greater access to the underwater environment. As soon as you descend in the water, or hold your breath, you are subjected to physiological changes for which you must compensate in order to dive comfortably and effectively. These changes are created by variations in water pressure and temperature, as well as the act of breath holding itself. A number of things about the underwater environment, such as weightlessness, can make life easier for the diver if proper advantage is taken of these factors. The scuba diver deals with the same environment as the breath-hold diver, and thus much of what is learned here will be of value as the underwater adventurer progresses toward the use of scuba apparatus.

SURFACE DIVES

Whether you are a skin diver or a scuba diver, your great underwater adventure truly begins with the surface dive that starts your descent into the depths. Several techniques are available, depending on the circumstances involved, and these techniques must be perfected in order to get your exploration of the underwater world off to a good start. Both skin divers and scuba divers have the option of a head-first or a foot-first descent.

Head-First Surface Dive

Also called the *pike* dive, the head-first dive from the surface is best begun while moving forward face-down, with legs, arms and body horizontal. Bend the body sharply at the waist, forcing the head, arms and upper half of the body straight down. Next, raise the legs vertically out of the water. The weight of the legs will

TUCK DIVE

drive you straight down. The key to this dive is to get as much of the legs out of the water as possible so that their weight forces the body downward. Begin kicking as soon as the fins are underwater. Arms and hands are extended forward to protect the head while descending. Hands are used to pull the diver downward.

This dive can also be done from a motionless position on the surface instead of moving forward.

A similar head-first method from a motionless position on the surface is to pull the legs into a tuck position and, when the upper body is vertical, straighten the legs above water to drive the body downward. Some divers find that in

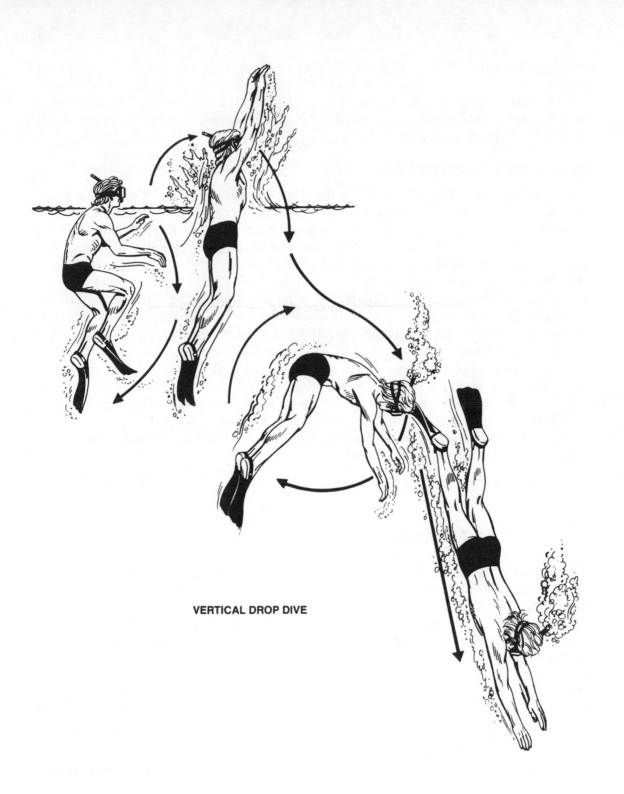

VERTICAL DROP DIVE

moving from the tuck to the vertical position the legs are partially submerged before they are straight up and down, thereby reducing the downward thrust.

Practice, timing and adaptation of either dive will result in splash-free, nearly effortless descent to a considerable depth (depending on buoyancy factor) before kicking is necessary.

Vertical-Drop Dive (Feet-First)

When practiced and perfected, this feet-first maneuver permits dropping nearly straight down from the surface. The feet-first attitude gives added protection when water depth is not known, or when obstructions or a heavy concentration of water plants exist in the dive area. Neutral or slightly negative buoyancy acquired during descent may eliminate the need for reversal of position and permit a continued feet-first drop.

Starting from a vertical position (as in treading water), give a strong kick with the fins and, if possible, a downward stroke with the hands to lift the body above the surface. Immediately after the lift, straighten the legs and body, and raise the arms and hands high above the head. Body and arm weight will provide the thrust to drive the diver downward as the legs do in a head-first dive. Also, the hands can be used in an upward sweep to increase the downward thrust.

This dive also makes it easier to clear the ears because there is less blood pressure in the head than with a head-first dive.

When surface-dive techniques have been mastered and the other basic skills have been developed to the point of minimum expenditure of effort, the new divers will be ready to prolong their underwater activities.

PRESSURE EQUALIZATION

Pressure increases rapidly as you descend in the water. As a rough rule of thumb, it increases about 1 lb per square inch (psi) with each 2 ft of depth. More exact figures are 0.445 psi per foot in sea water and 0.432 psi in fresh water.

We are already experiencing barometric pressure at the surface: 14.7 psi, or 1 atmosphere. Each 33 ft of descent in sea water (34 ft in fresh water) will add another atmosphere to the total, or absolute, pressure. The pressure at 33 ft of ocean depth is 2 atmospheres absolute, and so on. The atmosphere system is the easiest to use in considering many aspects of pressure. The volume of air and other gases will vary inversely in direct proportion to changes in pressure (Boyle's Law). That simply means that as pressure increases, volume tends to decrease proportionately, and vice versa.

Increase of Pressure With Increase of Depth

Depth (feet, seawater)	Pressure (atmospheres, absolute)	Related Change in Volume (given 1 cubic foot) at 1 atmosphere)
surface	1	1
33	2	$1/2$
66	3	$1/3$
99	4	$1/4$
132	5	$1/5$
165	6	$1/6$
297	10	$1/10$

The effects of pressure can be divided into "direct" (or primary) and "indirect" (or secondary).

The direct effects are largely mechanical and fairly obvious. The indirect effects are more subtle. They come about mainly through the partial pressures of the gases that the diver breathes.

The direct effects of pressure are produced either (1) by way of a pressure difference built up across some structure of the body, or (2) by way of a change in gas volume. In most cases, these two are actually very closely related.

Unless a pressure difference, or "differential," exists, pressure does not have noticeable direct, mechanical effects at common diving depths. For practical purposes, we can assume that living tissue behaves like the water of which it is largely composed: it transmits pressure throughout itself without being compressed.

The same is true of the body parts that are "solid tissues." For example, taking your legs from one depth to another produces no noticeable change whatsoever. But the body is not *all* a mass of solids and solutions like a leg. It contains certain *air spaces,* and others may be hitched onto its surface in the form of goggles, mask, etc. The following are all potential trouble spots:

1. Spaces associated with the ears.
2. The sinuses.
3. The lungs and airways.
4. Gas pockets in the stomach and intestines.
5. Any air space applied to the surface of the body.

The body will transmit pressure freely through all its "fluid" portions directly to, but not necessarily into, these air spaces. If the space has a soft, or supple, wall, this pressure will simply cause the space to collapse until the air

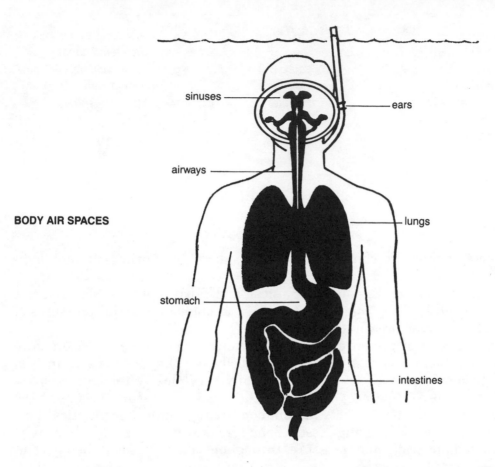

BODY AIR SPACES

sinuses

ears

airways

lungs

stomach

intestines

inside is compressed to the appropriate volume for that pressure (Boyle's Law). Once this volume is reached, nothing more will happen.

If the space has a semirigid wall and will not compress freely, the end result will be compromise—some compression of the gas and some pressure difference across the wall. If the space is walled by bone, for example, the pressure inside will remain what it was to start with, while the outside pressure goes up. Here, the whole surrounding pressure (above 1 atmosphere) can act as a differential. But if a rigid or semirigid space has an open connection to a source of air at ambient pressure, the developing differential will simply force air into the space until the pressure is *equalized*. The amount of air required to equalize also follows the pressure-volume relationship: if a rigid space is equalized at 33 ft, it will contain twice as many air molecules as it did at the surface, and so forth.

When the ambient pressure is reduced, these processes simply go into reverse. A flexible space will just re-expand, and nothing will happen unless the expanding gas overfills it. An equalized rigid space will simply vent the extra gas if the connection remains open. If there is overfilling or blockage, of course a differential will develop—higher pressure inside the spaces than outside.

All injuries resulting from pressure differences can be lumped under the term *barotrauma* (injury due to pressure).

Middle-Ear Squeeze

What can happen to the middle ear serves as a good example. Consider the space marked "middle ear." When you leave the surface, this contains air at surface pressure. As you descend, the ambient pressure increases, but the internal pressure does not. This produces a differential across the eardrum. In addition, the body is transmitting the pressure to the walls of the space as well: the blood pressure is going up along with the ambient pressure, and this means that the same differential is operating across the walls of every blood vessel in the membrane lining.

Normally, before any of the differentials get very high, you can get air at ambient pressure from the throat to go through the eustachian tube and equalize the pressure. But the tube does not always pass air very readily. You may have to

MECHANISM OF THE EAR

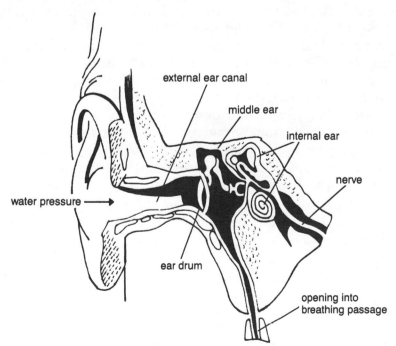

external ear canal

middle ear

internal ear

nerve

water pressure →

ear drum

opening into breathing passage

do some swallowing, jaw moving or other maneuvers to get the tube to open. A few people have voluntary control over certain muscles and can open it at will, but most aren't so lucky. It may be necessary to grab your nose and blow to get air started through; but if you blow too hard, the "trap door" may just shut tighter, and damage is possible. The blowing trick is called the *valsalva* maneuver.

A few people never can "pop" their ears because of some structural difficulty. Almost anyone will have trouble if a cold, infection or hay fever causes the membranes around the opening to swell. In these cases, using nose drops, spray, an inhaler or an oral decongestant may shrink the membranes enough to make equalization possible. But remember that it never pays to push yourself when you have trouble.

Sometimes when you descend too fast it becomes difficult to equalize pressure in your ears. When this happens, you may have to come up a few feet to equalize and then resume descent while continuing equalization.

If you cannot equalize by getting air to go through the eustachian tube, but continue going down, what happens then? The blood vessels in the lining of the middle ear are usually the first place trouble appears; and since the membrane lining continues over the inner surface of the drum, blood-vessel troubles appear in the drum also. The vessels are not designed to take much excess pressure, which will squeeze a lot of blood into them. Depending on how severe the squeeze is and how long it lasts, the vessels will swell, leak and finally burst. There will be bleeding, first into the lining and then into the space. The drum will become bloody in the process, but it will not necessarily be ruptured. Often, there will be enough bleeding into the space to reduce the air volume and equalize pressure, thereby keeping the drum from giving way. This process is not recommended.

Only a few feet of descent without equalization will cause discomfort and the beginning of trouble. Ten feet of such descent could cause serious damage, including rupture of the eardrum, something you should not take lightly, even though it usually heals without much trouble. "Equalization by bleeding" leaves free blood in the space, and this plus membrane damage could cause infection. Infection, in turn, may cause scarring and result in permanent deafness.

Without infection, even a ruptured drum will usually heal in a couple of weeks. Normally, the only treatment is "hands off"—which means keeping everything that might carry bacteria (including fingers, medicine, implements and especially water) out of the ear.

It is always advisable to see a doctor and let him or her keep track of an ear injury. You must see a doctor promptly if noticeable hearing loss, ringing of the ear or any kind of dizziness develops: such symptoms may indicate a much more serious form of injury involving the inner ear.

The beginning or continuation of pain later may indicate infection, as may the development of drainage from the external ear canal. Any sign of infection also calls for a prompt visit to the doctor. It is normal to have blood in your nasal secretion or to spit up traces for a few hours after injury because blood from the middle ear will drain down the eustachian tube. In case of rupture, you must not dive again until the doctor says the drum has healed.

Rupturing the eardrum when bareheaded in cold water can have very impressive effects. Cold water getting into the middle ear will cause a violent upset in the sense of balance, resulting in marked dizziness (true vertigo) and nausea. Although this will usually pass off as soon as the water warms up—a minute or so—things can be pretty tense in the meantime. You just have to hang on. Don't try to surface unless your diving buddy can take charge. You literally won't know which way is up until the effect subsides. If the nausea leads to vomiting, you may have a serious problem with your breathing apparatus.

Less obvious disturbances of equilibrium at times of pressure change (such as the beginning of ascent) are sometimes lumped under the heading of *alterno-baric vertigo*. This is thought to be due to abnormal pressures in the middle ear that have an effect on adjacent inner-ear structures. It often follows a descent marred by difficulties in equalizing.

The external ear canal is also subject to squeeze if it becomes blocked for any reason. This problem will be discussed under "suit squeeze" later in this chapter.

Sinuses

There are four pairs of paranasal sinuses: the *frontal* sinuses in the forehead above the bridge of the nose, the *maxillaries* in the cheekbones, the *ethmoids* between the eyes, and the *sphenoidal* sinuses back under the brain. These sinuses are cavities in the bones of the face and head. They are lined with a membrane continuous with that of the nose, running through the bony canals that connect the sinuses to the air passages of the nose. If this membrane swells up where it goes through a bony canal, it may shut off the sinus completely. This is not unusual during a bad cold, and it makes it impossible for the sinus to equalize.

Allowing for the obvious differences, almost everything said about the middle ear during the squeeze will also apply to the sinuses. Trying to take pressure when your sinuses won't equalize readily is asking for a serious case of sinusitis. Sometimes nose drops and the like will help. There is, however, the unfortunate possibility that the effect of medication will have worn off by the time you need it most. Sometimes a rebound effect—even more congestion than before--occurs. Vasoconstrictor products for oral use (tablets or capsules) are effective for ear and sinus problems in many people. Take note, however, that many such decongestants, especially those that may be purchased without a prescription, are combined with antihistamine compounds that can cause drowsiness.

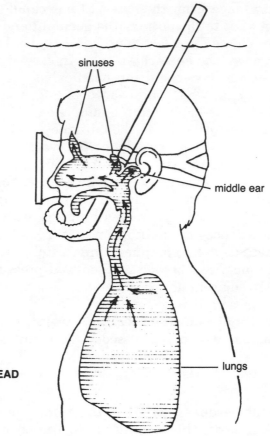

sinuses

middle ear

lungs

AIR SINUSES IN THE HEAD

Lungs and Chest

The lungs and airways won't give trouble during descent so long as you keep breathing and are able to get a plentiful supply of air from your scuba. But if you are deliberately making a breath-hold dive, or if your air is cut off on the way down, a form of squeeze becomes possible.

During descent without extra air for equalizing the lungs and airways, the existing lung gas is compressed in accordance with Boyle's Law. In this process, the lungs and chest (thorax) simply get smaller as they do during exhalation. But beyond a certain point, the structures start to resist further reduction of volume, and pressure within the lungs falls below the surrounding pressure. Further descent is possible, but if it continues too far, blood vessels in the lungs will burst. Bleeding into the lungs from this cause is what is meant by *thoracic squeeze,* fortunately an uncommon accident. A very similar situation can develop if you try to breathe through a snorkel from more than a foot or so of depth.

The maximum depth of descent on a "full breath" is a highly individual matter and depends on too many factors to be predicted with any accuracy. Records beyond 250 ft have been set by individuals with unusual lung capacities.

"Gut" Squeeze

Don't memorize this one! It doesn't happen. The structures in the gastrointestinal tract all have supple walls, so any air pockets are simply compressed with no local differences in pressure and no strain. The only possible trouble comes on ascent.

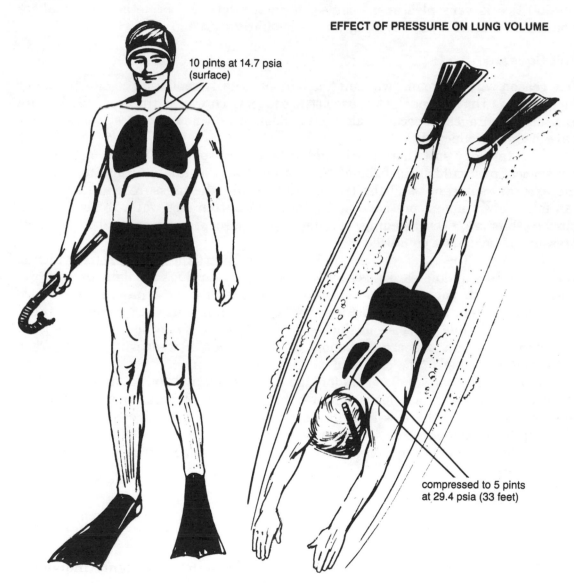

EFFECT OF PRESSURE ON LUNG VOLUME

10 pints at 14.7 psia (surface)

compressed to 5 pints at 29.4 psia (33 feet)

External Air Spaces

You have probably noticed that your face mask can exert suction on your face as you descend and that you have to let air into it through your nose to keep the sensation from becoming severe. The mask is just trying to give you a face squeeze.

The most easily damaged tissues within a mask are the membranes covering the surface of the eyeball and lining the lids and spaces around the eyeball. Hemorrhage can also occur behind the eyeball, in the socket. None of these possibilities is very pleasant. Goggles, normally having no method of equalization, are unsuitable for anything but very shallow diving.

Suit Squeeze

One reason why the foam "wet suit" has almost totally replaced the older types of "dry suit" is that it does not cause local squeeze. However, the wet suit has its own disadvantages, especially at greater depths; and new forms of the dry suit have been introduced.

Within a dry suit there are bound to be several more or less incompressible air spaces, particularly in folds of the material and at anatomical sites such as the external ear canal and the crotch. As a result, the pressure within the suit can fall below ambient pressure on descent. This encourages water to leak in; and pinches, blisters, even bleeding, can develop in susceptible areas unless the suit pressure is somehow equalized.

Closing off the external ear canal can cause an *external ear squeeze,* which is very much like middle-ear squeeze. For this reason, earplugs are dangerous. Suits made of smooth rubber can occasionally seal over the external ear; but more often external ear squeeze is just a part of overall suit squeeze. Not only is there a bigger irreducible air space at that point, but the ear is a lot more delicate than the skin; so a suit squeeze can show up there even if it doesn't appear very noticeable elsewhere. The cure and cautions are the same.

This form of ear squeeze can damage either the canal lining or the eardrum or both. The usual result looks like a bunch of blood blisters; and if one of the blisters has burst, there will be bleeding from the external ear. In this case bleeding to the outside *does not necessarily* mean that the drum is ruptured, as it does in the middle-ear squeeze. However, the drum *can* rupture under this circumstance.

Miscellaneous

Squeeze due to external air spaces may show up occasionally in unusual forms.

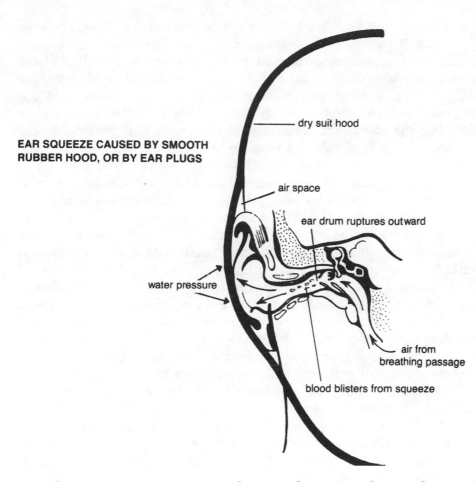

EAR SQUEEZE CAUSED BY SMOOTH RUBBER HOOD, OR BY EAR PLUGS

dry suit hood

air space

ear drum ruptures outward

water pressure

air from breathing passage

blood blisters from squeeze

As you can see, pressure changes that occur during descent can have many effects on the skin diver. The primary considerations are barotrauma, or "squeeze," and changes in buoyancy. Some of the indirect effects of pressure relate to breath holding and are discussed in the following paragraphs.

All of the pressure factors discussed above relate to the scuba diver, who is also subjected to other pressure-related phenomena as a result of breathing compressed air. These phenomena are described in a later chapter on scuba diving.

BREATH HOLDING

In order to descend beneath the surface of the water without the aid of some artificial breathing apparatus, the diver must obviously hold his or her breath.

The key to safe and effective breath-hold diving is to avoid excess. This is true in any breath-holding activity, even on the surface, but special problems are caused by the indirect effects of pressure associated with underwater activity. These effects relate mostly to scuba diving and are discussed in detail in the chapter covering that subject. It is enough for the breath-hold diver to know that the deeper he or she goes, the more oxygen molecules are made available to his or her tissues, thus offsetting the metabolic consumption of oxygen and prolonging his or her breath-holding ability *at depth*. Conversely, as the diver ascends, the drop in pressure sharply reduces the oxygen supply to the tissues. This process, of course, is accelerated by normal oxygen consumption during the breath-hold experience. The result for a diver who has "pushed it" while breath holding in deep water may be a sudden loss of consciousness during ascent. This problem can be avoided by limiting both the depth and the time for breath-hold dives and by being sensitive to your own limitations. Some breath-hold divers attempt to extend their limits by a process known as voluntary hyperventilation. This involves completely inhaling and exhaling several times in rapid succession prior to a breath-hold dive. In this way, a diver is able to blow off the carbon dioxide in his or her system. This causes a lessening of the desire to breathe but in no way increases the amount of oxygen available to the tissues. This is a dangerous practice, which can accelerate the process of hypoxia described above.

The real key to effective breath-hold diving appears to be relaxation. The relaxed diver is consuming less oxygen and building up less carbon dioxide during the dive, and is at the same time more sensitive to the cues that tell him or her that it is time to return to the surface for more air, rest and relaxation.

Divers who practice safe breath-holding techniques can spend many hours enjoying their free-diving freedom in the underwater world to depths of 20 ft and beyond.

BUOYANCY CONTROL

One of the keys to relaxed diving is buoyancy control. A skin diver usually will attempt to achieve neutral or slightly positive buoyancy on the surface. Through an effective surface dive, the free diver can quickly descend to a point where water pressure has reduced the volume of his or her wet suit, skin diver vest and lungs to a degree that enables him or her to drop easily to a greater depth. Since skin divers have no means of suddenly increasing their volume at depth in order to rise to the surface easily should a problem arise, they may wear a weight belt.

It should be sturdily constructed, flexible and wide enough to be comfortable when worn next to the swimsuit or over the exposure suit. It must be equipped with a quick-release buckle that permits positive release with one hand. The wire buckle is recommended because it is different from those used on other items of

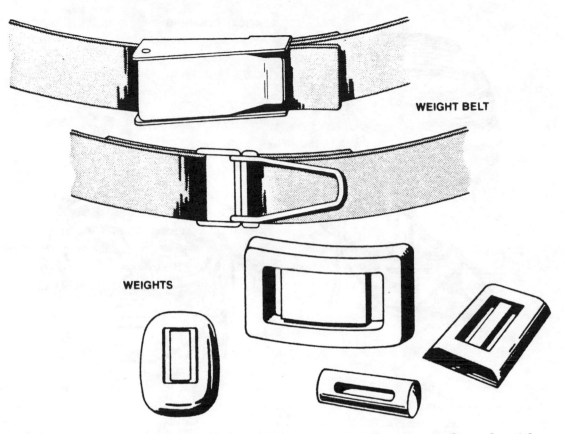

WEIGHT BELT

WEIGHTS

scuba gear. This allows the diver to release the belt by sense of touch without confusing its buckle with other buckles in case of need to dump the weights quickly. Belt-size (girth) adjustment methods are variable according to buckle design. Such adjustment is necessary, not only to fit the individual but also to provide for additional length when protective clothing is worn and weights added. *Do not tie any excess belt material.* Doing so will eliminate the effectiveness of the quick release. Elastic-type belts made of rubber are available and provide a snug fit in spite of girth variations caused by pressure when an exposure suit is worn.

Weights should be so constructed that they can be readily added to or removed from the selected belt. An even distribution of weight is desirable for stability.

Important: The weight belt goes on last and comes off first.

MASK AND SNORKEL CLEARING

Clearing a flooded mask involves displacing the water in it with exhaled air. The air, being lighter than water, will force the water out at the lower portion of the

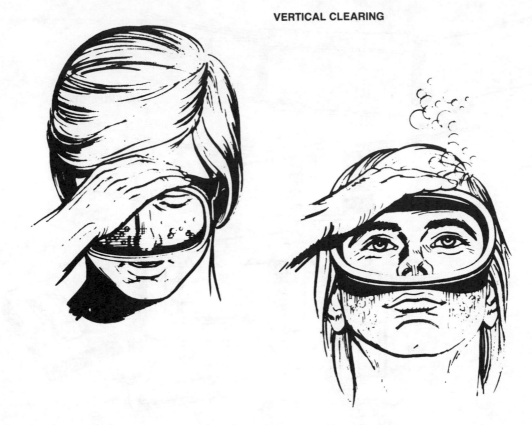

mask if the upper portion is held firmly to the face by hand to prevent escape of air at the top of the mask. The amount of hand pressure and the position of the hand will depend on the mask type and size. Head position during clearing will vary for the same reasons. Before trying to perform the following clearing methods at depth, don the flooded mask, have your dive buddy hold you slightly below the surface, and perform the clearing action. (Note: With varied head positions the uppermost portion of the mask must be held to the face so as to prevent the escape of air at the top.)

Vertical clearing for masks not equipped with a purge valve. With the mask flooded, hold the top rim firmly to the forehead (slight separation of the lower skirt from the upper lip may occur due to this pressure). Now, while looking down, start exhaling through the nose. The chin-down position will prevent the water in the mask from entering the nose because it is blocked by the air in the nasal passages. Continue exhaling while changing the incline of the face toward the surface. The displacement of water by air will be seen. Continue until air escapes at the bottom portion of the mask. The mask should then be free of water.

CLEARING WITH PURGE VALVE

The inclination of the head toward the surface during exhalation will vary according to shape and size of the mask. This variation will be greatly altered if the mask is equipped with a purge valve.

Vertical clearing for masks equipped with a purge valve. Because purge valves are usually located in the lower portion of the mask, it is generally only necessary to apply sufficient hand pressure to the top portion of the mask to prevent the escape of air at that point. Most types require little or no inclination of the face toward the surface while exhaling to clear the mask. Due to the size and location of the purge valve, experimenting to determine the best head position and hand pressure will be necessary to achieve the best results.

Horizontal roll clearing. This method is least preferred, but it is effective. Exert firm pressure on one side of the mask rim (right or left) with hand. Roll the body so that the shoulder opposite the side being held is toward the bottom. Exhale gently and continuously. This causes the water to be displaced by air. Continue the roll until all water is purged. This will generally be accomplished in the first 90° but may require a 180° turn until experience and practice indicate correct hand pressure on the rim and satisfactory exhalation rate. (*Note:* Failure to achieve complete clearing is usually due to change of body and head position to other than horizontal.)

It should be noted that many masks are designed to permit sealing of the nostrils by pinching or finger pressure. This convenience will assist measurably when attempting to prevent middle-ear squeeze by sealed-nose exhalation. (*A*

HORIZONTAL CLEARING

skills note at this point is desirable: Early introduction of higher pressure into the eustachian tubes *before* the need is felt, rather than when indicated by discomfort or pain, may make descent easier.)

The "puff" or "blast" snorkel-clearing method has been described earlier in this book for use by snorkelers. For breath-hold divers, the easiest clearing method, both to learn and to perform, is the water displacement ("downhill") action. The action is simple and its advantages many. Clearing becomes a part of the ascent procedure of looking up to see that the way to the surface is unobstructed.

The ascending diver, snorkel in mouth, looks upward. This puts the open end of the snorkel below the mouthpiece. Just before surfacing (2 to 5 ft deep), the diver starts to exhale gently into the tube. Water is cleared by air and gravity. The head-back position is held until the chin is clear of the surface. This will usually result in the open end being out of water also. You may now inhale and assume normal surface position. During initial practice the diver should make the first inhalation with caution in case water displacement was incomplete or the open end was not pointed down until above the surface.When properly performed, this displacement method is natural and effortless regardless of bore size.

SPECIAL ACTIVITIES AND EQUIPMENT

Many individuals are content to spend their time underwater as basic skin divers, using the equipment and techniques described so far in this book.Others pursue specialized activities, such as underwater hunting, in which breath-hold diving holds certain advantages over the use of scuba and certainly provides more challenge from a sporting point of view.As they progress into the sport, skin divers may utilize a variety of special equipment also employed by scuba divers. Many consider a sharp diving knife to be essential equipment for any divers who hold their breath underwater.Some skin divers utilize full wet suits, depth gauges and other items associated with scuba activities. Information on this equipment and its use in both skin diving and scuba diving is included in the next chapter.

FOUR

BASIC SCUBA DIVING

Since the dawn of history man has had to go into and sometimes under the water. From the times of Homer, Alexander the Great, Aristotle, Julius Caesar and down through the centuries, men have sought ways to extend their diving time and to go deeper into the waters of the world. During these centuries, except for the past decade or two, the primary objective of the diver could be relatively expensive.The techniques of diving practiced then, as well as the equipment itself, required several men in a diving crew, yet diving was still economically feasible because it was being done for gain.

The sport diver, however, receives no gain from using the equipment except pleasure and possibly a limited amount of food. To this diver, one of the primary considerations in the purchase of equipment is cost. Because of this the trend in sport-diving equipment has been away from complex equipment.

Self-contained underwater breathing apparatus, from which the word SCUBA comes, has long been used. The first such equipment, designed by William H. James in 1825, was a thin copper or leather helmet fitted with a window. To this was attached a short diving dress or suit, having elastic waist and armholes. Air was carried in an iron reservoir in the form of a cylindrical belt. The iron container was charged to about 450 psi, a tremendous pressure for those days.

In 1943 Jacques Yves Cousteau tested a combination of a mask with a demand regulator and a high pressure diving tank worn on the back. It was the world's first successful fully automatic self-contained underwater breathing apparatus.

Self-contained underwater breathing apparatus is available in two basic types. One is *open-circuit,* in which air is breathed from the compressed-air tank and exhausted into the surrounding water as the diver exhales. The other is *closed-circuit,* in which the breathing gas is exhaled into a closed system, filtered,

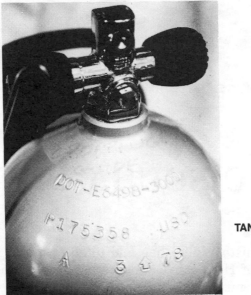

TANK MARKINGS

recirculated and rebreathed by the diver. Closed-circuit scuba requires special training and maintenance and is not recommended for sport diving.

Early models of open-circuit scuba included the *continuous-flow* system. As its name suggests, this type sends a constant stream of compressed air from the tank past the diver's mouth, whether or not he or she is using it. Such steady flow of air is so wasteful and so sharply limits time underwater that it is impractical and seldom used.

Diving apparatus actually used for breathing below the surface is composed of three main items of equipment, each of which is essential. They are the *compressed-air tank,* the *tank valve* and the *demand regulator.* There are numerous different types and manufactures of these items on the market, many of which have proved to be excellent in actual service. No one manufacturer or model, however, is necessarily ideal for all divers. Each diver will have individual requirements and preferences and should consult the diving instructor and other experienced divers before making a final selection.

EQUIPMENT

In addition to the equipment used by snorkelers and skin divers, scuba divers must be trained in the use and maintenance of a number of items.

TANKS

Scuba tanks are available in a number of sizes and are made of either steel or an aluminum alloy. Until the early 1970s, nearly all compressed-air diving tanks were steel. Since that time the aluminum tank has become increasingly popular. A tank of either material is acceptable as long as it conforms to the requirements of the U.S. Department of Transportation.

Tanks in common use in sport diving vary in capacity from 18 to 80 cu ft and a working pressure from 1800 to 3000 psi. The 71.2-cu-ft steel tank, used by more divers than any other, weighs about 28 lbs empty and 35 lbs full, and is about 2 ft long and 8 inches in diameter. Depending on design, it will take internal pressure up to 2475 psi. When full, a "seventy-one," which has a capacity of about 1/2 cu ft, will contain approximately the same amount of uncompressed air as a telephone booth.

Many modern tanks are made of aluminum alloy. Two advantages of the aluminum type are a capacity of 80 cu ft and a working pressure up to 3000 psi, also depending on design. Another desirable feature of the aluminum tank, unlike the steel tank, is its rustproof nature.

Steel and aluminum tanks are equally durable if kept free of damage and clean and dry inside. Steel tanks should be galvanized outside to protect against rust. A number of other coatings are also used on tanks for appearance and protection, but because they are easily scratched their chief contribution is color. Size of tank is often a matter of diver size, individual preference and type of use.

Compressed-air tanks are made in many sizes and to various specifications, as defined in Title 49, Code of Federal Regulations, U. S. Department of Transportation, Parts 100 to 199.

Each tank must have the tank type, working pressure, date of manufacture, manufacturer, for whom manfactured and a serial number stamped into the material of which the cylinder is made. In addition, the stamped information will indicate any subsequent inspection dates and whether the tank is approved for overpressure filling.

The data stamped into the shoulder of a scuba tank will usually begin with either DOT (Department of Transportation) or lCC (Interstate Commerce Commission). Tanks properly cared for and not damaged or over filled can be used for years.

The data stamped into a tank are:

1. Federal controlling agency (DOT or ICC),
2. Type of metal tank is made from (3A, 3AA, etc.),
3. Allowable pressure (psig),

4. Serial number for identification,
5. Manufacturer's identification,
6. Date of first hydrostatic test,
7. Manufacturer's or distributor's symbol,
8. Pressure test history.

Of these data, the most important for a diver are generally the type of tank, allowable pressure and the most recent test date. Other data required include the words *spun* or *plug* when an end closure has been made by one of these methods, and the identity of the inspector. If the data contain a symbol between the month and year stamped on the tank, that mark identifies the inspector in each case.

A plus sign (+) after the date of manufacture indicates that a 10 percent overfill at 70°F is permitted, but only during the first 5 years after the manufacture date. Dates appearing below the date of manufacture indicate when the tank was tested hydrostatically for further service. Tank markings will appear as shown in the illustration.

Although most scuba tanks are made of steel, aluminum tanks are becoming increasingly available. One advantage of the aluminum tank is its relatively light weight. Like steel tanks, their manufacture and maintenance are carefully controlled by DOT.

The Department of Transportation requires that scuba tanks be hydrostatically tested (underwater) for pressure safety every 5 years from the date the tank

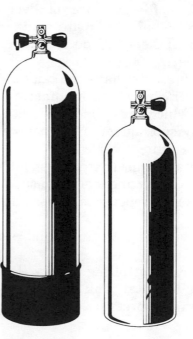

TWO TYPICAL TANK SIZES 80 cu ft 50 cu ft

was manufactured. It is advised, however, that sport divers have compressed-air tanks tested hydrostatically at least every 3 years, and inspected internally every year. Any time a tank is suspected of being damaged in any way, it should be inspected and tested regardless of how recently the last test was made.

If a tank fails to meet test requirements, it is considered unsafe for further use and no new date is stamped on it. No reputable vendor will fill a tank if more than 5 years have elapsed since the last date stamped on the tank—whether or not it was used for diving during that period.

Scuba tanks come in a variety of sizes depending on capacity, ranging from 18 cu ft to about 80 cu ft, and from 1800 psig to about 3000 psig. Manifolds and pack frames are available for mounting two or more tanks as a single dive unit. Tanks outside this capacity range may be used provided they are classified by an ICC or DOT rating as 3A or 3AA and can pass inspection and hydrostatic testing.

A diver should not invest in any tank without some thought as to the size best suited to the type of diving he or she plans to do. An old tank, or one that shows scratches, nicks or signs of corrosion, should not be purchased without proper certification that it is still serviceable. Foreign-built tanks may not be refilled by compressed-air vendors because they cannot be proved to meet DOT materials and manufacturing requirements. Also, many foreign tanks have metric threads in the neck, and standard valves will not fit them. Neck threading may also be a problem with some tanks that were not built to diving-tank specifications.

The Compressed Gas Association (CGA) has established certain practices and procedures to be followed by its members. These guidelines comply with the controls set by state and federal regulatory agencies and are available to all compressed-gas vendors and to the general public at small cost. If divers plan to inspect and fill their own tanks, copies of the appropriate CGA pamphlets should be acquired for ready reference. They may be had by contacting the Compressed Gas Association, 500 Fifth Avenue, New York, New York 10036.

Pamphlet C—6, "Standards for Visual Inspection of Compressed Gas Cylinders," identifies a high-pressure cylinder as one having a working pressure of 900 psig or higher. Most diving tanks are in this category. As suggested earlier, tanks should be carefully examined for signs of pitting, corrosion, dents, cuts, scratches or nicks, and for heat damage. If a tank shows evidence of fire damage (charred paint) or a burn by an arc or torch, it should be taken to a reliable service shop to be inspected and tested hydrostatically.

To further inspect the tank it should be cleaned so that all surfaces are visible, whether bare metal or coatings that are made to adhere tightly to the outside of the tank. If general corrosion or pitting is visible, the tank should be taken to a reliable service shop to determine the extent of the damage.

If the tank has a "boot" on the bottom to help it stand in an upright position, the boot should be removed to permit inspection of the tank metal beneath it.

Gouges and nicks caused by sharp edges on the tank bottom can cause metal stress and should be repaired even if the damaged tank passes a hydrostatic test. A retest is required after the repair.

A general guideline on dents is that they are acceptable up to $\frac{1}{16}$-inch deep if the diameter of the dent is at least 32 times the depth. Sharper, deeper dents could mean stress damage that affects the safety of the tank under high pressure.

As a good rule, damage that displaces or removes tank wall material to the point where the thickness of the remaining wall is close to the minimum specified for that tank in the Code of Federal Regulations is evidence enough to retire the tank.

Pamphlet P—5 offers "Suggestions for the Care of High-Pressure Air Cylinders for Underwater Breathing." These and the following suggestions will help ensure a long and safe service period for your diving tanks.

1. Never pressurize a tank above its rating. Tank pressure ratings are established for filling at 70°F. Before filling at temperatures much above or below 70°F, seek reliable professional advice.
2. Recharge with pure air only. Impure air may be contaminated with toxic or corrosive gases harmful to both you and your equipment.
3. Use only air. Even mixtures of pure oxygen and nitrogen in improper amounts can cause no-decompression diving problems or oxygen poisoning.
4. Keep water out. Keep the tank valve closed after air pressure gets down to 25 psig. A tank that shows 30 psig at the surface is "empty" at about 35 feet in either fresh or salt water.
5. Handle the tank carefully and avoid dropping it. Lay it on its side when unattended, particularly where people are moving about. When transporting a tank be sure it cannot roll or move about. Check that other objects which might damage tank or valve cannot shift during transportation.
6. Check for moisture or oil. Remove the valve and examine interior for liquids at the end of each diving season. If contaminated it should be thoroughly cleaned and dried before storing. Any time a tank has been emptied during a dive or left empty with the valve open or unseated, check it for moisture.
7. Prevent corrosion. Internal corrosion can be prevented, or held to a minimum, by the inspection procedures above. If the tank has an internal coating that has been penetrated and is peeling off, it should be removed. (This is not a "do-it-yourself" project. Have a qualified professional do it.) Do not allow a tank to lie around with other wet gear. Rinse off the tank as soon as possible after an ocean dive to remove salt, and after a fresh water dive to remove all possible contaminants.

8. Do not lubricate. Lubrication may contain toxic materials that could be inhaled. Also, hydrocarbon lubricants (most oils and greases) can combine with air or oxygen under pressure to form an explosive mixture. Oil products often hasten the deterioration of natural rubber in diving equipment. Tank threads and other fittings are designed to make leakproof connections under normal tightening without the aid of lubricants.

9. Keep the tank cool. Do not store or transport tanks under conditions that may expose them to excessive temperatures. If overheated the safety valve may be actuated, causing loss of tank charge and requiring replacement of the safety device.

Remember, the scuba tank is your only source of air underwater. Take good care of it and it will take good care of you.

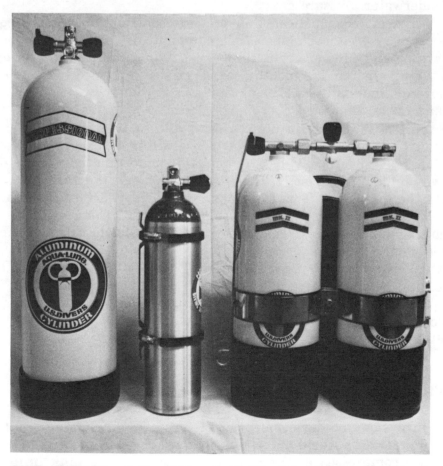

SCUBA TANKS: 80 cu ft; 15 cu ft "Pony Tank"; 50 cu ft double tanks with boots

TANK VALVES

Tank valves are used to control the flow of air from the compressed-air tank to the diver's breathing regulator and are made to be screwed into the threaded neck of the tank, where they remain until removed for replacement or tank inspection. Two types may be had. One automatically signals the diver when the air reserve is down to a certain pressure. The other only opens or closes to release or stop air flow.

"K" valve. This is a simple on-off valve that operates like a kitchen faucet. When it is turned to the on, or open, position, air will flow to the demand regulator until internal tank pressure equals water pressure or the air supply is exhausted.

Because the "K" valve lacks a signal for warning the diver that his air supply is about to run out, it is recommended that this type of valve be used only with an underwater pressure gauge.

"J" valve. A more sophisticated air-pressure control, the "J" valve contains a spring-operated reserve mechanism that automatically shuts off the flow of air when internal tank pressure falls to 300 psi. When the diver experiences difficulty in taking air from the mouthpiece, he or she is warned that the reserve is running low and manually pulls down the lever on the "J" valve to again release the flow and begin the ascent.

Both types of tank valve contain a *burst disk* or *blowout* plug that releases tank pressure harmlessly in the event of overfilling or expansion of the tank contents due to overheating. Valves without this important feature are not legal. Some valves have a small safety hole drilled through the threaded part that screws into the tank neck. This is an additional safety factor that allows air in tank to escape slowly and easily before the valve is fully removed. Unscrewing a valve from a tank could be extremely dangerous and should never be done except by a professional.

Tank valves use a high-pressure black "O" ring as a seal between tank neck and valve, and between valve and regulator attachment. Without an "O" ring between valve and regulator attachment, because of loss or damage, the valve is useless. For this reason it is advisable to carry a spare "O" ring in case one needs to change the regulator attachment.

DEMAND REGULATORS

It was the invention and development of the *open-circuit demand regulator* that made our underwater world accessible to the sport diver. With it he or she breathes pure compressed air from a high-pressure scuba tank in exactly the

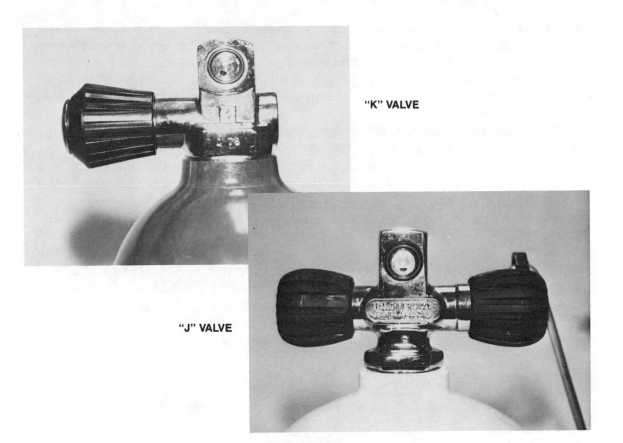

"K" VALVE

"J" VALVE

amount wanted, as it is wanted and at precisely the same pressure as the water pressure at any given depth. The air is then exhaled into the surrounding water without being recirculated and rebreathed. Only open-circuit demand scuba is recommended for the sport diver.

Demand regulators may be either two-hose or single-hose models. In either case, air pressure is reduced from tank pressure to ambient pressure in two stages.

The *two-hose* model operates as follows:

First-stage operation. In the first stage, high-pressure air from the tank flows through a spring-operated valve into an intermediate air chamber at about 120 psi above the ambient water pressure.

Second-stage operation. In the second stage, ambient water pressure acts directly against a flexible rubber diaphragm. As long as the diver doesn't inhale, the diaphragm remains stationary. As the diver draws in a breath, he or she creates a suction and reduces the air pressure in the second stage. Ambient water pressure then forces the diaphragm inward against a mechanism that opens the spring-operated valve in the first stage, and air flows from the tank to the diver through a semirigid, flexible air hose running from the regulator to the right side of the diver's mouthpiece.

When the diver stops inhaling, pressure on both sides of the second-stage diaphragm is again balanced and the valve closes off the flow of air from the tank. As the diver exhales, air from the lungs is forced from the left side of the mouthpiece, through a similar hose, to the regulator, where it is exhausted into the surrounding water.

Although the double-hose demand regulator is seldom used today for recreational diving, it does have certain advantages over the single-hose type: exhaust bubbles from the diver's mouthpiece are vented at the regulator behind the diver's back, thus allowing uninterrupted vision through the mask; and it is less likely to freeze up in special, cold-water diving than is the single-hose type.

In the *single-hose, two-stage* regulator, the first stage, like the two-hose type, is located at the tank valve. The second stage is built into the diver's mouthpiece. Air is carried from the first stage to the second stage by a high-pressure hose.

SINGLE-HOSE TWO-STAGE REGULATOR

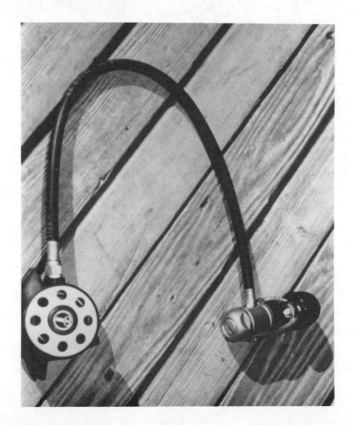

First-stage operation. The first stage of the single-hose, two-stage regulator is available in two designs, either a diaphragm type like that of the two-hose model above, or one using a piston valve. In both types air from the compressed-air tank is sent from an intermediate air chamber, through the high-pressure hose, to the second stage at about 120 psi above ambient pressure. It is this high internal pressure that requires a high-pressure hose to carry air from the first stage to the second.

Second-stage operation. In the second stage, air in the single hose is reduced from the higher pressure of the first stage to exactly the ambient water pressure at the level of the diver's mouth. There a second air chamber is separated from the surrounding water by a flexible diaphragm. As the diver inhales, a partial vacuum is created inside the chamber, allowing ambient water pressure to force the diaphragm inward. This activates a movable lever that opens an inlet valve connected to the high-pressure hose. As the diver stops breathing in, air pressure from the hose forces the diaphragm outward and the valve is closed when air pressure inside the chamber equals water pressure outside. It is this action of the second-stage regulator that balances air pressure and water pressure at any depth and allows the diver to breathe naturally.

The flow of air through the second stage can also be controlled manually by pressing inward on a *purge button* attached to the outside of the diaphragm. This action also opens the intake valve and allows air to enter the second-stage air chamber.

Exhaled air is released through the lower part of the regulator. As the diver breathes out, the increased pressure in the chamber opens a nonreturn exhaust

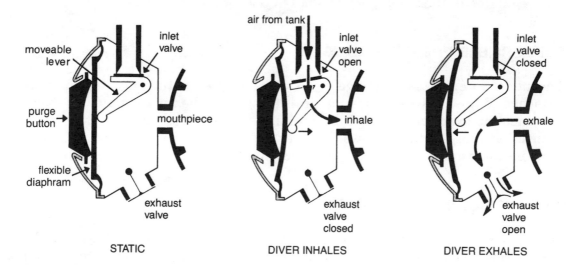

SINGLE HOSE REGULATOR, SECOND STAGE

valve and the air is forced out into the water. This completes the breathing cycle. The regulator is then ready for the next cycle.

SUBMERSIBLE PRESSURE GAUGE

The underwater pressure gauge is an absolutely essential piece of equipment. Attached to the tank valve or high-pressure part of the air regulator, it shows at all times the exact pressure within the tank. A high-pressure hose 2 to 3 ft long connecting gauge to tank allows the diver to attach it to a tank strap or buoyancy compensator where it is readily accessible underwater.

BUOYANCY CONTROL DEVICES

Buoyancy control is critical to anyone underwater, particularly the scuba diver who carries a tank and other related equipment underwater. Because the scuba diver is constantly confronted with buoyancy variations caused by depth changes, it is important that a precise method of buoyancy control be available.Such a method is provided by means of a buoyancy control device, or BCD, which is tied into the air supply from the scuba tank.In modern sport diving, the BCD has become an integral part of a diver's scuba equipment.

All BCDs generally have several things in common.In addition to the air supply from the tank, referred to as an auto-inflator, all BCDs have a large hose for oral inflation and for quickly dumping air. They also include a valved purging system for reducing buoyancy, and most have a third gas supply provided by CO_2 cartridges or a small air bottle.

These needed features have been provided in several formats:

1. *Standard BCD*. This is the "horse collar" type of vest which circles the head and covers the chest. This type of vest is the most common in use today and is available with the widest range of features, including separate air cylinders for filling the vest.
2. *Back-mounted BCD*. This device has an inflatable bladder that circles the tank and does not attach directly to the body. It has met with wide acceptance for some specialized applications, such as cave diving, but is controversial among many ocean divers. Generally, the back-mounted BCD lacks a backup inflation system and will not support the diver in a face-up position.
3. *Vest or jacket BCD*. Problems with the back-mounted type led to the development of a new generation of BCDs that combines many of the best features of both the standard and the back-mounted models. These BCDs look very much like a suit vest. They have backup inflation systems and will support the diver with his or her head well out of the water.

STANDARD BCD

BACK-MOUNTED BCD

A good buoyancy compensator should provide at least 25 lbs of lift and should float an unconscious diver in a face-up position on top of the water.

After each dive the BCD should be partially filled with fresh water and rinsed thoroughly inside and out and drained. The flexible hose should also be flushed, making sure that the mouthpiece valve is clean and clear of salt water. The CO_2 cartridge, if the vest has one, should be rinsed and its mechanism properly lubricated to resist corrosion.

If the diver is wearing protective clothing, the vest is donned after the clothing and before any other equipment. If the diver is not wearing protective clothing, the vest is donned next to the skin. *Harnesses must be adjusted so as not to restrict inflation of the vest.*

The number of possible uses and the variety of BCDs available make practice mandatory. In using scuba, oral inflation while submerged—to provide greater buoyancy and the necessary release of this expanding air upon ascent—must be practiced. This use will probably be the most common. Slightly positive buoyancy throughout the descent is maintained by periodic oral inflation.This requires complete familiarity with the oral-inflation mechanism. Preventing overinflation of the vest due to expansion of air introduced into the vest involves manual operation of the bleed-off mechanism. Familiarity with diving physics will indicate the need to relieve the expanding volume during ascent.

Inflation from the air supply or a supplementary tank is less difficult than oral inflation, but involves the same principles.

Due to the variety of vests, diving buddies and teams should familiarize themselves with the types worn by others so that they can be operated successfully in the event of emergency. This procedure should be practiced in a pool or in shallow water before making deep dives.

EXPOSURE SUITS

Another item that must be considered essential equipment for all but the most hardy scuba divers and the warmest climes is a suit worn to protect the diver against heat loss during underwater excursions.Some of these suits, in fact, tie into the scuba diver's air supply much like a buoyancy compensator and are used for that purpose in addition to thermal protection.During their training, scuba students should become familiar with the type of exposure suits they are likely to use in open water. These suits generally take two forms: wet and dry.

Wet Suits

The wet suit is the most common form of thermal protection used by the sport diver. It is a snug-fitting suit made of neoprene rubber consisting of small closed-cell bubbles filled with a gas. The wet suit allows a thin layer of water inside which is trapped next to and warmed by the skin. The snug fit of the suit reduces

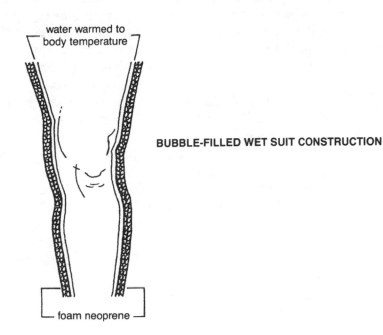

water warmed to body temperature

BUBBLE-FILLED WET SUIT CONSTRUCTION

foam neoprene

WET SUIT

or prevents circulation of water through it from the outside, and the gas-filled bubbles further reduce heat loss through the suit material by conduction.

Today the wet suit is one of the most important pieces of equipment used by a diver. Thickness of suit and amount of body coverage required depend on surrounding temperature and length of time spent in the water. In addition to providing warmth, it protects against sunburn, bruises, cuts and abrasion of the skin.

The gas-bubble construction of the wet suit increases the buoyancy of the wearer, which must be controlled by proper use of weights on the weight belt. As the diver descends, compression of the closed gas cells in the suit reduces buoyancy, and this effect must in turn be offset by a buoyancy compensator.

Wet suits vary in construction and are available in different thicknesses, from $1/8$ to $1/4$ inch. The thin diver will need a thicker suit than a heavy diver does because of the difference in the amount of body heat produced by each. A very active diver will also need less insulation because of the body heat generated during the dive. Absolutely necessary is a proper, snug fit to reduce flow of water next to the skin, to avoid air or water pockets and to allow maximum freedom of movement, breathing and blood circulation.

Zippers, used at different places on some wet suits for convenience in donning and doffing, can also reduce water tightness and increase chilling. Nylon lining that stretches four ways will often increase the life of the suit, as will thorough rinsing in fresh water and airing after each use. In drying and storing, wire hangers should be avoided because they may rust and damage the suit.

It is suggested that the prospective buyer of a wet suit, as with all important items of diving equipment, consult the instructor and other experienced divers before making a final selection of this valuable and important piece of gear, whether custom made to the user's individual requirements or a standard size and name brand.

Dry Suits

Another type of suit designed to protect the human body from heat loss, which is 25 times greater in water than in air, is the dry suit. As its name implies, this suit is designed to keep water from entering. It uses a layer of air inside the suit plus the suit material itself to insulate against cold. Dry suits are generally more effective in protecting the diver against heat loss than are wet suits. At the same time, dry suits are more expensive and more complicated to use. The dry suit is affected by pressure, not only by the compression of the suit material itself but also by the reduction of air volume inside the suit as the diver descends. Dry suits are designed so that air can be added to the inside of the suit from the diver's scuba. Regardless of their level of training in other areas, scuba divers contemplating the use of a dry suit should receive special training for this equipment before using it in open water.

BACKPACK

BACKPACKS

The diver's scuba equipment is rounded out with the backpack, which is used to hold the tank, and sometimes the buoyancy control device, next to the diver's body. Backpacks are made in a variety of styles, with two adjustable straps fitting over the shoulders and one around the waist. The waist strap and at least one shoulder strap usually have a quick-release buckle for fast removal of the pack. A retaining band designed for ease in changing tanks locks the tank to the pack frame. All parts are made of corrosion-proof materials and can be maintained by rinsing and seeing that all fittings are secure. Some types of quick releases may require occasional lubrication. When a backpack is not in use, the straps should be wrapped and secured to keep them from getting in the way during transport.

DIVE PREPARATIONS

A successful scuba dive depends not only on what the diver does in the water but also on the effectiveness with which he or she prepares for the dive. Divemasters, charter boat operators and fellow divers often make preliminary judgments about an individual's diving ability based on the way in which he or she prepares for the dive. Predive activities should be learned and practiced by students of diving with the same diligence with which their underwater activities are pursued.

FILLING THE TANK

Air is the natural atmosphere of the earth. It is an odorless, colorless and tasteless mixture of nitrogen and oxygen, and contains small amounts of water vapor, carbon dioxide and several other gases in very tiny amounts. For practical purposes breathing air is considered to be 78 percent nitrogen and 21 percent oxygen by volume. The traces of other gases, being so small, are included in this ratio.

Compressed air for breathing may be prepared by compressing atmospheric air or by mixing 78 parts of pure nitrogen with 21 parts of pure oxygen. Where it is made by compressing the air, filters are used to remove hydrocarbons, CO_2, CO, water vapor and other harmful gases. Because some of these contaminants may be present in the compressor itself, filters are required between the compressor and the tank to screen them out. The filters should be inspected regularly to make sure that they are in good condition and not saturated with the contaminants, thereby losing their effectiveness.

Most companies that manufacture pure air from nitrogen and oxygen do so in large volume for special and industrial use. Some, however, make limited quantities available for breathing purposes as a community service to divers. This type of air may vary slightly from the 79/21 mixture but will always be within 1 or 2 percent and is considered by some vendors to be the purest form of breathing air. However, do-it-yourself mixing should not be attempted. Oxygen under pressure is much more dangerous to handle than compressed air. Getting the correct mixture is also tricky. High or low concentrations of oxygen could cause problems with oxygen poisoning, or with nitrogen narcosis or bends, respectively.

A number of organizations and institutions, all of a nonfederal nature, have been working on standards of air purity for many years. The Compressed Gas Association publishes the *Handbook of Compressed Gases*. The American National Standards Institute, which is concerned with standards for all aspects of scuba diving, issues a *Minimum Course Content for Safe Scuba Diving Instruction Z86*. Additional copies of this publication can be ordered from the Institute at 1430 Broadway, New York, New York 10018. The diver who is concerned with the purity and safety aspects of compressed breathing air is advised to consult these publications.

Divers should always buy breathing air from a reliable dive shop or compressed air dealer. If you maintain your own compressor, keep it in good repair and always change the filters before they become overloaded. Most compressed-gas dealers and many dive shops will analyze your air supply for a modest charge if you have any reason to question its purity.

Small portable compressors are available that are designed for charging scuba tanks. They may be driven by either electric motors or gasoline engines. Such pumps usually compress air at rates from 0.3 to 1.5 cu ft per minute, making the filling time relatively long. These small compressors are not designed with the capacity of filling 3000 psig tanks. Compressors with greater pump rates and higher pressures can be purchased, but because of their size they are not easily portable.

When using a compressor driven by a gasoline engine, be sure that the exhaust fumes are downwind from the intake side of the compressor and that proper filtering of the compressed air keeps exhaust fumes from entering the scuba tank.If an oil-lubricated compressor is used, similar precautions must be taken to prevent oil vapors from contaminating the breathing air.

As air is being compressed, its temperature rises. This happens when tanks are being filled. If they are filled slowly the surrounding air or water will cool the tanks off. Because water cools better than air, tanks are often placed in water while they are being filled. If the tank is allowed to stay hot while it is being filled, it will not contain as much air (measured in cu ft) as if it were filled cool, even though the gauge reads the same pressure for the hot tank. As the hot tank is allowed to cool the pressure will drop.

Tanks should be filled and gauged at 70°F to get a full tank.

If a tank is suddenly drained the reverse can happen. Turning the tank valve wide open to drain it may cause water and ice to form on it as it cools. The danger is that water may condense on the *inside* of steel tanks, causing rust to form. To avoid this, don't drain tanks quickly.

An economical way to fill scuba tanks is the "cascade" system, which uses several large cylinders (or tanks) having as much as 360 cu ft capacity and 3500 psig each. These large containers can be supplied by a compressed-air manufacturer or dealer in various combinations of volume and pressure. The type to be used is determined by the size and frequency of diving refills as well as the working pressure of the tanks to be refilled.

When using a cascade system you buy only the air, not the large cylinders. Most suppliers allow a reasonable time for using the air purchased. After that period, rent, or "demurrage," is charged on the containers. For that reason the greatest economy is achieved by efficient use of the rented system in terms of capacity and frequency.

For efficiency in recharging, at least three large cylinders should be set up in a bank and connected one to the other by a main line, or manifold. Little advantage is gained by using more than three or four cylinders. The main line is in turn connected to the charging line for the scuba tank. This line should have a bleed valve for relieving pressure after charging the small tank and before disconnecting it from the system. The scuba tank should be immersed in water to keep it at room temperature, preferably at 70°F, as it is being filled.

Each large cylinder is connected to the main line by a separate valve. To fill a scuba tank the valve on one of the cylinders is opened, allowing high-pressure air to bring the small tank to the desired pressure. After one or two small tanks have been filled, the pressure in the large cylinder being used may be reduced to 1600 psig or less. The valve on the first large cylinder used is then closed, and the valve on the second cylinder is opened and other small tanks filled at high pressure. This process of shifting from one cylinder to another is followed until the pressure in all the large cylinders is down to a point at which they can no longer bring small tanks to the desired pressure. This will allow the filling of some diving tanks to a relatively low pressure for shallow-water or pool use, but not below 300 psig because that might allow moisture to enter the tanks. It is this process of using the higher pressure in the other tanks as the pressure in each is reduced, like a waterfall, that gives the cascade system its name.

This efficient combination of three large high-pressure cylinders joined together allows approximately 80 to 85 percent use of the air purchased. Also, using a three-cylinder manifold system can mean a saving of as much as 60 percent of the cost of sending the individual cylinders back to a plant for refill.

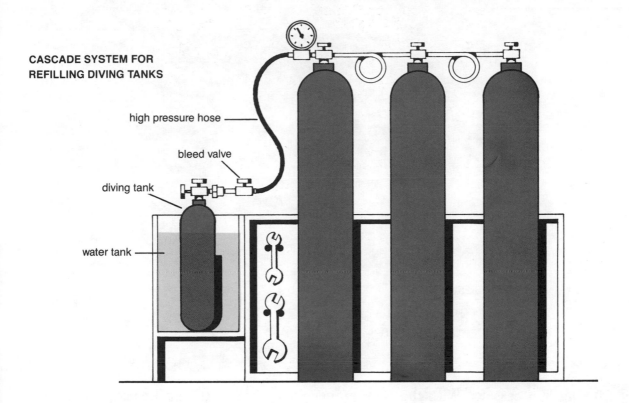

CASCADE SYSTEM FOR REFILLING DIVING TANKS

high pressure hose ————

bleed valve ————

diving tank ————

water tank ————

SCUBA ASSEMBLY

As you begin to assemble your scuba gear, stand the tank in an upright position and make sure that the backpack is securely attached so that no slippage can occur. With the backpack properly positioned, the tank valve should extend far enough above the pack for easy assembly of the regulator to the valve, but not so high as to interfere with free motion of your head while swimming.

During the scuba assembly process, never leave the tank standing upright in a situation where it may be knocked over or fall over with the motion of the boat.

If the scuba tank has been completely refilled following its last use, which should always be the case, a piece of tape should be wrapped around the valve outlet. As the first step in attaching the regulator to the tank valve, remove the tape from the valve and examine the valve opening. This opening should be surrounded by a black rubber ring, called an 0 ring. Inspect this high-pressure seal to make sure that it is securely in place within its groove in the valve and that it is clean and free from cuts or nicks. You should be prepared to replace this

**TANK WITH
BACKPACK**

0 ring if necessary. With the tank properly attached to the backpack, the valve opening should face toward the backpack, toward the back of your head.

Before attaching the regulator to the valve, crack the valve open briefly, allowing escaping air to blow any accumulated water or dirt out of the valve opening. Remember, your valve knob operates like any other, turning on counterclockwise and off in a clockwise direction.

The air inlet to your regulator is covered by a dustcap, which should be removed by backing off the yolk screw. Next, slip the yolk down over the tank valve, matching up the tank outlet with the regulator inlet. Make sure that the regulator hoses are positioned properly, with the hose leading to your primary second stage located so that it will hang over your right shoulder. Next, securely seat the regulator inlet into the valve outlet, and gently tighten the yolk screw. This screw should be centered in the small indentation on the tank valve provided for this purpose.

Make sure that the face of the submersible pressure gauge is turned away from you, and then slowly turn on your air. If the regulator is properly attached to the valve, you will hear air entering the system and the hoses will stiffen slightly. If you hear continuously escaping air, simply shut the valve off, purge the system and repeat the assembly procedure. After you have opened the valve all the way, turn it back about half a turn to avoid damage to the valve should it strike an object during the dive. Once your scuba system is "charged," you should check the reading of your submersible pressure gauge and inform your dive buddy and dive master of the amount of air available to you for this dive.

Test your regulator and any backup regulator by first depressing the purge button and then breathing on this system. Make sure that you exhale into the regulator during this test to check the exhaust valve. Air should flow freely in both directions through your regulators.

SUITING UP

Although a wet suit or a dry suit is the first thing to put on when suiting up, be sure to perform whatever gear assembly and other predive chores are necessary before donning your suit. This item, designed for comfort underwater, may make you uncomfortably warm if worn too long on the surface. A rubber suit should be put on carefully, gripping large handfuls of material and stretching the suit, particularly at the seams, as little as possible. Work into the legs, sleeves and boots a little at a time, pulling the sleeves and legs fully up the limb before proceeding further. Even when a wet suit or a dry suit is not necessary because of comfortable water temperatures, a diver would be well-advised to wear a shirt to

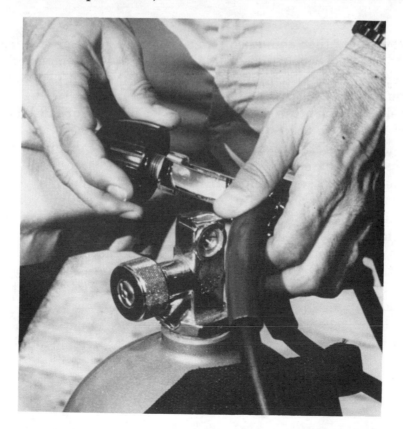

"ATTACHING THE
REGULATOR"

keep tank straps and other equipment from chafing. If you are wearing a BCD not attached to the backpack, this should be donned next. Remember, the straps of your BCD should be adjusted for proper fit before you put on your wet suit.

Before you slip into your scuba harness, make sure that you have positioned your weight belt, fins and mask in an accessible location. Your movements will be somewhat restricted once the tank is positioned on your back.

Several methods are available for donning scuba gear, all of which begin with arrangement of the shoulder and waist straps for accessibility and placement of air hoses to prevent accidentally strapping them into your harness. Perhaps the most common and versatile method for slipping into your harness is to have your dive buddy hold the tank at the appropriate level while you place your arms in the shoulder straps. Once you have taken the weight of the tank on your shoulders, your buddy can then hand you each end of your waist strap for you to buckle together. When it is convenient to stabilize the tank against some object, you can often strap on the backpack in a seated position. You then roll to a kneeling position before standing upright.

BCD stabilizer jackets, which are attached to the scuba backpack, make it possible to don your scuba gear with appropriate support from behind just as you would put on an ordinary jacket.

DONNING FINS

ASSEMBLED SCUBA HARNESS

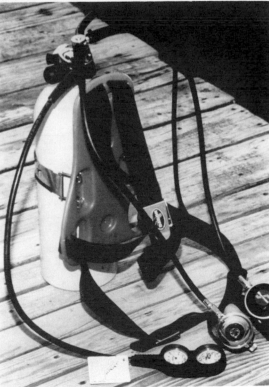

DONNING SCUBA HARNESS WITH BUDDY

70

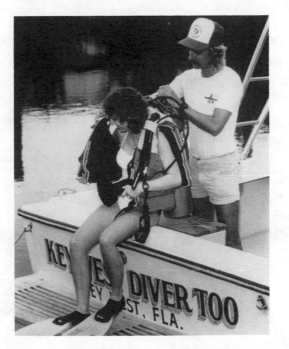

A weight belt must go over all of the other straps so that it may be removed easily. Always hold the weight belt by the end without the buckle to avoid having weights slide off the belt. To get the weight belt in the proper position, you may have your buddy hold it for you, hold it by both ends and step through it, or swing the belt behind you. In the latter case, be sure you have the space to perform this maneuver safely. Once the weight belt is positioned across the small of your back, lean forward slightly to relieve the tension on the front of the belt and make it easier to tighten it into position. It is wise to position your weight belt so that the quick-release buckle throws in the opposite direction from the buckle on the scuba waist strap, making it possible to discriminate easily between these equipment items when removing your gear.

After all of this, don't forget your mask and fins. This does happen. Find a stable position near the water's edge before donning the fins. It is dangerous and very poor form to move about on land or on a dive vessel with your fins on your feet. The key to putting on your fins with a heavy scuba tank on your back is to stabilize yourself and then pull the left fin on with the right hand and the right fin with the left hand. This crossover maneuver is less awkward and eases tension in your back and legs.

Don't forget that your mask should have been defogged before you slipped into your scuba harness. If you have forgotten this until the last moment, ask

someone who is not yet suited up to rinse your mask for you. Make sure that the mask is securely in place before entering the water, and do not remove the mask from your face until you are back on the boat or on dry land following the dive.

The final step in suiting up is a gear check. First, check your own equipment to make sure that your air is on, that you have plenty of it, and that everything is working properly. Then, inspect your dive buddy's gear while he or she inspects yours. Remember, a diver's predive behavior reflects how he or she will perform in the water, so examination of your buddy's gear for correctness and function helps you to familiarize yourself with his or her diving competence as well as the equipment. A buddy gear check will also permit you to assist each other more efficiently should it become necessary during the dive.

The scuba diver should enter the water with sufficient air in his or her BCD to provide slight positive buoyancy, using one of the entry techniques described earlier in this book. At this point, the diver should make final adjustments in the suiting-up process, tightening straps and positioning equipment to conform to the weightless environment. Upon completion of these finishing touches, the fully equipped scuba diver is ready to begin his or her underwater adventure.

**LEAN FORWARD
TO TIGHTEN
WEIGHT BELT**

STRAIGHTEN UP AND BUCKLE WEIGHT BELT

BREATHING COMPRESSED AIR

The direct effects of pressure on the descending scuba diver are the same as those described earlier for the breath-hold diver, with the exception of lung volume, which is maintained at its normal level by compressed air regulated according to depth. The pressure of air in the lungs is maintained at a level equivalent to the surrounding water. Because of the presence of pressurized air in the lungs, the scuba diver must consider some special factors in order to ensure his or her safety underwater. These factors include the direct effects of pressure during ascent and the indirect effects of pressure while at depth.

AVOIDING LUNG DAMAGE (PULMONARY BAROTRAUMA)

Few of the air spaces in the body are likely to give a diver trouble during ascent. Even an ear or sinus that gave you a bad time on the way down will usually behave. Air in suits, face masks and other equipment normally escapes freely as it expands.

Very rarely, gas pockets in the gut will cause some trouble. This might happen if you swallowed air while at depth—or if you'd had some potent beans for lunch. If the resulting gas were too far from either end of the alimentary canal to escape readily, it might overfill the gut and cause pain. It would probably work its way out one way or the other without harm, but ascent should certainly be slowed down if abdominal pain develops.

Similarly, compressed air in the lungs which expands during ascent will escape without any problems, as long as the diver breathes normally during ascent. However, a diver can be in big trouble if he or she fails to exhale properly while ascending. *A scuba diver must never hold his or her breath while underwater.*

Remember, if a diver is at 99 ft and ascends, the air in the lungs will undergo a fourfold expansion by the time he or she surfaces. The volume will double between 99 ft and 33 ft, and it will double again between 33 ft and surface. The actual rate of expansion becomes more and more rapid as he or she approaches the surface even if the rate of ascent remains constant. If the diver has even a normal volume of air in his or her lungs when starting ascent, this expansion can fill the lungs completely, and any excess must be exhaled—or else.

Failure to let this expanding air escape promptly and adequately will cause the pressure in the lungs to rise above that in the rest of the body and on the outside.

Once the lungs are fully expanded, the resulting differential will increase directly with the distance of further ascent. Since the lungs are very delicate, it does not take much excess internal pressure to cause serious damage.

What, exactly, can happen? The most obvious thing is simply a *burst lung*—an accident which is about as ugly as it sounds, but which isn't necessarily fatal in itself. The most serious possibility is *air embolism*. With or without an obvious, " burst," a pressure of around 4 ft of water can force air from the air sacs or *alveoli,* into the blood vessels which surround them. Once the air is in the vessels, it is carried rapidly to the heart. From there, it is pumped out into the arteries which supply the whole body. And these are so arranged that some of the air is almost bound to go up the arteries which supply the brain.

Arteries look like the branches of a tree splitting and resplitting into finer and finer branches and twigs. Therefore, a bubble of any size much larger than a red blood cell is bound to get stuck eventually. It will then form a plug *(embolus)* which will keep blood from flowing any farther in that particular branch. The brain tissue beyond the plug will be deprived of its blood supply and can survive total deprivation for only a few minutes without permanent damage.

A person who has suffered this kind of accident may be unconscious even before reaching the surface, or he or she may climb out and appear normal for as long as a minute or two. It is possible to have a very small embolism with only limited symptoms, but this is rare. Usually, the victim collapses, loses consciousness and may go into convulsions. Other signs, such as showing bloody froth at the mouth, breathing difficulty and turning blue, will depend mainly on the extent of lung damage and the presence or absence of other consequences of overpressurization of the lungs. Sometimes the respiratory center will be involved in the embolism, and breathing will cease.

The only treatment with real hope of success is *recompression*, but even if this is done promptly, it carries no absolute guarantee. The desired effect is to reduce the size of the bubble-plugs to the point where substantial blood flow can resume. This phase may be rapid, but considerable time is then required to ensure that the bubbles are absorbed and will not simply re-expand when the pressure is returned to normal.

Other possible consequences of overinflation of the lungs are usually far less serious than air embolism, but they deserve mention.

Mediastinal emphysema—air forced into the tissue spaces in the middle of the chest. Symptoms may include chest pain, trouble in breathing, trouble in swallowing, shock.

Subcutaneous emphysema—air under the skin, usually around the base of the neck. This is not serious in itself, but it is often associated with mediastinal emphysema. Air in the neck region may interfere with talking, breathing or swallowing.

Pneumothorax—air in the space between the lungs and the lining of the chest wall on either side. This will cause the affected lung to collapse at least partially and may interfere with breathing. If pressure builds up in the pneumothorax, the lung will be completely collapsed and the contents of the chest will be pushed over to the other side. Both breathing and heart action may be affected.

Prevention is the key word in lung accidents. As a cause of death in scuba diving, these probably run a very close second to drowning. Many cases are probably not recognized as such even in autopsy.

In normal ascent with scuba, all you need to do is breathe normally throughout ascent. This keeps your "pipes" open.

Many lung accidents like air embolism occur during emergency ascents in which the scuba is out of air or not working properly. Here, the essential rule is to let the expanding lung air come out freely as you ascend. It is very important to have detailed plans for emergency ascend, to think them through and discuss them thoroughly in diving classes—and to practice them if appropriate safeguards can be provided.

In order to avoid the possibility of lung damage on scuba, whenever a scuba diver's regulator leaves his or her mouth, it should be followed by a chain of bubbles. The scuba diver should always exhale lightly and continuously when the air supply is interrupted, either by the removal of the regulator from the mouth or by depletion of the air supply. This will prevent what is unquestionably the most serious problem resulting from the direct effects of pressure on the scuba diver.

PARTIAL PRESSURES

So far we have dealt with the *total* pressure or air and how it varies with the changes in volume. Air, however, is a *mixture of gases,* each of which has its individual pressure. Although we commonly speak of it as oxygen, air, by volume or number of molecules, is 78 percent nitrogen,* 21 percent oxygen and 1 percent other gases, including carbon dioxide. Thus, oxygen accounts for about 1/5 the total pressure exerted by air, and nitrogen about 4/5. These fractions are called the *partial pressures* of the various gases. This is an important factor in diving, because the functions of the body are more directly influenced by the individual, or partial, pressures of metabolically active gases (such as oxygen or carbon dioxide) than by total pressure.

The composition of air is generally consistent everywhere, and precise values are given below. These values may vary in special cases. The exact composition is

*Although nitrogen makes up 78 percent of the air we breathe, from the atmosphere or compressed air tanks, it serves us mainly by carrying and diluting oxygen for use by the human system.

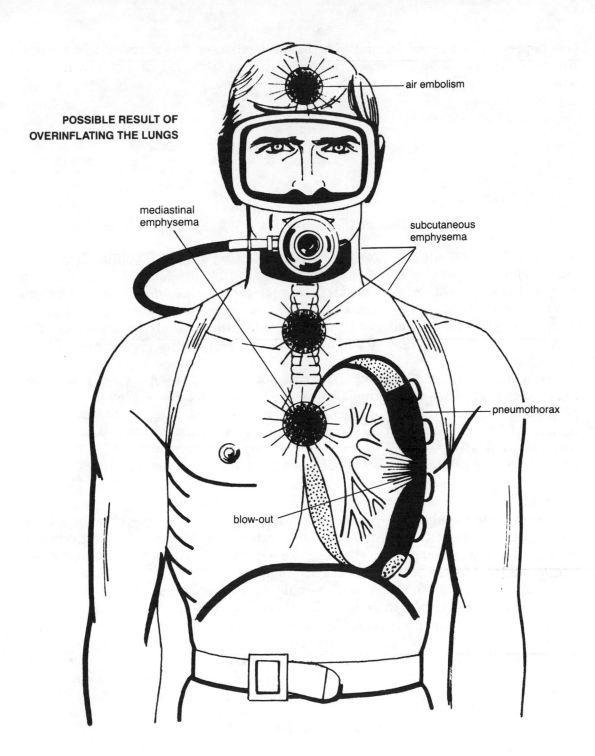

POSSIBLE RESULT OF OVERINFLATING THE LUNGS

air embolism

mediastinal emphysema

subcutaneous emphysema

pneumothorax

blow-out

also dependent upon the humidity, or amount of water vapor present in the air. Air analysis is usually expressed in percentages of "dry" air unless stated otherwise.

Composition of Dry Air

Gas	Percent of air (by volume or number of molecules)
Nitrogen (N_2)	78.00
Oxygen (O_2)	21.00
Carbon Dioxide (CO_2)	.03
Others, combined	.97
	100.00

Breathing too much oxygen over a period of time can be harmful, depending on how much is breathed, for how long, and at what pressure. John Dalton, in what is known as *Dalton's Law*, stated: *in a mixture of gases the pressure each gas exerts is proportional to its percentage of the total mixture*. This means that at sea level, where the air pressure is 1 atmosphere (1 atm), the nitrogen partial pressure is 0.78 atm (78 percent of 1 atm), and the oxygen partial pressure is 0.21 (21 percent of 1 atm).

When pressure on the air changes, the percentage of composition of each gas does *not* change. Thus, when the air pressure in a scuba tank is 2250 psi, it is still 21 percent oxygen, and the oxygen partial pressure of the air in the tank is 21 percent of 2250 psi, or 472.5 psi. In air used for breathing, the partial pressure of nitrogen will always be 78 percent of the total air pressure, and the partial pressure of oxygen will always be 21 percent of the total air pressure.

We have stated that breathing an excess of oxygen can be harmful. How is it possible to get too much oxygen if its percentage of the various gases that make up air does not change, even under increased pressure? One way is by breathing 100 percent oxygen for too long a period. Another is by breathing pure oxygen at a pressure of 2 atmospheres absolute (29.4 psia) for a much shorter time. A similar effect will be had by breathing compressed air at 297 ft in sea water where 21 percent of 10 atmospheres equals 2.1 atmospheres, or 30.9 psi.

This is in keeping with *Henry's Law*, which states that *the amount (concentration) of a gas that can be absorbed into a liquid is in proportion to the partial pressure of that gas*. Our bodies are composed mostly of liquid, and all liquids can absorb gas "into solution," meaning that the gas changes into and becomes a part of the liquid. For example, an unopened bottle of carbonated, or "soda," water contains carbon dioxide in solution under pressure. Before the bottle is opened, the contents look like plain water. Then, when the bottle is opened the pressure is relieved and the carbon dioxide comes out of solution in fizzing bubbles. The amount of gas that can be absorbed into any liquid depends on:

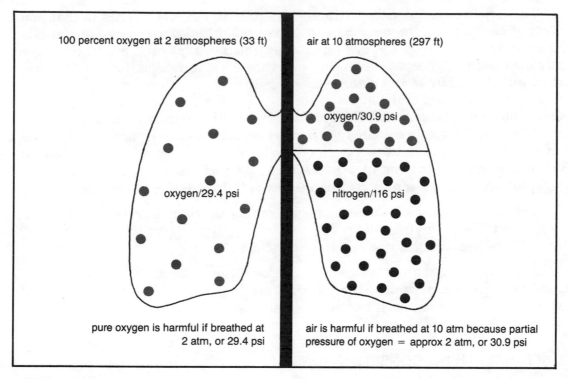

100 percent oxygen at 2 atmospheres (33 ft)

air at 10 atmospheres (297 ft)

oxygen/30.9 psi

oxygen/29.4 psi

nitrogen/116 psi

pure oxygen is harmful if breathed at
2 atm, or 29.4 psi

air is harmful if breathed at 10 atm because partial
pressure of oxygen = approx 2 atm, or 30.9 psi

OXYGEN POISONING

1. The chemical natures of the gas and the liquid.
2. The partial pressures of the gas (see Dalton's Law).

Thus, in the case of one gas (nitrogen) and one liquid (oil in the fat cells of the body), for example, the amount of nitrogen that can be absorbed by the liquid is in proportion to the nitrogen's partial pressure.

We are constantly taking the various gases that make up air into solution in the liquids that compose most of our bodies. At sea level this poses no problem. But when the partial pressures are raised excessively, problems such as muscular spasms, blurred vision, nausea, labored breathing, disorientation and fatigue can occur.

Keep in mind that it takes time for gas to be dissolved and absorbed, just as it takes time to dissolve sugar in water, so that sometimes the effects of excessive partial pressures of air or other gas mixtures may be subtle or slow to appear when diving. Obviously, it can be dangerous to dive with pure oxygen, even to as little as 33 ft, or to use regular air at a depth of 297 ft. This is one of the reasons for the rule limiting safe sports diving to a depth of 100 ft with clean scuba air.

The importance to scuba diving of Dalton's and Henry's Laws is that *some* effects of each gas on the body depend on its *individual partial pressure,* and not the total pressure or on the gas's percentage of the total mixture. These effects are called *indirect effects of pressure,** and they are the reason, for example, that breathing air at 297 ft is a dangerous practice.

The need to keep scuba air even purer than the air we breathe on the surface is also shown by Dalton's and Henry's Law. Poisons become more deadly in higher concentrations. For this reason a poisonous gas, such as one in the exhaust fumes of a gasoline engine, might represent only a small partial pressure at the surface. But, if included in the air in a scuba tank, its increased partial pressure and absorption could represent a real danger as you dive deeper. Remember:

1. Poisonous gases become more dangerous as their partial pressures increase with diving depth.
2. Pure breathing air is required for scuba.

Both the maximum amount of gas absorption (per Dalton's and Henry's Laws) and the rate at which it is absorbed are important when discussing medical problems of diving, such as decompression sickness.

OTHER BREATHING CONSIDERATIONS

The amount of air that has to be moved in and out of your lungs depends on the amounts of oxygen (O_2) and carbon dioxide (CO_2) to be transferred. These amounts depend mainly on how much muscular work you are doing at the time. The amount of carbon dioxide produced is usually just slightly less than the volume of oxygen consumed. At complete rest oxygen consumption can be as little as half a pint (one measuring-cupful) per minute.

During heavy exertion, oxygen consumption can reach 15 to 20 times the resting value—more in exceptional athletes. The maximum amount of oxygen a person can consume per minute is called the *aerobic capacity* and is one of the best indicators of physical fitness. Every person has an upper limit, usually set by the ability of the heart to pump blood and the blood's ability to carry oxygen to working muscles. The amount of oxygen consumed and carbon dioxide produced during a dive can vary tremendously. It can be as low as the resting rate or as high as the diver's aerobic capacity, depending on what he or she is doing.

The body has no real ability to store up oxygen as a reserve, but it does have a mechanism, *anaerobic metabolism,* that lets you work beyond your aerobic

---

*Indirect effects of pressure depend on the partial pressure of the individual gases and their concentration in the body.

capacity for short periods in emergencies. Calling upon the anaerobic energy source involves production of *lactic acid,* increased breathing, an *oxygen debt* that must be repaid quickly, and unusual fatigue. For many reasons, divers should train themselves to economize on exertion whenever possible.

Lung Ventilation

The volume of air that must be moved in and out of the lungs is ordinarily about 20 times the volume of oxygen being provided and of carbon dioxide being removed. For example, a very approximate average value for oxygen consumption in underwater swimming at sustainable speed is 1.5 quarts per minute; and the corresponding lung ventilation would be somewhere around 29 quarts per minute, or very roughly 1 cubic foot per minute. This makes a handy example, but individuals and conditions vary so much that it can be misleading and hazardous to employ such an estimate for practical purposes, such as calculation of air-supply duration in scuba. The actual value can be much more or much less.

The effect of depth on air-use rates is extremely important. Oxygen consumption and carbon dioxide production involve the same number of gas molecules per minute at a particular work rate regardless of depth. In contrast, adequate removal of carbon dioxide at any given rate of production requires the same volume of lung ventilation (as measured at depth) regardless of depth. A diver who is working hard enough to use 1 cubic foot of air per minute at the surface will continue to breathe about as deeply and about as often if he or she keeps up the same work rate at depth. But at 33 ft, each cubic foot of air will contain twice as many air molecules, and the diver's tank will be drained twice as fast. At 99 ft, where the pressure is 4 atmospheres absolute, the air supply will last only about 1/4 as long as at the surface.

Overexertion

Production of lactic acid during anaerobic metabolism causes a sharp increase in ventilation beyond what would otherwise be required. This is one reason why excessive exertion is hazardous in diving. It is also a reason why poor physical fitness limits activity and endangers a diver. One of the things that slows people down when they begin to reach their aerobic limit is "running out of breath." Unfortunately, the time-lag in this reaction allows you to go well beyond comfortable limits before you realize that you've done so.

Marked breathlessness is unpleasant enough on dry land. Underwater, even with the best-breathing scuba, it can be extremely disagreeable. Especially for a novice, it can be terrifying. In fact, this may be one of the most frequent causes of panic, and thus of serious accidents in diving. It can happen as a result of something as simple as trying to keep up with a better swimmer who believes in the "same-ocean buddy system." (If you and this diver are diving in the same ocean at the same time, you're buddies—enough to satisfy him.)

Hyperventilation

Hyperventilation, or breathing more than enough, is also possible. It can be done voluntarily, as before a breath-hold dive (see below), or it may happen involuntarily as a result of anxiety or fright. Beginning divers are likely to hyperventilate to some extent. The main result of hyperventilation is a lowering of the carbon dioxide level in arterial blood. Depending on the degree of lowering, this can cause such symptoms as lightheadedness, shaking, tingling in hands or feet, muscular spasms and impairment of consciousness. Such effects can be accompanied by increased anxiety, and a vicious cycle may result.

Carbon Dioxide Retention

In contrast to hyperventilation, a tendency to ventilate the lungs inadequately and thus to retain carbon dioxide exists in an unknown proportion of divers. This becomes evident principally during exertion; and in some individuals, subnormal ventilation and elevation of arterial carbon dioxide levels can be demonstrated even under good working conditions on dry land. Almost every effect of diving tends to aggravate the problem. The main consequences involve loss of orientation, alertness, response to stimuli, judgment and consciousness. Especially when carbon dioxide retention and nitrogen narcosis are combined, serious problems— including loss of consciousness–may occur.

As yet, there is no generally accepted way of testing divers so as to identify those who retain too much carbon dioxide. Clues almost certainly include using less air than others doing the same work underwater, and having severe headaches, especially after dives. Headaches are a common aftereffect following a period of high CO_2.

Breathing Patterns

The best pattern of breathing in diving is a relaxed, slow, regular rhythm that soon becomes second nature. A diver who becomes acutely conscious of his or her breathing is probably working too hard and should try to slow down and be more relaxed. Rapid breathing often involves shallow breaths and may use too much good air just to ventilate dead air space, while barely meeting the body's needs. "Skip-breathing" and artificial ways of trying to save air are not recommended because they tend to increase carbon dioxide retention and may be responsible for producing or aggravating that tendency. It is far better to reduce air use by conserving energy. Easy, relaxed habits of swimming and work usually permit the diver to do just as much as could be done with rapid movements and bursts of heavy effort.

Scuba with unnecessarily high breathing resistance will reduce a diver's capacity for comfortable work, and the increased density of air at depth not only increases the work needed to move air through both the scuba and the diver's own airways but also lowers the maximum amount that can be moved with any degree of effort. As a result, divers must be particularly careful to try to avoid doing too much at depth. Divers who smoke have been shown to be at a particular disadvantage because of the airway restrictions. As has been explained, poor physical fitness leads to low limits of physical effort, increased air use, and therefore to unacceptable hazards during work done at depth.

INDIRECT EFFECTS OF PRESSURE

The direct effects of pressure are those involving compression or expansion of gas or unequalized differences of pressure that affect the body structures. In many other situations in diving, it is the *partial pressure* of a gas that is crucial. This is the case, for example, in hypoxia and carbon dioxide excess. The partial pressure of the gas is what determines whether its "level" is too low, normal or too high. The matter is more complex in the case of carbon monoxide; partial pressure competes with that of oxygen. Under the heading of "indirect effects of pressure," we deal with additional problems where increased pressure has its effects primarily through the partial pressures or the gases concerned.

Oxygen Poisoning

Oxygen is essential for life, so it may seem surprising that it can have poisonous effects; but this is important for divers to understand. The normal partial pressure of oxygen in air is 0.21 atm, equivalent to 21 percent oxygen at sea level. Above about ½ atmosphere (e.g., 50 percent oxygen at surface or 25 percent oxygen at 33 ft), lung damage will develop within hours or days depending on the oxygen "dose." This is a recognized problem in treating hospital patients who need extra oxygen, but it seldom affects divers except in prolonged periods at depth in saturation diving or in extended recompression with oxygen breathing.

More important for most divers is the fact that oxygen can cause convulsions, like the fits or seizures of grand mal epilepsy. Drowning is the usual result of an underwater convulsion, but the risk of convulsion seldom arises unless the partial pressure of oxygen approaches 2 atmospheres. Such a dose is reached with pure oxygen at 33 ft, 50 percent at 99 ft, 20 percent at 297 ft, etc. Convulsions may occur at lower pressures with excess carbon dioxide either inhaled or retained.

There should be no possibility of oxygen poisoning in the use of open-circuit scuba unless charged with something other than compressed air. In most closed circuit scuba, only pure oxygen can be used; and the depth of safe diving is severely limited. Special closed- and semiclosed-circuit apparatus designed for gas mixtures must be used with great care to avoid oxygen poisoning. The severity of the limits is illustrated by U.S. Navy rules which normally restrict the use of 100 percent oxygen for working dives to no more than 25 ft, with a 75-minute time limit at that depth. Limits permitted for unusual circumstances extend to 40 ft, where only 10 minutes are allowed.

Nitrogen Narcosis

Air contains about 78 percent nitrogen. The high partial pressure of nitrogen encountered when breathing air at depth has two principal effects: narcosis (anesthetic and stupefying) and decompression problems.

Nitrogen narcosis was identified and named in the United States in the early 1930s. When Captain Jacques Cousteau and his associates "discovered" it much later, they called it "rapture of the depths." A less poetic but more accurate translation from the French would substitute drunkenness for rapture.

How narcosis works is not clearly understood, but it is probably similar to the way gases are used for anesthesia work—also incompletely understood. Nitrogen can probably be thought of as an anesthetic gas like nitrous oxide (laughing gas), * but much weaker. In any event, the effects can be compared with something a lot more familiar: alcoholic intoxication. The relationship to alcohol has been expressed in what might be called Martini's Law: the mental effects of each 50 ft of descent, while breathing air, are approximately equivalent to those of one dry martini.

At 100 ft ("tee martoonies"), for example, you may not be aware of reduced ability unless you try to do something that requires a quick response or accuracy of thought or motion, like reading a depth gauge, figuring decompression or handling an emergency. As with alcohol, it is difficult to realize—or be concerned about—how impaired you are. A diver breathing air at 150 ft or more may

*Nitrous oxide has become a drug of abuse in some circles. Divers should be aware that such use is extremely hazardous, especially because of the likelihood of hypoxia during administration. Deaths from nitrous oxide abuse have been documented. Additional hazards include habituation. Prolonged or repeated use can lead to damage to the blood-forming bone marrow and to degeneration of the spinal cord.

scarcely remember what job he or she descended to do, may care less and will generally be a menace to self. Susceptibility to narcosis varies considerably among individuals, but no one is immune. The risks are generally much greater for the scuba diver than for his or her counterpart in a hard hat—protected as this diver is by the suit, airhose, lifeline, communication circuit and tender.

Retention of carbon dioxide does not cause nitrogen narcosis, as some have claimed in the past; but excess carbon dioxide can greatly magnify the effects of nitrogen and other narcotic inert gases.

Helium has no apparent anesthetic action at depth, and this is the main reason for its use in deep diving.

Decompression Sickness

When the body is exposed to an increased partial pressure of any gas, increased amounts of that gas will go into solution in the blood and tissues. The gas gets in by diffusion through the membrane that separates the lung air spaces (alveoli) from the blood that flows around them. This blood becomes charged with the gas and then carries it to the tissues. When the body remains exposed to the same pressure, gases taken up in this way will remain in solution.

When the pressure is reduced, the gases will start leaving the same way they got in: through the circulating blood and the lungs. But getting all the dissolved gas out in this way takes a long time; and if the surrounding pressure is reduced too rapidly, the unloading process will fall seriously behind. The partial pressure of the tissue gas can then be quite far above the total (external, ambient) pressure, and a state called *supersaturation* will exist. A small degree of supersaturation can probably develop with little or no formation of bubbles, and some degree of bubble formation can apparently be tolerated. However, symptoms will appear if the process goes beyond a certain point.

Because it is constantly being consumed, oxygen seldom attains very high pressures in the tissues, and tissue oxygen pressure alone seldom starts bubble formation. But "inert" gases like nitrogen or helium—which the body does not utilize—can cause serious difficulties. Opening a bottle of carbonated beverage provides a good demonstration of the principle. Before the cap comes off, the liquid holds the gas quietly in solution. But removing the cap drops the pressure. The liquid becomes supersaturated and starts to bubble.

In bringing a diver up, the objective is to keep the degree of supersaturation from becoming great enough to cause the formation of bubbles. The guide for managing such safe ascent is called a *decompression table*. Following is an example, taken from the *U.S. Navy Diving Manual*. The ascent rate of 60 ft/min and

A CASE OF NITROGEN NARCOSIS—
"TEE MARTOONIES"

U.S. Navy Standard Air Decompression Table

Depth (feet)	Bottom time (min)	Time to first stop (min:sec)	Decompression stops (feet) 50	40	30	20	10	Total ascent (min:sec)	Repetitive group
							0	0:40	*
							2	2:40	N
							7	7:40	N
							11	11:40	O
							15	15:40	O
							19	19:40	Z
40	200	0:30							
	210	0:30							
	230	0:30							
	250	0:30							
	270	0:30							
	300	0:30							
							0	0:50	*
							3	3:50	L
							5	5:50	M
							10	10:50	M
							21	21:50	N
							29	29:50	(
							35	35:50	(
							40	40:50	
							47	47:50	
50	100	0:40							
	110	0:40							
	120	0:40							
	140	0:40							
	160	0:40							
	180	0:40							
	200	0:40							
	220	0:40							
	240	0:40							
							0	1:00	
							2	3:00	
							7	8:00	
							14	15:00	
							26	27:00	
							39	40:00	
							48	49:00	
							56	57:00	
						1	69	71:00	
60	60	0:50							
	70	0:50							
	80	0:50							
	100	0:50							
	120	0:50							
	140	0:50							
	160	0:50							
	180	0:40							
	200								
							0	1:10	
							8	9:10	
							14	15:10	
							18	19:10	
							23	24:10	
							33	34:10	
						2	41	52:10	
						4	47	59:1(	
70	50	1:00							
	60	1:00							
	70	1:00							
	80	1:00							

the specifed stops are *intended* to allow enough gas to depart naturally through the lungs to prevent trouble in almost all instances.

No stops are required for relatively short or shallow dives as a look at the table shows.The "no-decompression" limits as specified by the standard airdecompression table are of great interest to most scuba divers and are presented in the table below. As will probably become very clear, scuba divers are well advised to stay within these depth-time limits and to avoid the necessity of making decompression stops. Even so, it is necessary to consider the prescribed rate of ascent and to be fully aware of the implications of *repetitive dives* (see point 4 below).

"No Decompression" Limits

Depth (ft.)	Bottom Time* (min)
(less than 33)	(no limit)
35	310
40	200
50	100
60	60
70	50
80	40
90	30
100	25
110	20
120	15
130	10
140	10
150 to 190	5

Be sure to understand these important points about use of the decompression table and "no-decompression" limits:

1. *Depth* is tabulated in 10-foot steps. Unless your greatest depth corresponds exactly to one of these tabulated depths (and you must be sure of this), use the *next greater* depth in selecting your decompression schedule.
2. Remember that *bottom time* means the number of minutes that elape from the moment you leave the surface to the moment you start your ascent not just the time actually spent at maximum depth. Times are tabulated

Bottom time is the total elapsed time between leaving the surface and starting ascent—not just time spent at the maximum depth. Note that it would rarely be possible to make a dive to 150 ft or more, accomplish any useful work there and be ready to start up—all within five minutes; so attempting to make such deep dives on a "no-decompression" basis is seldom advisable.

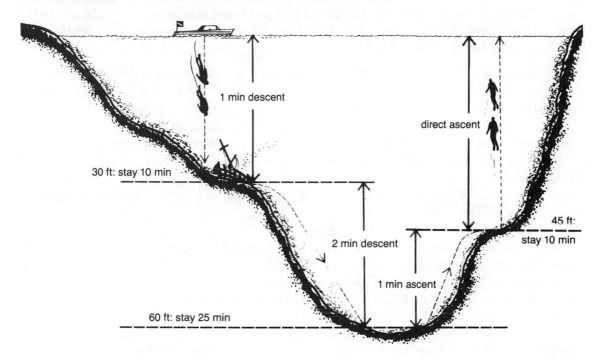

1 min descent

direct ascent

30 ft: stay 10 min

45 ft:
stay 10 min

2 min descent

1 min ascent

60 ft: stay 25 min

in 5-or 10-minute steps, and unless your time is exactly equal to one of the tabulated times, you must use the next greater one. *Example:* a 26-minute dive to 102 feet requires use of the schedule for 30 minutes at 110 feet.

NOTE: If a dive involves exceptional cold or hard work, add a safety factor by using the schedule for the depth and time beyond that which would normally be used.

3. *Rate of ascent.* The table was calculated and tested for an ascent rate of 60 ft/min (1 ft/sec), and this should be followed. If you come up faster you are omitting some of the decompression that ascent at the specified rate provides. If you come up slower, this amounts to spending more time at depth (and thus taking up more nitrogen) than was expected. If your dive was close to the stated depth and time of the schedule you are using, either mistake might result in decompression sickness.

4. *Repetitive dives* are defined as successive dives made within a 12-*hour* period. Every dive, whether or not it requires decompression stops, leaves some excess of nitrogen in the body. It leaves gradually while you are at the surface, but it is not completely cleared out in less than 12 hours.

Therefore, if you make another dive within a 12-hour period, your body will contain more nitrogen when you start up from the dive than it would have if the previous dive or dives had not been made. As a result, you will need more decompression—or will be able to spend less time at depth on a "no-decompression" basis.

The *U. S. Navy Diving Manual* provides a system for safe and sensible determination of limits and decompression schedules for repetitive dives, giving credit for nitrogen lost during the time at surface between dives.

Having to make decompression stops on ascent obviously makes scuba diving much more complicated, especially when there is a chance of running out of air during the stops, as is often the case. So, unless there is a very good reason for doing otherwise, the scuba diver is much better off to stay within the "no-decompression" limits and to make sure that he or she does not unwittingly go beyond those limits by making repetitive dives.

Diving in the decompression range, the suit-and-helmet diver has a lot of advantages: unlimited air supply; tenders who keep track of the time, depth and stops. Proper decompression can be accomplished with scuba, but it requires more planning and preparation and more attention to details than most scuba divers are willing to put into it. Mistakes are easier to make and more likely to be serious.

Many people have either or both of two serious misconceptions about decompression in scuba diving. One is that you will always run out of air before you can get into decompression trouble. This is not true even with ordinary single-cylinder rigs; and it is quite untrue with larger models and with unusually high charging pressures. If a successful "liquid-air" scuba ever becomes available, its duration will invite grave decompression problems.

Misunderstandings about air supply duration and decompression limits stem in part from improper use of round numbers on air-use rates. It is substantially true that an average diver doing moderate work near the surface will use about one cubic foot of air per minute. This provides a very useful illustration and example. But the same diver can use either a lot more or a lot less air if the work rate changes, while another may use considerably more or less air even at the same work rate.

The second misconception is that the U.S. Navy decompression tables include a large margin of safety and are so unnecessarily conservative that you can violate them recklessly. This impression has probably arisen from the fact that serious violations are occasionally committed with no apparent harm. The real truth comes out in a broader view: there is no great safety factor built into the tables at all. Any team that does a lot of diving will see its share of decompression sickness, including some serious cases, even if it follows the tables very closely.

Another myth concerns the *"un-bendable" diver,* who is under the impression that his or her extraordinary qualities of physical condition or spirit are a sure defense against bubble formation. It is true that susceptibility to decompression sickness can differ considerably among individuals.It can apparently vary also in the same individual from one time to another. Old "bubble-proof" may one day push his or her luck too far.

Unusually deep or prolonged air dives present difficult problems in decompression. The U. S. Navy schedules provided for such dives admittedly have a rather high incidence of bad results and should be avoided whenever possible.

The U. S. Navy tables are designed for diving in the ocean. Anywhere above sea level, "surfacing" puts the diver at a lower ambient pressure and under greater risk of bubble formation than was contemplated when the tables were calculated and tested. Diving in mountain lakes, for example, involves considerable risk if these tables are applied literally. Various rules, systems and tables have been put forward for dealing with this problem, but none has yet had adequate experimental validation, to this author's knowledge.

There is some evidence that even small elevations, such as the 600 to 800-ft altitudes found around the Great Lakes, may affect the outcome with some schedules.

Even after an uneventful "no-decompression" dive, divers will have significantly more nitrogen in their tissues than they had before. Lengthy exposures to altitude might bring about symptoms of bubble formation. Again, final evidence is lacking, but a simple rule that is almost certainly reliable is to put a 24-hour interval between surfacing from a dive and flying.

The foregoing discussions should have made it clear that decompression problems can complicate scuba diving greatly. Staying within no-decompression limits simplifies the process, and observing the general rule of not diving below 100 ft would also eliminate a number of problems.

The need for prolonged decompression is one of the most serious limiting factors in diving to greater depths and in tackling time-consuming jobs at any depth. Decompression time lengthens greatly as time increases at any given depth, but eventually (probably within 36 hours) the body becomes saturated with nitrogen (or helium) at the pressure of depth. Saturation means that the pressures of dissolved gas in all of the tissues have come to equilibrium with the external pressure of the gas, and no more gas will be taken up. Beyond this point of time, the decompression time needed on ascent will no longer increase. It will be very long—on the order of a half-day or more per 100 ft of depth—but a diver who has reached saturation would require no greater decompression time if he or she remained for a week or a month.

The saturation principle is the basis of the "undersea habitation" idea put into practice in U.S. Navy Sealab projects and similar enterprises. The same principle is equally important in systems that keep divers under pressure in a comfortable pressure chamber on a surface ship and send them to depth in a connecting submersible chamber. At the moment, the latter system is used more often, but improvements in equipment may make sea-floor living more attractive in the future.

Symptoms

The most frequent manifestation of decompression sickness is *pain*. This dominates the picture in about 90 percent of the cases. (Strictly speaking, "the bends" refers only to the painful form of decompression sickness, but the term is commonly used to refer to any manifestation and will be so used here.) Pain may occur anywhere, but it is usually confined to one well-localized part of the body, with joints in the limbs being most commonly affected.

A diver who has a real bends pain isn't likely to call it a mild symptom. However, there are some symptoms—fortunately less frequent than pain—that are really serious. These are produced by bubbles in the central nervous system (brain and spinal cord) or in the lungs. The lung symptoms are called "chokes." They may involve such things as shortness of breath, pain on deep breathing, coughing and the like, and should be given prompt treatment. The condition is probably caused by obstruction of lung blood flow by bubbles. Circulatory collapse and death may occur rapidly in untreated cases.

The central nervous system symptoms can include a great variety of disorders. The following list will give some idea of the possibilities:

1. Dizziness.
2. Weakness or paralysis anywhere in the body.
3. Numbness—loss of feeling anywhere.
4. Collapse and loss of consciousness.
5. Blindness or other disorders of vision.
6. Ringing of the ears or other defects of hearing.
7. Convulsions.

Any such development indicates that some part of the nervous system has been deprived of its blood supply or disrupted by pressure from a bubble in the tissue itself. Nerve tissue usually can't survive such abuse for very long, so treatment must be both prompt and sufficient to relieve the symptoms.

Serious symptoms do not necessarily follow only deeper, longer dives or more serious violations of tables. They can occur after relatively mild exposure with decompression that would ordinarily have been fully adequate.

The possible variety of symptoms of decompression sickness is so great that almost any abnormality which shows up after a dive has to be considered a possible "bend" unless it is obviously caused by something else. This can be misleading. For instance, a diver who develops a sore knee after a dive may know that he hit it on a rock during the dive—but such injuries may increase the chance of a bend in the affected location. The fact that a dive was within the "zero-decompression" limits or that proper decompression was given doesn't mean very much either.

Milder symptoms of decompression sickness, not usually treated by recompression, include *itching, rash* and *unusual fatigue.* Such symptoms may precede or accompany more serious manifestations, and divers experiencing them should be watched closely. Occasionally, rash may include or become a corpselike mottling. Rarely, swelling *under the skin* may become severe enough to require recompression. *Abdominal pain* deserves special mention. It may represent local bubble formation deserving treatment in its own right. More alarmingly, it may warn of impending spinal cord manifestations such as paralysis of the legs and lower trunk.

Even an experienced diving medical officer may have a difficult time deciding whether a certain symptom is due to decompression sickness. Frequently, a "test of pressure" has to be given; and, if this is inconclusive, the patient may have to be treated just to be safe.

Almost every bend, if untreated, will produce permanent injury of some degree. Whether this will be minor or serious depends on the location and severity of the case. The disability may not become evident for some time

Two commandments about decompression sickness are worth considering: (1) remember that almost anything can happen, and (2) when in doubt, treat—and treat adequately.

Additional information on the treatment of decompression sickness is provided in the first-aid section of this book.

WHAT TO BREATHE

Deciding what breathing gas to use in scuba is seldom a problem. With open-circuit equipment, compressed air is the only logical choice. With simple closed-circuit oxygen-rebreathing scuba, pure oxygen is the *only* choice. Nevertheless, there seems to be a lot of interest in the possibility of breathing something different, so the subject is worth some discussion.

The risk of hypoxia in a closed-circuit rig charged with something other than oxygen has already been explained.

Why not use oxygen in open-circuit equipment? There are several good reasons:

1. Danger of explosion on charging. Oil and oxygen will cause explosion if they combine under pressure. Oil may have gotten into the diving gear either during manufacture or repair, or as a residue of oil vapor from a previous air charge.

2. Danger of oxygen poisoning. Use of oxygen imposes severe depth-time limits that are not normally associated with open-circuit gear.
3. There are absolutely no advantages. Oxygen does not decrease the amount of gas you use, and you can't go deep enough to get any decompression advantage from it.

Nitrogen-Oxygen

Air is a nitrogen-oxygen mixture. Its main drawback is the amount of nitrogen it contains and what this means in terms of decompression. The most obvious way to remedy this is to boost the amount of oxygen present.If you cut the nitrogen percentage in half (40 percent nitrogen, 60 percent oxygen), you could theoretically double your absolute depth as far as decompression limits are concerned. But the corresponding increase in oxygen pressure would lead to oxygen poisoning long before you could take full advantage of the mixture.

In any event, using such a mixture in open-circuit scuba would hardly be advantageous enough to warrant the trouble of mixing and analyzing or the expense of buying the mixture. The short duration of gas supply at depth would keep you from getting much benefit from any extension of depth-time decompression limits.

Helium-Oxygen (heliox)

Granting that the breathing mixture has to contain oxygen and that the oxygen has to be diluted if you are going deep, the question boils down to what you can use for this dilution. Besides nitrogen, helium is almost the only practical possibility today. The compelling advantage of helium is its lack of narcotic effects. Its lesser density is desirable from the standpoint of respiratory effort at greater depths. Disadvantages include the effect of helium on voice intelligibility and more rapid loss of heat from the body. While helium-oxygen mixtures are essential for deep commercial diving, there are few advantages that would warrant their use in sport diving.

Hydrogen

The danger of explosion makes diving with hydrogen a specialized process, but most of the risk can be eliminated. Availability and cost compared to helium are the main reasons for continuing interest in hydrogen. Low density may make it the only suitable gas for extreme depths. Its small but definite narcotic effect may also be desirable for physiological reasons.

Rare Gases

Gases other than helium have been tried, but *argon* and *krypton* are more narcotic than nitrogen, and *xenon* is as potent an anesthetic as nitrous oxide. *Neon* lacks narcotic properties, but it is relatively dense. "Crude neon" is a mixture of neon and helium, a byproduct of liquid air production. It has been used for moderately great depths in commercial diving.

According to what is now known, any inert gas usable for diluting oxygen will entail much the same decompression problems as nitrogen. The idea of using combinations of inert gases may have some merit, and alternating them is part of one accepted deep-diving procedure. However, certain switches of inert gases can provoke bubble formation even with no reduction of pressure.

Breathing Apparatus for Mixed Gas

As mentioned above there is not much point in using nitrogen-oxygen or helium-oxygen mixtures in open-circuit scuba, and they absolutely must not be used in simple closed-circuit rigs because of the danger of anoxia.

The drawback with open circuit is the limitation of gas-supply duration. This can be overcome by using a system in which part or all of the gas is rebreathed. But safe rebreathing of mixtures requires apparatus which is far more complicated than the simple oxygen-rebreathing circuit. Such equipment is available and is in use for military and commercial diving, but its high cost and complexity place it outside the realm of practicality for sports use. The complexities are formidable, meticulous maintenance is essential and the potential hazards are very great. This is true even of the best equipment from experienced and reputable firms. A diver with a personal mixed-gas scheme on the drawing board is flirting with death.

The greatest potential for development of self-contained diving apparatus lies in the direction of mixed-gas scuba, but it is difficult to predict whether or how soon this sort of equipment will become practical for sport diving or whether it will ever be used widely where simpler systems could be used widely where simpler systems could be employed.

Special Problems of Women

Differences between males and females include much more than the obvious contrasts, and none of the differences that might be important in diving have been investigated systematically. Decompression tables and oxygen limits have been worked out for male divers and may or may not be fully satisfactory for women. Menstruation probably presents no special problems. Present information suggests that the risks of diving during pregnancy are unacceptable for the fetus in terms both of developmental defects arising very early and of decompression injury later on. It will be difficult to define safe limits and appropriate precautions. Women who are or may be pregnant should be discouraged from diving.

Drugs and Diving

Many diving fatalities and near-misses are thought to have occurred because of an unexpected effect of some drug or medication. Little is known scientifically except that the effect of diving on drug actions is largely unpredictable and often quite surprising. Divers should not only avoid self-medication but also be cautious about compounds prescribed by a physician. Alcohol and its aftereffects are known to complicate most of the medical problems of diving. Reports on marijuana and other drugs of abuse indicate that these regularly turn good dives into bad trips. The hazards and implications are obvious.

AIR CONSUMPTION

At times it is important to know how long to stay down on your air supply. For example, can you swim underwater to a shipwreck and still have enough air to look around, or should you snorkel there on the surface to save air? A common question asked by beginning divers is how long they can stay down with a tank of air. Once divers understand the relationship between pressure and volume as it relates to lung inflation at depth, they then understand that the diver's air consumption rate at depth (ACRD) is affected not only by breathing rate but also by depth. Although the volume of air required to fill the lungs and air passages of the body is the same at depth as it is at the surface, it will take more air to fill that volume at the higher pressure experienced underwater. For example, at 33 ft in sea water the absolute pressure is 2 atm, and at 99 ft it is 4 atm. Therefore, your air consumption rate at 99 ft would be twice that at 33 ft.

The amount of air in a tank is proportionate to the tank pressure. If you have 80 cu ft of air in a tank at 3000 psi at the start, and the pressure is reduced to 1500 psi, you will then have 40 cu ft of air left in the tank.

A diver's breathing rate will be affected by the water temperature, exertion and other factors, including level of experience. Any diver can obtain a rough approximation of his or her breathing rate simply by noting the depth of the dive, the time underwater and the pressure change during the dive. For example, let's suppose that the diver who reduced the tank pressure in his or her 80-cu-ft tank at 1500 psi hits a depth of around 33 ft during a dive that took approximately 20 minutes to complete. During those 20 minutes, the diver used approximately half of the 3000 psi, therefore half of the 80 cu ft of air in the tank, or 40 cu ft of air.

Since the diver was in 33 ft of water and less than approximately 2 atm of pressure, he or she required twice as much air to fill the lungs at that depth as would have been needed at the surface. Since the diver used 40 cu ft of air at 2 atm, he or she would use only half as much, or 20 cu ft of air, at the surface. This particular diver would ordinarily consume 20 cu ft of air in 20 minutes at the surface, giving him or her the breathing rate of 1 cu ft per minute. Using this breathing rate, the diver can now estimate the amount of breathing time he or she will have on a 100-ft dive under similar conditions of exertion, temperature and so on.

This diver, who uses approximately 1 cu ft or air per minute at the surface, will use four times that amount at 99 ft, or 4 atm. This diver then needs only to divide his or her air consumption at depth (4 cu ft per minute) into the number of cubic feet of air available with the tank (80 cu ft) to estimate the availability of 20 minutes of air during this dive.

A dive that will completely exhaust a tank should never be planned. There are two reasons for this: first, the diver should always allow a margin of safety in reserve air for unexpected changes in the dive plan and for emergencies; second, an "empty" tank is more likely to become contaminated than one with a small amount of pressure left in it. A good rule, which will be repeated elsewhere in this book, is to always have at least 300 psi in reserve at the end of the dive, and more for deeper dives.

A diver's air-consumption rate will vary from day to day, and from dive to dive, for various reasons. Some are difficult to predict—such as how cold you are, how strenuously you swim or work, and whether you breathe faster than usual because of anxiety. Divers come in all sizes, shapes and ages, varying degrees of physical fitness and diving experience, and may be of either sex. All these factors help determine the metabolic rate, which in turn controls the amount of air the lungs require per unit of time. Persons in good physical condition are generally more efficient in their use of energy, and those with a reasonable amount of fat under the skin are better insulated against heat loss in the water. Beginning divers, because of nervousness and lack of experience in conserving energy, use more air than they will need later on, and cold water tends to make many people overbreathe.Because of these and other factors—which differ sharply from person to person—the "average" diver is more a statistical figure than a real person. The individual diver may vary in breathing requirements depending on such things as amount (if any) he or she smokes, proper rest and level of anxiety.

UNDERWATER SWIMMING

Most divers are built in such a way that they can easily maintain a level attitude in the water without the counteraction of weights, or air in the BCD. This is an

ideal condition for swimming, both underwater and at the surface. Weights on a weight belt tend to drag the lower body and legs downward, and if this effect is compensated for by inflating the BCD, the tendency toward a head-up attitude, or tilt, is increased. In addition, the downward drag of the weight belt at the waist and the upward pull of the BCD can make the diver feel as if he or she were in the middle of a tug-of-war.

Advances in the design of modern BCDs allow the diver to achieve greater trim in the water to eliminate the head-up, feet-down attitude and thereby conserve the energy needed to correct an undesirable body tilt. Some BCDs are shaped to allow greater air volume in the mid-body area and less at the neck in order to make it easier to achieve a neutral attitude. Certain devices have the buoyancy compensator and the weights mounted on the backpack to eliminate the uncomfortable pull of the scuba tank and weights in one direction and of the BCD in the opposite direction. Exhaust valves are being designed to let air out of the buoyancy compensator more easily, and are placed so that the diver does not have to disturb neutral attitude in order to operate them.

Ideally, proper trim of BCD and weight belt will bring about a balance between the two without requiring additional air or additional weight. If an

adjustment is necessary, it is usually better to reduce the amount of air and weight used rather than continue to increase either or both.

Body attitude can also be determined by the use of hands and feet. In swimming with the feet below the body, the kick will be upward as well as forward, which is undesirable. Beginning divers often unconsciously adopt this attitude to try to compensate for negative buoyancy, but it is more tiring than taking off some weight or adding air to the BCD.

In swimming close to a muddy bottom, trim should be adjusted to achieve slightly positive buoyancy. With the use of the hands, this will put the feet above the head and avoid stirring up the mud with the fins and reducing visibility. At the same time the kick can be used to keep the body close to the bottom. This technique, often used by cave divers, can be useful to marine biologists, underwater photographers and others who need maximum clarity of surroundings.

A neutral state of buoyancy is generally the safest and requires almost no effort to maintain when diving. Neutral buoyancy is best achieved by adding only as much weight to the body as is needed for descent and then adjusting the amount of air in the buoyancy compensator. It is a mistake to add more weight than is needed and in turn balance its effect by increasing buoyancy. The result will be increased resistance to movement underwater, physical discomfort and poor trim.

Most divers without a wet suit may need no weight, or only a few pounds, to achieve neutral buoyancy. The average wet suit composed of jacket and bottoms will have a positive buoyancy of about 12 lbs near the surface in fresh water, and more in salt water. The extra weight needed for neutral buoyancy in salt water will be about 3 percent of your total weight—body, wet suit and other equipment being worn—in addition to whatever you needed in fresh water.

Any part of the body or equipment that is above the surface is dead weight and tends to press you down. Thus, if you swim with the scuba tank out of the water you will require a considerable amount of air in the buoyancy compensator in order to float on the surface. For this reason it is often easier to swim to your destination and back underwater. When swimming on the surface, try to keep as much of the body and diving equipment in the water as possible for support and use the snorkel for breathing rather than trying to hold your head out of the water.

Although the swimming pool and other shallow-water training areas do not provide the depth necessary for practicing major buoyancy changes and control, they do allow the beginning diver to become familiar with basic procedures. To do so, partially inflate the BCD by mouth before entering the water. This step also serves as part of the predive check. After entry, deflate the BCD (method depends on make and design) until descent can be easily and comfortably accomplished.

Slight positive buoyancy is the safest. When diving in deep water, do not rely on the buoyant effect of the BCD to counteract an excessive amount of weight on the weight belt. Proper addition of weight to the belt is an important part of the predive procedure. In shallow water, such as a pool, deep-water procedures can be simulated by donning a slightly excessive amount of weight and descending to the bottom. Then inflate the BCD orally or from the air tank until neutral or slightly positive bouyancy is achieved.

Practice valving off air from the BCD and lungs during *simulated* long ascents. Do not attempt rapid buoyant ascent at any time while using scuba. The ever-present threat of lung damage rules it out as a training proceedure.

EQUIPMENT FAMILIARIZATION AND PROBLEM SOLVING

Given the principles outlined above, routine use of scuba equipment underwater is relatively easy.At the same time, the competent diver should be familiar enough with his or her equipment and the techniques involved in its use to deal comfortably with small problems that could occur during an underwater experience, thus avoiding situations that could escalate into larger problems.

A diver with even the most basic competence should be able to deal with having a mask accidentally kicked off by another swimmer, becoming momentarily entangled in a submerged fishing line or unexpectedly encountering some underwater turbulence, in a relaxed and efficient manner that confines such situations to being incidents rather than crises.

A variety of training procedures are available for developing confidence and competence in the use of scuba equipment.

The following orientation, best practiced in a swimming pool, is offered as a suggested procedure. Instructors develop techniques and progressions that adapt to their individual programs. This suggested procedure is, however, the product of many of these adaptions.

After completing predive checks and assembly of equipment, buddy teams should, in shallow water, each don all equipment with the assistance of the other. This initial donning should emphasize the BCD position, proper fastening of quick-release devices and the positioning of the weight belt so as to permit instant doffing if necessary.

Special care must be taken during the following exercises to prevent unvented ascent after breathing compressed air while submerged. Even in the shallow end of the pool there is potential hazard, and such an ascent could cause some form of lung injury.

Recheck the regulator function before submerging. With the mouthpiece in place, breathe normally. Lie on the bottom of the pool, face down. Alter the breathing volume and note the change in buoyancy which results. Roll to the side and to the face-up position. In using the single-hose regulator, free flow does not occur, regardless of position, so it is not a problem.

After completing the initial breathing exercise, the trainee should surface while breathing normally. Return to the bottom, remove the mouthpiece and surface while exhaling continuously.

Clearing the flooded mouthpiece and resuming breathing are the next phase. The flooded single-hose regulator may be cleared after inserting the mouthpiece by pushing the purge button or by puffing into the mouthpiece. Inhalation following either method should be of the cautious, trial type rather than a full breath.

Clearing methods are simple and usually accomplished on the first attempt. Ridiculous as it may seem, however, the beginning diver must be impressed with the fact that inhalation cannot occur if the lungs are already full. Complaints of regulators not functioning, no air, or inability to breathe after mechanically purging the mouthpiece are, in many instances, traceable to this human failure. The trainee should practice the appropriate clearing procedures until complete ease is achieved with each.

After initial orientation, trainees will benefit from swimming several lengths of the pool while on the bottom, breathing normally. If they so desire and are comfortable enough, they should flood and clear the mouthpiece and mask several times during this exercise. Experimentation with and regulation of breathing volume during the exercise will demonstrate the desired buoyancy control.

Utilization of the foregoing skills (and their necessity) will be featured in the next exercises, involving donning and doffing scuba while underwater.

DONNING

Before attempting don and doff procedures underwater, a full demonstration of both should be given on pool deck or shore. Again review the nature and function of all harness, because underwater don and doff practice will involve feeling, rather than seeing, much of the equipment. Initial performance of the exercises underwater will be easier if done in shallow water and while wearing the mask.

Overhead Method

After the scuba has been positioned on the bottom, with the weight belt placed over the tank near the base and the single-hose regulator attached, dive to the scuba. Grasp the valve, holding it close to the chest so as to maintain bottom position. Clear the regulator and breathe. While still face down, grasp the tank and move it, parallel to the bottom, to the area of the thighs. Roll to your back and sit up. If using fins, they may be donned before putting on the scuba harness to permit greater freedom of the body while leaning forward. Place the scuba on or between the thighs with the backpack on top. Transfer the weight belt to your lap. Make up the shoulder harness to fit the upper body. Insert the hands and forearms into the straps and grasp the air tank. Be sure that the right arm is *outside* the single hose before inserting the arm into the harness—otherwise the hose will be caught under the armpit when the tank is swung over the head. If hose is caught under harness or arm, this may be corrected by removing the mouthpiece and repositioning the hose. Next, insert and clear the mouthpiece and continue breathing.

The tank is now lifted through an arc into position on the back. Position the shoulder straps. Grasp and pull the waist strap into position and fasten it. If a crotch strap is part of the harness, it may be used to pull the bottom of the tank into position. The crotch strap may be held until needed by anchoring it beneath the buttocks or between the legs.

With harness in place, adjusted and fastened, the weight belt may now be donned. This can be done while still in the sitting position, but is better accomplished in a face-down "knee-chest" position which allows snug fastening without a lot of juggling.

The latter part of the overhead procedure may be practiced by standing erect

OVERHEAD DONNING METHOD

4

5

in the shallow end of the swimming pool and swinging the scuba tank from pool edge over the head and into position on the back. This will permit easier adjustment of tank, hose and harness, and make these steps more natural when donning underwater.

Side Donning Method

The initial contact and clearing is the same as in the overhead method. While in prone position, draw knees forward to the area of the scuba valve, keeping the body inclined forward. Pull the tank and weight belt up between the thighs with weight belt in the right hand. Raise the right knee and swing it to the right. You are now kneeling on the left knee only. Place the weight belt across and high up on the right thigh for ballast. Mask and harness may now be donned. Next, insert the right arm into shoulder harness, making sure scuba hose is *above* the right arm. Using both hands, scuba tank is moved up and around the right shoulder to the back. Insert the left arm through harness and fasten shoulder harness. Kneeling forward, fasten weight belt around the waist. Don fins by raising each knee and bringing the foot forward.

Both the overhead and side donning methods work more easily when the diver is bare-skinned than when wearing a wet suit or other protective clothing. When such equipment is worn, shoulder straps and other harness may have to be maneuvered into position because they do not easily slip over rougher materials.

There are numerous variations of these two basic donning methods, including kneeling on both knees and lying on the back. All have merit and are dictated by physique, buoyancy, dress and equipment design. Individual preference and experience of the instructor will help determine which method best suits the individual diver.

DOFFING

Doffing of scuba tank, harness and regulator hose is performed by reversing the donning procedure. Because side doffing is easier and safer than the overhead method, only it is recommended. Side doffing should be done from the side from which the regulator hose comes. However, the underwater doffing of scuba is an exercise of very limited usefulness and is meeting with increasing resistance at the teaching level, as are emergency-ascent training exercises. The reason is that practicing emergency procedures often subjects the diver to the same hazards as the actual emergency does.

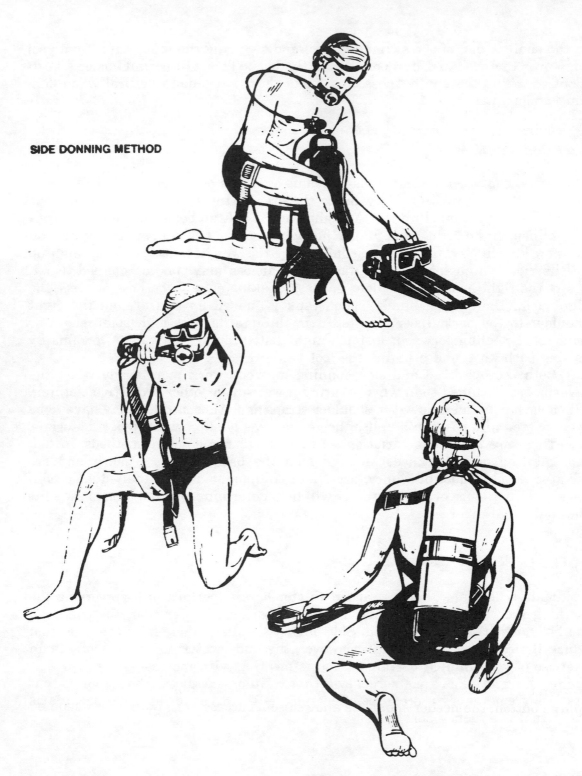

SIDE DONNING METHOD

On the other hand, a very practical maneuver to be perfected by the basic scuba diver involves doffing gear on the surface of the water prior to exit. Exit to an area higher than the surface while wearing full scuba equipment can be a difficult maneuver without assistance. With a diving buddy, or with others available to help, doff and pass the heavier pieces of equipment upward. It is advisable to keep fins on during the process for greater lift and holding of position. To reach a surface at or near water level, while still in a horizontal, floating position, pull yourself forward with one hand and push with fin action. When aboard to waist level, roll to a sitting position to rest or remove gear.

BREATHING ALTERNATIVES

Air Sharing

This is an emergency procedure. Sharing air with a buddy should be done only because of a regulator failure, exhausted air supply or some other situation that rules out the use of the scuba. Any of these conditions will make ascent for the airless diver, the "needer," necessary, either with or without the buddy. If ascent is with the diver who still has air, the "donor," the sharing will have to begin immediately. In either case, the needer must remember to exhale steadily while rising in order to prevent lung damage.

On discovering that he or she is not getting air, the needer should promptly make it known to the buddy by using the out-of-air signal—drawing a finger or hand across the throat. The donor then takes charge, maintaining control of the regulator mouthpiece by keeping a firm grip on it at all times. The donor must also control breathing rate and ascent rate. If necessary, the donor will have to remind the needer to exhale and even slow the ascent rate as required to prevent lung damage. He or she should try to get into position so as to be able to take physical control of the assisted diver if conditions warrant, but must use good judgment in this respect. Nothing will be gained by both buddies being out of air. The donor must protect his or her own safety as well as that of the buddy.

If the airless diver should be to the left side of the donor, each should have a hold on the other's tank harness to prevent separation, or the donor may choose to use his or her left arm to help maintain position or direction. The donor extends the regulator mouthpiece with the right hand and does not let go of it. The needer puts his left hand on top of the doner's to help guide the regulator to his mouth. The sharing is begun by passing by the regulator back and fourth between them at regular intervals as they ascend the surface. If the regulator has a purge button, the needer should be allowed some access to it. Both divers should exhale slowly and steadily when the regulator is being used by the other.

SINGLE-HOSE SHARING

OCTOPUS ATTACHMENT

Easier than sharing a single regulator and mouthpiece between buddies is the use of an additional second stage attached directly to the air tank. Called an "octopus" because its use gives the scuba an appearance of having many arms, it has a longer hose for easier use by the needer. To keep it from dangling when not in use, it can be secured to the tank with a shock cord so as to come free with a firm pull, or held to the harness or BCD with velcro.

Spare Air

Another alternative to the diver's primary air supply is to carry small quantities of additional compressed air for emergency use. A commonly used alternative for such an air supply is the pony bottle, a very small compressed air bottle, usually strapped to the diver's primary scuba tank. This small scuba cylinder is usually utilized with a separate two-stage, single-hosed regulator. A newer form of the pony bottle is a small scuba cylinder with the demand regulator attached directly to the valve with no intervening air hose. This system is usually carried in a separate holster so that the diver may remove the bottle and hold it to his or her mouth during ascent.

Another source of emergency breathing air for the diver lies within the

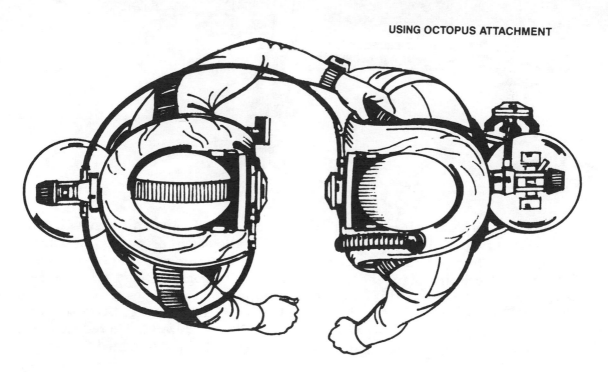

USING OCTOPUS ATTACHMENT

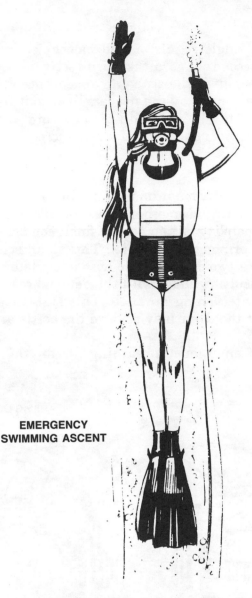

**EMERGENCY
SWIMMING ASCENT**

buoyancy compensator. An even partially inflated BC often contains enough air to sustain a diver while he or she is rebreathing the same air during an emergency ascent. The diver can learn the technique of breathing air from his or her BC through the oral inflator hose after clearing it properly. This takes some practice, and a danger of this kind of training exists in the form of possible bacterial infections from the interior of the buoyancy compensator. BCs used for this training purpose should be properly treated with a disinfectant to reduce this danger. Recent equipment developments include a mouthpiece designed for emergency breathing from the buoyancy compensator oral inflator hose. Divers interested in spare air should consult with their instructors and equipment retailers for information on the latest designs.

EMERGENCY SWIMMING ASCENTS

Well-trained divers should rarely, if ever, allow themselves to get into a situation where they have lost their primary air supply and have no other breathing alternatives available to them. In such situations, the diver may have to perform an emergency swimming ascent, an ascent with no breathing supply. The key factor in the emergency swimming ascent procedure is to avoid pulmonary barotrauma by allowing expanding air to escape from the lungs during the ascent. This is accomplished by light but continuous exhalation throughout the ascent. Remember, *scuba divers should never hold their breath at any time while underwater*. Continuous exhalation is not the same as breath holding, nor is it an attempt to breathe. For this reason, a diver performing an emergency swimming ascent should retain a regulator in his or her mouth during the ascent, exhaling through the regulator on the way up and attempting to breathe air as it expands within the air supply system during the ascent. Attempts to breathe should be accomplished with an open airway and at no time should involve breath holding. The ascent rate should be controlled and not fully buoyant. The practice of emergency swimming ascent procedures during training is considered risky by some instructors, diving physiologists and physicians.

If practice is considered essential, ascents of the continuous-exhalation type can be made in *shallow* water for a variety of distances within a noncritical depth. Even this simulation should be well supervised. Some experienced (and most basic) divers find it difficult to keep their cool when they reach the "empty lung" point with some distance still to go. Having the regulator mouthpiece readily available and usable in case of an abort may seem to be a crutch, but it's still better than panic.

A practice ascent can be made by having a fully dressed scuba diver snorkel to a flag and free-dive 15 ft or so to an instructor, drop the weight belt and make a *simulated* free ascent—"blow and go." The diver does not breathe on the scuba and thus carries only a 1-atmosphere lungful of air down with him or her. This procedure assures the instructor that the student has gone through the drill and has met some stress in an underwater situation, while ensuring that embolism problems will not occur.

FIVE

ENJOYING THE ENVIRONMENT

The true essence of the sport of skin and scuba diving lies in the application of the skills and knowledge presented in the pages of this book to the unique environment of inner space. Both the challenges and the opportunities presented by that environment are covered in this chapter.

Because approximately three-quarters of the earth's surface is covered by water, fresh or salt, there is a body of water convenient to nearly every sport diver. The variety of environmental conditions existing in the earth's waters is noted, studied and recorded in detail by word and photography in countless volumes. World-traveling divers become veritable storehouses of environmental lore. Instructors, books, experienced divers, watermen and guided personal experience will, in time, broaden the basic knowledge set forth here. Knowledge of a specific environment and its influence on diving activity in a given locale must be acquired by consulting available data and local divers. Observance of safety, local laws, regulators, regard for the rights of others, preservation of nature's balanced community and upholding a high standard of conduct and performance are all required of a good diver. Respect for and care of our relatively new environment will help to make each entry into it a pleasant and memorable occasion.

WEATHER

Continuous changes in barometric pressure and air-mass movements bring about a variety of conditions broadly referred to as *weather*. Divers are not expected to be meterologists, but they should study predicted conditions (weather forecasts and maps) when planning dives.

Seasonal changes of temperature, probable weather conditions, plant growth and marine creatures' habits are more or less predictable. Dependent on the earth's climatic zones, weather conditions and temperature (water and air) follow a general pattern for a given area. The seasonal changes often influence planned diving activities. Temperature variation (air and water) and atmospheric changes create situations of physical importance to the diver.

WATER TEMPERATURE

Variation of water temperature in the oceans and connecting inland seas is far less dramatic than that of air. Divers readily adapt to water-temperature changes

WATER TEMPERATURE VARIATION

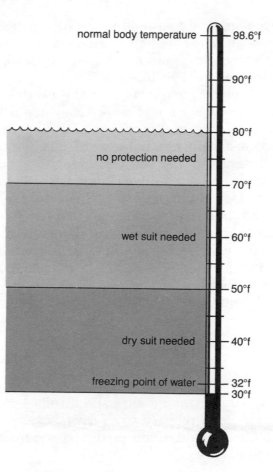

normal body temperature — 98.6°f

90°f

80°f

no protection needed

70°f

wet suit needed — 60°f

50°f

dry suit needed — 40°f

freezing point of water — 32°f

30°f

114

THERMOCLINES

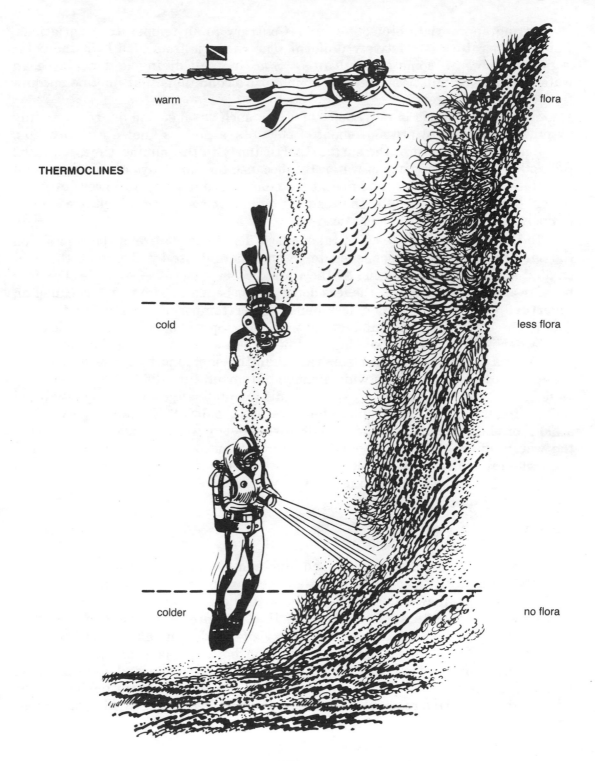

warm

flora

cold

less flora

colder

no flora

by wearing appropriate protective suits. Contrary to air-temperature variations, water temperature is relatively uniform. The range is from 28.5°F in the polar regions to 85°F in some tropical areas. Since not all diving is done in ocean waters, the diver must consider the temperature conditions that may be encountered in inland waters.

Heat is exchanged in still bodies of water, such as lakes and quarries, mainly by upward and downward movement of currents, a process known as *convection*. When sunlight penetrates the surface, particularly in the summertime, it warms the upper levels of the body of water. But because the sun's rays cannot penetrate the water deeply, no great temperature change results at the lower levels in waters of considerable depth. The result is often a *thermocline,* which is a sudden temperature change felt as you descend.

In the fall the opposite effect takes place. The temperature of the cold air on the surface causes the upper levels to become more dense by absorbing the heat created in the summer months. As the water becomes more dense it also becomes heavier and sinks, replacing the less dense water beneath. The result is called an "overturn," with the warmer, less dense water temporarily rising to the top. Again, the convection currents, circulating from top to bottom, are in effect.

Water is a much better conductor of heat than air is, meaning that it absorbs heat from a diver's body at a faster rate than the surrounding air does. For this reason we cannot tolerate as wide a range of temperature difference underwater as on the surface. Without an exposure suit for protection, most people will get cold during a typical dive when the temperature is below 80°F; and if the water is at 90°F or above, overheating will occur during heavy work or exercise. In most of the waters of the world, it is only a matter of time before a diver feels chilled, even when wearing protective clothing. However, the time this takes may be a lot longer than the diver was planning to stay in the water.

WAVES

Waves generated by wind, currents and high-and low-pressure atmospheric conditions may drastically alter the surface and bottom contour of dive sites located in the relatively shallow waters adjacent to ocean beaches. Planning dives in such areas should include a study of prior weather and predicted dive-time weather, both local and general. Dives planned for visits to deeper offshore sites, where surface-wave action has little or no effect on bottom topography, should still include assessment of weather conditions. Surface travel to and from the site, mooring at the site, entry and exit can be made miserable, even dangerous, by wind and waves. Divers should obtain specific knowledge relative to their areas before diving.

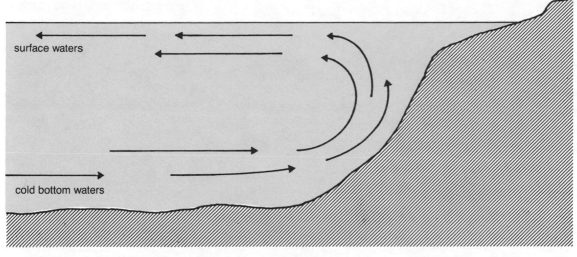

OVERTURN ACTION OF WATER AS A RESULT OF TEMPERATURE

CURRENTS

Entry and exit for shore-based dives should be planned to prevent exhausting battles with tidal flows. A diver's horizontal speed generally averages less than 1 knot. Thus, trying to gain distance against a 1-knot current could be an exhausting and losing battle. Work with the current, angling into or at cross angle to it as desired. Obviously, a longer walk on land is safer than a short but exhausting swim.

Local peculiarities in current caused by jetties, coves, prominences, reefs and bars should be a part of planning for entrance, exit and diving activity. This knowledge, coupled with the advice of divers having experience in the area, should be a part of planning and execution.

Regular water flows, such as those caused by rise and fall of tides, should also be a part of every diver's environmental knowledge. Tide tables are available for practically every body of water having a tidal rise and fall. Tides are attributed to the gravitational pull of the moon and sun that causes bulges in the sea's surface. Though not so pronounced in deeper waters, tidal influence is obvious in the more shallow areas adjacent to land masses. Tidal movements of water are to be expected and included in operational dive plans. Ebb (falling) and flood (rising) of tides is accompanied by a slack period (no motion). Slack tide is usually within one hour of high and low tide.

Ocean currents along the shore (parallel to, or nearly so) should be observed prior to making an entry. Such currents are often generated by waves. Waves

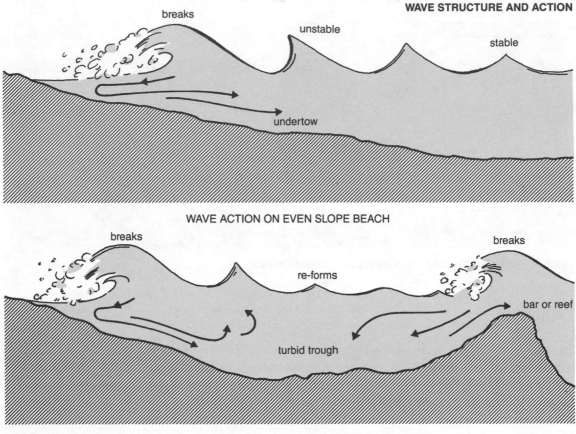

breaks

unstable

stable

undertow

WAVE ACTION ON EVEN SLOPE BEACH

breaks

breaks

re-forms

bar or reef

turbid trough

WAVE ACTION INDICATING OFFSHORE BAR OR REEF

arriving obliquely to the shore generate a current that runs before them and parallel to the shore. Determination of such flow should dictate entry and exit points so as to prevent exhausting swims against the flow. Observation of water surface prior to entry is a must for the safety-minded diver. Bottom contour charateristics, currents, wave height and patterns should be determined by visual observation for 5 or 10 minutes before making entry.

Surface-water movements in rivers and streams can generally be determined by watching floating objects. However, water movement below the surface is often sharply influenced by bottom contours. Knowledge of such conditions should be obtained from experienced sources prior to diving. If such information is not available, adequate safety lines should be rigged to permit remaining at the proposed site during the dive and to provide direct exit to the dive base.

Water movement near dam spillways, level control valves or gates (at or below surface) can be dangerously swift and should be avoided. Attempts to

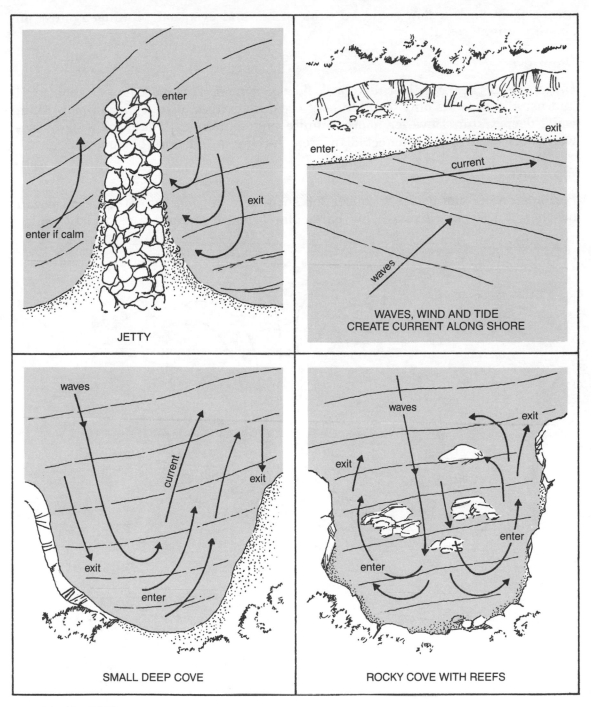

JETTY

WAVES, WIND AND TIDE
CREATE CURRENT ALONG SHORE

SMALL DEEP COVE

ROCKY COVE WITH REEFS

ENTRIES AND EXITS

escape from such a flow could be exhausting, and eventual pinning against an opening might result.

Undertow

Undertow might better be called back flow or run off. This back flow is shortlived and usually extends only to the line of breaking waves, usually in no more than waist-deep water. However, more definite and sometimes troublesome flow seaward may occur and be detected in areas having an offshore bar or reef.

Rip Current

Perhaps one of the greatest causes for swimmers getting into trouble off ocean beaches is the rip current. This particular type of current is caused by water

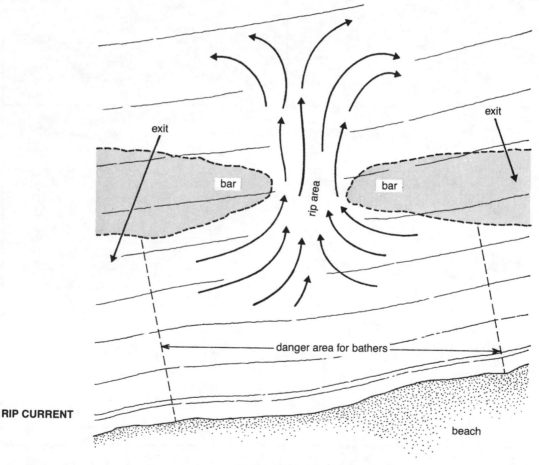

RIP CURRENT NEAR BEACH

flowing seaward through a gap in a bar or reef, setting up a swirling action inshore leading into a strong current outward, which carries the unwary or inexperienced diver or swimmer rapidly away from the safety of shallow water. Experienced divers often use these "rips" as an easy, fast way to get out beyond the reef or bar.

The rip current can usually be recognized by watching for a gap in the continuous line of breakers over a reef. Closer inshore some turbulence may be noted in the area of the rip, accompanied by an interruption of the general pattern of waves.

Fortunately, the rip current continues beyond the reef or bar only a short distance, then splits and dies out. If you are caught unexpectedly by one, relax, angle cross the rip and return with the waves well to either side of it.

Rip currents may also occur close to the beach when waves breaking near the beach deposit large volumes of water on it. The resultant back flow may cut a channel in which water flows seaward rapidly back to the breaker line. Strong currents may also result when obstructions interrupt the flow of lateral currents.

Currents, regardless of cause or location, tend to carry silt, minute marine life and debris—all of which reduce visibility in varying degrees and make the water turbid (murky), depending on their concentration.

VISIBILITY

Seeing underwater would be nearly impossible for divers if there were not some way to provide an air space between the eye and the water. Our eyes are made to function in the medium of air; underwater that problem is overcome by providing an air space between the lens of the diving mask and the eye. Air in the mask, which also covers the nose, is provided by exhaling through the nose.

As light enters any medium it is absorbed by the medium and its speed is slowed, which has the effect of bending the light rays at an angle, known as *refraction*. As light passes from the denser water through the air in the mask to the eye, it is bent and distorts the vision in two ways. It makes objects appear 25 percent closer than they actually are, and ⅓ larger than they are. As divers gain experience underwater they learn to correct for this condition; otherwise they are constantly fooled by reaching for something that turns out to be farther away and smaller than it appeared. Also, in the same refraction process, light waves are bent by the water. Thus, a fish that appears from the surface to be in a certain spot would be missed by a spear gun because it is actually a number of degrees away from that line of sight.

Light is absorbed much faster in water than in air, and the warm colors are absorbed first. Red light is taken up after passing through only a few feet of

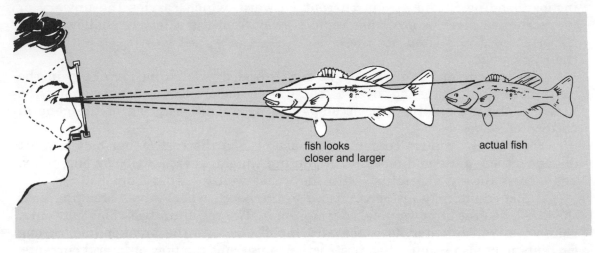

fish looks
closer and larger

actual fish

water, orange by the time it has passed through 25 ft, and green by 60 ft. Below 60 ft most of the sunlight that has *not* been absorbed is blue. To observe "true" colors it is necessary to use an underwater light. Color photography underwater requires the use of strobe lights to restore the warmer colors.

Light penetration is often reduced and altered by dyes present in the water in fresh-water diving. For this reason the predominant color underwater may be green or brown instead of blue.

Visibility may also be sharply reduced by the amount of extraneous matter in the water, such as dirt or plankton. This effect, known as *turbidity,* can be so strong that in otherwise crystal-clear water as much as 75 percent of the sun's light rays can be cut out in less than 20 ft of depth.

Many divers wear their prescription eyeglasses inside the diving mask. Those who prefer contact lenses may wear them when diving. However, the chance of losing a lens is the same as in other sports, particularly in the unexpected flooding of a mask. The use of either eyeglasses or contact lenses is not ideal. Masks with lenses in which the diver's own prescription can be ground are available in several colors and include a nosepiece for both scuba diving and snorkeling.

Open water and silt-free lakes and streams are often very clear, but, again, they can become dangerously dark when currents or streams stir up or carry in with them small particles that reduce the penetration of light. Harbors, rivers, estuaries and the open water in their vicinity are often near zero in visibility and not conducive to safe diving. These murky waters may carry products of pollution that could be injurious to the diver. Sharp jagged metal or glass, old pilings, rocks and long-abandoned sunken hulks endanger skin and equipment. If circum-

EFFECT OF WATER ON COLORS

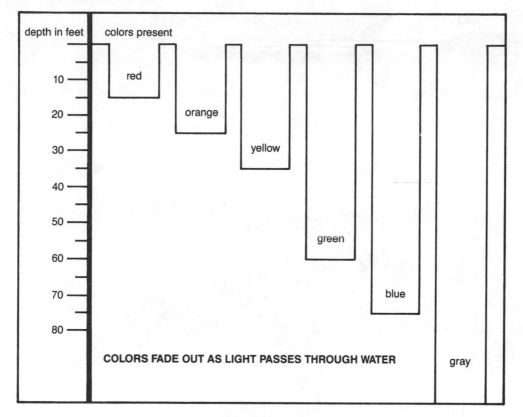

stances demand diving in water of poor visibility, extreme caution before, during and after diving should be taken. Dive buddies should maintain contact by a short length of line. Waterproof lights should be used. A lookout topside with boat or float and diver's flags to keep surface craft clear is a safety must. It is better to travel a little farther to get to clear water than to risk injury or infection in dirty, dark water. Even open water can be dangerous when visibility is poor.

SURFACE TRAFFIC

"Stop, look up and listen when ascending" is a good rule during dives anywhere. Surface-craft users will be unaware of the location of divers unless the area is adequately indicated with diver flags. Even then the diver must exercise caution, because not all surface-craft operators know the meaning of the flag. Avoid diving

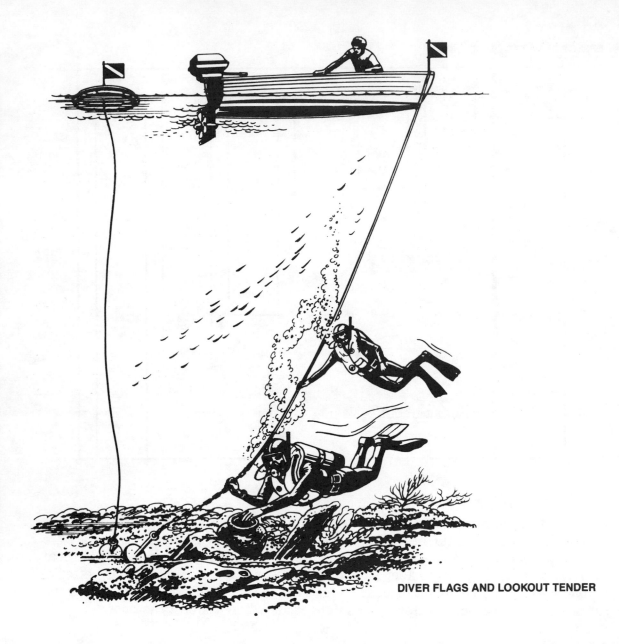

DIVER FLAGS AND LOOKOUT TENDER

in areas of surface-craft travel. Maintain a plainly visible surface safety and lookout tender. Post the area adequately with diver flags, stay within the posted area and obey prearranged signals for caution, surfacing or recall to base. Skin divers must be even more cautious. Delays in ascent are limited in time. Plan for safety and dive the plan.

UNDERWATER SOUND

In 1953, Jacques Cousteau published his well-known book *The Silent World,* depicting the pleasures of scuba diving. Despite the impression left by this title, the underwater world is not silent. In some areas it is extremely noisy. The sounds heard beneath the surface come from waves, surf, shifting sand and stones, boat engines and marine life such as fish, shrimps and crabs.

Sound travels four times faster in water than in air, and certain noises, such as the whine of a boat motor, may be heard for greater distances underwater. In spite of this, it is diffcult to use the human voice for satisfactory communication underwater. Because of the difference in viscosity of air and water, and other deadening effects, only about 1 in 10,000 parts of the sound generated in a diving mask actually enters the water. The rest are mixed up with the noise of escaping scuba air.

Recent developments have lowered the price of underwater communication equipment that can more effectively send spoken words through the water. Before these devices were developed, divers often sent sound signals to each other by banging on a scuba tank with a knife handle or a stone. But at any real distance this custom is often not very effective, partly because determining where a sound is coming from is difficult due to the high speed of sound in water. To compensate for this condition, divers must learn to look around and detect the sources of sound by other means.

UNDERWATER OBSTACLES

Submerged trees, wreckage, cable, rope, nets and fish line (particularly monofilament) present entanglement hazards even in relatively clear water. The surge of waves, or careless passage while maneuvering through or around such areas in which this occurs, may result in entanglement and the need to use your knife. Careful and methodical disentanglement or removal with minimum motion gives best results. Areas of poor visibility and possibly having bottom trash should be avoided as diving sites.

MARINE LIFE

The continental shelf, although much of it is beyond the reach of most divers using present-day equipment, supports an abundance of the ocean's available supply of food, from the smallest to the largest forms of life.

One-celled plants called *diatoms,* microscopic in size, live on the silica

LOBSTER

SEA ANEMONE

OCTOPUS

SEA URCHIN

SCORPION FISH

SPIDER CRAB

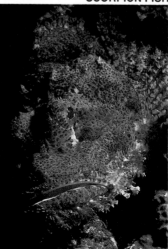

DIVER IN KELP

EEL GRASS

FIRE CORAL

BARRACUDA

MORAY EEL

STING RAY

GREY NURSE SHARK ▲　　　　　　　**▼ BLUE SHARK**

MAKO SHARKS ▲

◄ TIGER SHARK　　　　　　　**▼ WHITE TIP SHARK**

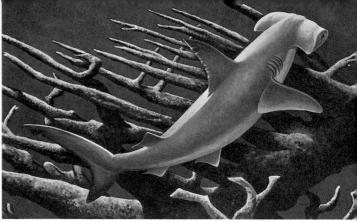

▲ HAMMERHEAD SHARK

BULL SHARK ▲   WHALE SHARK ▼   ▲ GREAT WHITE SHARK

washed down by the rivers. Other microscopic organisms called *dinoflagellates,* animal larvae and a myriad of small floating animals that feed on the diatoms are collectively called *plankton.* Plankton is the food of larger sea life, even for some whales and members of the shark family. Most of the inhabitants of the sea feed upon one another, which prevents overpopulation. Thus is established a balanced community in the sea.

As on land, the variety and abundance of life are determined by environment, temperature and the availability of food. Even slight temperature changes have a marked effect on sea life; therefore most forms are restricted to certain areas. There are many varied pursuits open to divers in the underwater world. Geology, photography, zoology, marine biology, archeology, spear fishing, treasure hunting or just sightseeing are full-time paying jobs for many. Whether professional or amateur, all divers should become acquainted with the creatures of the underwater world. The following descriptions, though not in any order of importance, will serve as basic background for study.

Rather than attempting to introduce all the undersea creatures, only those considered to be potentially harmful to the diver will be covered. Some are nonaggressive and only cause injury when disturbed by accident or intentionally. Others, by nature of their habits, may be aggressive and a threat to the safety of a stranger in their underwater world.

Rays

The ray family, though not all venomous or equipped with a specialized defense mechanism, comprises a large portion of the harmful sea creatures. Rays have a cartilaginous skeleton and, for the most part, feed on plankton and crustaceans. The larger forms, such as the manta ray are rarely seen by the average diver. The smaller forms are very numerous in species. Because it is responsible for a number of injuries to divers reported annually, the *sting ray* will receive some attention. Most of these rays can be found in relatively shallow water. They are bottom feeders and may be observed lying on or partially submerged in the sand or mud with only their eyes, breathing holes and a portion of the tail exposed.

Their defense mechanism consists of a barb or barbs located on the tail adjacent to its junction with the body. When disturbed or molested, the barb is raised by erectile tissue from its normally flat position. The barb is bony, grooved in the center, sharp and with serrated edges.

The sting ray is not aggressive and, by nature, is easily frightened. A diver seeking to avoid puncture by the barb can cause the ray to flee by shuffling his fins on the sand or mud nearby. The sting ray, if disturbed, will generally swim a short distance away and again bury itself in the sand or mud. Rays are difficult to detect in murky water, and divers should proceed with caution over the bottom when they are known or expected to be in the area. The barb is sufficiently strong

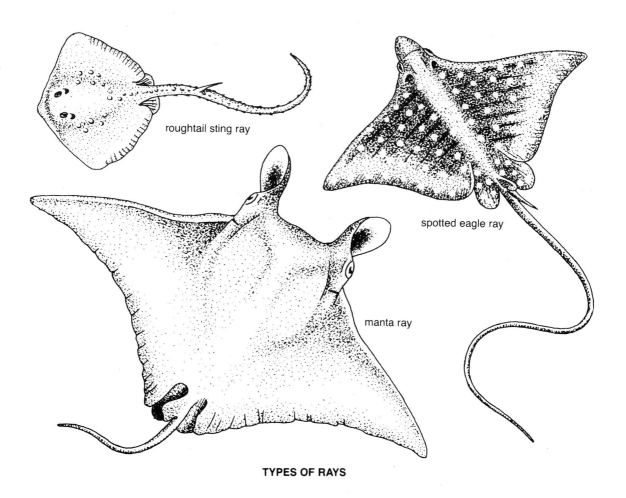

roughtail sting ray

spotted eagle ray

manta ray

TYPES OF RAYS

and sharp to cause a severe laceration or puncture in the foot, hand or body. The unfortunate diver so injured should leave the water immediately and receive first aid.

Another species known as the *torpedo ray*, often found on the sandy bottom off northern California, is equipped with an organ capable of giving an electric shock severe enough to stun a large fish.

Despite these defenses, however, the entire ray family is nonaggressive and will avoid contact with the diver when possible.

Coelenterates

The coelenterates (see-lent-er-rates) are invertebrates that are dangerous because of their numerous stinging cells. They are grouped into four major categories;

hydroids, jellyfish, corals and sea anemones. The major portion of this group of dangerous or harmful animals probably is coral. Coral exists in practically all the warm waters of the seas.

Coral, with its many brilliant hues and its varied and beautiful formations, is made up of many millions of living and dead polyps of the coelenterate family. Using calcium deposits in the water, a small shell-like cup is built at the base. This is the living polyp's home. As the polyps reproduce and die, successive layers of these shells are deposited in a variety of formations. Concentration of these coral growths may result in the formation of reefs and atolls.

Beautiful as coral may be, it becomes a menace to the diver when contacted with bare skin. Stings and lacerations resulting from contact with coral may vary from annoying to serious. The lacerations and stings must receive first aid and, when necessary, medical treatment. Prevention of such injury should be practiced by avoiding contact or wearing protective clothing and gloves.

Fire coral, often called *stinging coral*, is not a true coral. It is a colony of hydroids that grows among true corals and may be recognized by its bright yellow color and branching colonies.

Portuguese Man-of-War

This is a colony hydroid. The specialized organisms make up what appears to be a single individual. The stinging cells in the tentacles are particularly dangerous to man because they cause extreme pain, partial paralysis and systemic reactions that may make hospitalization necessary. Having been once stung, a victim may be more seriously affected if stung again.

The Portuguese man-of-war is easily identified by the brilliant, iridescent float which appears above the surface and supports the tentacles, which may attain a length of many feet. The stinging tentacles, even when broken away from the main colony, should be avoided, since they are still capable of inflicting severe stings.

Jellyfish

These free-swimming coelenterates are quite numerous in rivers, bays and open water during late spring and summer in temperate zones. In the warmer seas they may be found at any time. Jellyfish vary in size from 1 inch to many feet in diameter, with tentacles streaming down several inches or even feet below the umbrella-shaped body. Because they are capable of moving up and down in the water, they may be found either near the surface or quite deep.

Contact with the tentacles of a jellyfish can cause a wide variety of discomforts to the diver. These vary from mild, local stinging to violent systemic disturbance. The latter is rare, but as jellyfish are difficult to avoid, especially in limited-visibility areas, adequate protective clothing should be worn if their presence is suspected.

The *sea wasp* is an extremely dangerous jellyfish that inhabits the warmer waters of Australia, the Philippines and the Indian Ocean. An apparently less deadly but closely related form may be found in northern Australia, the Indian Ocean and the Atlantic Ocean from Brazil to North Carolina (cf. Halstead's *Dangerous Marine Animals)*. It may be identified by its dome-shaped bell, which may grow to heights of 10 inches or more, but is usually much smaller. The sting of this species is capable of causing death in less than 10 minutes. Recently reported in *Skin Diver* magazine by James Mead is another deadly jellyfish closely resembling the sea wasp but apparently not the same. Mead refers to it as a *box jelly*. This species can be as large as a man's head and is transparent, except for a bluish tinge. It originated in the Timor Sea and spread through the islands of southeast Asia and into the tropical waters of Australia.

Sea Anemones

Sea anemones are marine animals of the same family as jellyfish, hydroids and coral. They may look very much like brightly colored flowers. Size varies from less than an inch to more than a foot in diameter, and some are capable of inflicting a venomous sting that can be harmful to divers.

Mollusks

These shellfish broadly include clams, mussels, oysters, snails, abalones and cone shells. Though not venomous, with the exception of the cone shell, many have sharp or serrated edges that are capable of inflicting painful and easily infected wounds. Gloves should be worn when collecting specimens of them. Some mollusks are inedible, particularly in specific areas. This may be determined by consulting local sources of information or government bulletins. Certain cone shells possess a venomous stinging apparatus that can produce a variety of systemic effects and in some cases may even result in death.

Barnacles and Tube Worms

These creatures have hard shells that, in many cases, are sharp and capable of inflicting easily infected wounds when contacted.

Sea Urchins

Sea urchins belong to the family of the starfish, sand dollar and the sea cucumber, but they are considerably more dangerous. The spiny burr may be found on the bottom, on and under reefs and wrecks in warm waters. They are equipped with spines which, in some instances, are long and needlelike. Because of their sharpness, the spines of the sea urchin may penetrate skin or light clothing and often break off. Every effort should be made to extract each spine as soon as possible, and the puncture wound should be immediately cared for to prevent infection.

Crabs and Lobsters

Many of these crustacea have large claws for capturing their food. Unwary divers may find themselves painfully attached even to one of the smaller species. The larger species are capable of breaking a finger with their large claws. When attempting to collect them by hand, wear heavy gloves and know how to capture your prey lest you be caught instead. Local divers usually develop safe procedures and will generally share their knowledge with you.

Octopus

The octopus has been the villain in many an ancient sailor's tale, with its size enormously magnified and its aggressiveness said to be so great that whole ships were pulled under by its tentacles. Skin divers have found no evidence to support such tales. The octopus is nonaggressive and—except for the largest of the species, which may measure 20 ft from arm tip to arm tip—is usually small, timid and, because of its nocturnal habits, seldom seen. Handling an octopus should be done carefully so as to avoid the center-placed beak, which in some species secretes a venom that paralyzes its prey.

Squid

The squid has ten arms, two longer than the others, and, unlike the octopus, swims about. It is capable of inflicting severe bites with its beak when annoyed or caught. The giant squid grows in excess of 50 ft.

Scorpion Fishes

The venomous scorpion fishes have been divided into three main groups. Halstead in his *Dangerous Marine Animals* groups these fishes on the basis of the structure of their venomous organs as follows: zebra fish, scorpion fish proper and stone fish. Zebra fish are beautiful and inhabit coral reefs. The scorpion fish proper are not nearly so beautiful and may be found in a variety of species in practically all the oceans and seas. The stone fish, the most venomous of all, is found along coastal areas in shallow, warm waters of the Eastern Hemisphere.

These fish are equipped with venomous spines in various numbers in the dorsal, pelvic and anal fin areas. Due to the extreme effect of the venom, the utmost caution should be exercised when moving about in areas known to be inhabited by them.

Sea Snakes

Sea snakes are usually brilliantly colored with flattened tails. They may be seen in tropical waters, particularly the Pacific and Indian Oceans. They secrete a venom similar to but stronger than cobra venom. Regardless of their reputed tameness, handling and contact with them should be avoided. If bitten, avoid exercise and seek immediate medical help.

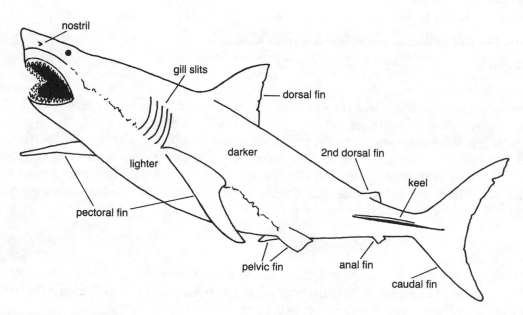

SHARK EXTERNAL ANATOMY

Sharks

Although considered by many experienced divers as not being worthy of the considerable space given it in discussions and descriptions, the shark still remains one of the most popular subjects of conversation during talk of diving by nondivers and new divers. The existence of the technical and nontechnical volumes written about sharks attests to the importance of this creature of the sea.

The Smithsonian Institute has documented accounts of shark attacks around the world numbering over one thousand in the last 50 years. The majority of the attacks were on persons in waist-deep (2 to 4 ft) water or who were involved in sea disasters. Relatively few authenticated unprovoked attacks have occurred involving divers. From available data it appears that most attacks occur during daylight hours between 10 A.M. and 6 P.M., in water of 70°F or warmer. It cannot necessarily be assumed, however, that the night would be less dangerous. Night can be even more dangerous because of greater feeding activity and because the human in water is perceived by the shark by lateral-line sense and smell. These shark senses are more acute at night, probably because their night vision is reduced.

Before describing some of the members of the shark family assumed to be most dangerous, it may be advisable to present some preventive measures. The following are expressed as personal opinions in Cousteau's *The Shark:*

Every species of shark, even the most inoffensive, is anatomically a formidable source of potential danger. . . . The youngest sharks—and therefore the smallest—are the most brazen. Even a small shark, two feet in length, can inflict dangerous wounds.

Sharks race in from great distances to devour any fish in trouble. They can perceive the fish's convulsive movements by the rhythm of the pressure waves carried to them through the water. At a short distance, sharks are also extremely sensitive to odor, and particularly to the odor of blood. For both these reasons, underwater fishermen should not attach their catch to their belt.*

A buddy team, when confronted by sharks, can best keep sharks in view and achieve protection by working back-to-back. Although many measures have been put forth to prevent attack, such as striking the water forcefully, shouting underwater, directing a stream of bubbles or banging on air tanks, their collective worth is questioned by authorities. A solid object 2 or 3 ft long, such as a shark billy, may provide effective protection against the shark. The end of the shark billy should be studded with short points or nails so as to prevent slipping off the shark's skin. It serves the purpose of repelling the shark and, at the same time, increases the distance between the diver and the shark. In order to avoid any aggressive reaction, the shark billy should not be used with the intent to strike or wound the shark.

The best protection lies in ease of movement when diving, swimming slowly and softly, and avoiding any abrupt change of position. Observe the area behind and to the extreme sides. Do not try to outswim a shark. Face the menace, extend the shark billy and, when possible, keep the shark in view while you quietly retreat to your boat. If there is blood in the water from speared fish or from human injury, leave the water immediately. Do not carry speared fish close to your body. Tow your catch on a minimum of 20 ft of line or, better yet, remove it from the water immediately.

There are 250 or more identified species of shark. Because of their variety,

*Jacques-Yves Cousteau and Philippe Cousteau, *The Shark: Splendid Savage of the Sea* (New York and Garden City: Doubleday, 1970).

TROUBLE!

size, distribution and unpredictable behavior, no hard-and-fast rules which apply in every case can be given for handling an encounter with a shark. Remember that all sharks, even the smallest, possess the ability to inflict harm, with or without provocation.

Here are some brief descriptions of the better-known sharks (lengths given represent full growth).

White Shark. Length: 30 ft. Black or slate gray dorsally and white on the belly, but may occur as leaden white entirely. Feeds on large fish and turtles. Generally found in temperate seas in deep water, but often comes into shallow water. Aggressive and considered most dangerous. More attacks on men and boats have been attributed to this species than to any other. The majority of these were unprovoked attacks.

White-Tip Oceanic Shark. Length: 11 ft. Bluish gray or brown above, yellowish to white below. Fins are white-tipped and mottled with gray. Has very large fins. Authenticated reports of unprovoked attack are on record.

White-Tip Reef Shark. Length: 8 ft. Color is gray above, white below, and the fins are conspicuously white-tipped. Although we have no reports of attacks from this species, its abundance around reefs makes it potentially dangerous.

Tiger Shark. Length: 12 to 15 ft. Distinguished by a large head, convex snout and wide overhanging jaws full of sickle-shaped teeth. Smaller members may have conspicuous color patterns on back, and fins of dark brown blotches or bars on a gray or gray-brown background. These markings fade with growth so that larger specimens may be patterned on the caudal fin or not at all. This shark ranges throughout tropical and subtropical areas of all oceans, both inshore and offshore. It may be found in temperate belts during the summer. There are authenticated unprovoked attacks on record.

Mako Shark. Length: 12 ft. It has a pointed snout and is streamlined and fast. Its color is dark blue or blue-gray above and white below. It has a bilateral keel forward of the caudal fin. There are authenticated reports of attacks on men and on boats.

Whale Shark. Length: 35 to 40 ft. The largest fish in the world. Unlike most sharks, its mouth is at the front of the head instead of being underslung. Brownish, with a closely spaced pattern of yellowish or white dots over entire body. Generally considered harmless in spite of its extraordinary size.

Hammerhead Shark. There are several types of hammerhead shark. The largest is known as the Great Hammerhead and may exceed 17 ft in length. Hammerhead sharks are found in most warm waters throughout the world. They are easily distinguished by their unusual head, shaped like a tack hammer with eyes and nostrils at the outer portions. Because of their nostrils in front of the hammer, they are, if nearby, the first on the scene where blood is spilled. There are authenticated records of unprovoked attacks on men.

Blue Shark. Length: 12 ft. This shark is indigo blue above, lighter on the sides and snow-white below. Found in tropical, subtropical and warm temperate seas of all oceans. There are numerous authenticated reports of unprovoked attacks on men and on boats.

Black-Tip Shark. Length: 6 to 8 ft. This shark is gray or bronze-gray above, white to yellowish below. Fin tips are dusky to black, particularly in the smaller specimens. Occurs in all warm waters of the world. Authenticated reports of attack are meager.

Lemon Shark. Length: 11 ft. Color is varying shades of brown above, paler brown below—sometimes yellowish. Characterized by second dorsal fin almost as large as the first. This species' identified range is strictly inshore in enclosed sounds, bays and river mouths, New Jersey to northern Brazil in western Atlantic.

Barracuda

Next to sharks (or ahead, depending on how you feel), these are probably the most feared of the undersea predators. This fear is not altogether unwarranted. There have been many authentic reports of attacks by the barracuda. However, in almost all cases it can be assumed from the evidence that the attacks were due entirely to the presence of blood from an injured fish or a human being, bright or shiny lurelike equipment, mistaken identity because of poor visibility, or disturbance and bubbles caused by surface swimming. The barracuda will swim over, alongside of or around the diver and may be tempted to rush in only when a fish is speared. Then it is not so respectful, and if the catch is disputed it may easily remove a diver's finger or adjacent parts along with the fish.

Barracuda will usually retreat from the presence of a diver if the diver makes a bold advance. The larger the fish the less easily it scares; and sometimes a slow retreat of the diver is the better part of valor.

Stick to the rules concerning visibility, clothing, equipment, blood and injured fish. If you don't panic, the barracuda will probably be just another inquisitive member of the underwater population.

There are twenty or more species of barracuda, but only one, the *great barracuda,* is of concern to the skin and scuba diver. Ranging from 3 to 10 ft in length, the fish is long and cylindrically built for speed. Its wedge-shaped head (about one-fourth of the body length) is half occupied by the knife-edged front and rear teeth. These are displayed almost constantly since the barracuda has two mouth vents which permit it to swim with mouth open. The coloring, though changeable with environment, is usually dark green or blue on top, the sides are silver or yellow, and the belly is white. Dark bars and blotches mark the back and sides. It may be found around wharves, buoys, coral beds and wrecks, usually near the surface.

Moray Eel

The 6-foot *green moray* is covered with thick, leathery skin. The basic color is bluish, but this is covered with a yellow mucus blending to green. Some specimens are brownish or slate-colored because of an absence of yellow, in the mucus. They are usually found in holes or crevices of the reefs of the West Indies and Florida Keys.

Three species of spotted morays are found as far north as Charleston, South Carolina. Still another which inhabits deep water may be found as far north as New England. The Pacific moray eel ranges off the southern coast of California.

The moray eel poses no problem to skin divers unless they carelessly put their hand into a hole or crevice without first cautiously assuring themselves of its contents. If the eel does bite, it is tenacious and capable of producing severe lacerated wounds.

Some of the tropical species are known to be poisonous if eaten. Consult local fishermen and divers as to the edibility of local eels.

Aquatic Mammals

Whales, Dolphins and Porpoises. These acquatic mammals are generally not considered to be a menace to the skin or scuba diver. One of the dolphin family (*Grampus orca*), known as the "killer whale" because of its size and hunting habits, usually in schools, can be dangerous. They are characterized by a bluntly rounded snout, high black dorsal fins, a white patch just behind the above the eye, and the striking contrast of jet-black color of the head and back with snowy white underparts. Records of their attacks on herds of seal and other large creatures indicate their danger potential. It would be wise for divers to leave the water if killer whales are sighted.

Seals and Sea Lions. Although these animals are not normally a menace to divers, they may be aggressive to the danger point if they are guarding a harem or if the herd is nearby. Avoid areas in which there are large groups and stay out of trouble.

Plant Growth

Plant growth in the form of seaweed or kelp, particularly in heavy concentration, can be annoying or even dangerous to the inexpeienced or panic-stricken diver. Rising from the bottom, kelp may spread out and cover large areas of the surface. A diver coming up from kelp should keep his hands overhead, part the kelp, look for a clearer area, then drop feet first and move to the clearer area underwater. Eel grass may be long enough to entangle equipment in heavy surge.

If entangled in either kelp or grass, remain calm and methodically disentangle or cut away the plants, drop below and swim to a clearer area.

Food Fishes

Food fish of particular interest to the spearfishing skin or scuba diver are so numerous in species and habitat that local divers should be consulted or Fish and Wildlife Service booklets obtained and read before diving so as to comply with custom and law. Also, fish that are good to eat in one area may not be edible in another. A planned activity usually gives best results.

Fish Poisoning

This is internal poisoning due to consumption of fish, and resembles food poisoning. The symptoms can occur at any time from shortly after consumption of the meal to 10 hours later, and may vary in intensity, depending on how poisonous the fish was and how big the meal. Nausea, vomiting, abdominal cramps and diarrhea, even numbness, paralysis or impairment of the senses may occur.

Little is known of this particular poisoning, and the best treatment is prevention. Consult local sources to learn the presence of poisonous species. If symptoms appear, large quantities of water by mouth will help flush the alimentary tract and speed recovery. All cases should be brought to the attention of a physician as soon as possible.

Parasites

A parasite known as the flat-fish tapeworm has one of its intermediate life cycles in the muscle tissue of freshwater fish. It is dangerous to human beings only if the fish is eaten raw. Cooking destroys the parasite.

ADDITIONAL EQUIPMENT

In order to deal adequately with the environment, divers may add additional equipment to their basic scuba gear. This equipment, in turn, becomes part of the divers' personal environment during their sojourns underwater. During their basic training, divers become familiar with special equipment items that they are likely to use in the underwater environments that they will frequent. Some equipment items are applicable to all environments, while others have more specialized uses. Some of the more common items of equipment beyond basic skin and scuba gear are on the following pages.

DIVER FLAG

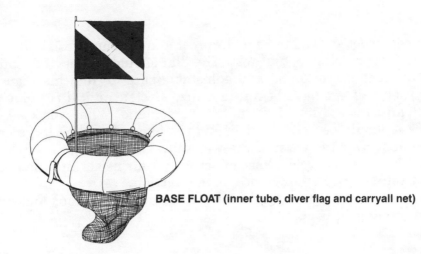

BASE FLOAT (inner tube, diver flag and carryall net)

Diver Flag

A red flag with diagonal white stripe from upper staff to lower outside is widely accepted and used by divers to denote the area in which diving is in progress. Its use has been widely advertised to boaters through diving clubs and through individual diver effort. Some states have enacted a law that forbids surface-craft operators to approach closer than 100 ft to the displayed flag.

The flag is to be displayed on a staff of sufficient (not less than 3 ft) height to be clearly visible and in sufficient numbers so placed as to define the area of diving operations. The placement of the flag(s) must govern the sphere of activity of the diver as well as the boat operator. This is a precautionary device to protect both diver and boat operator. Neither will benefit from its display if its meaning and restrictions are not known and obeyed.

Float

The float, whether an inner tube, inflated raft, inflated boat, modified surfboard or other satisfactory improvisation, should be brightly colored on its above-the-water surface and equipped with a diver flag. The flag staff should be sufficiently high to permit adequate visibility.

This float can be used as a surface base, a resting station and, in an emergency, as a rescue device. Suitable racks or holding devices can be rigged to attach equipment and to provide out-of-the-water storage for speared fish. If random coverage of a large area is anticipated, and if conditions permit, a tow line from the float to the diver will assure its proximity when desired.

Watch

The watch is constructed so as to be waterproof and pressure resistant to at least 220 ft, or 8 atmospheres, by actual test. The dial should be easy to read, have a clearly visible sweep second hand and adjustable bezel to indicate elapsed time.

Recently, some divers have begun to utilize electric digital readout watches, which provide all the necessary information on demand. Whatever kind of watch is used, the case should be noncorrosive, and the band should be large enough to permit attachment over the wrist of the wet suit. Time passage is of the upmost importance to the diver in every phase of activity. Your needs and the price of the watch will, of course, greatly influence your selection.

"Bottom timers" that start automatically upon submersion, and stop upon surfacing are gaining in popularity.

DIVING WATCH

Depth Gauge

Depth, equally important as time, is an essential factor to be known and controlled in practically all diving activity. The depth gauge is available in three basic types:

1. *Capillary.* This consists of a small-diameter plastic tube, open to the water on one end, mounted on or in the perimeter of a calibrated dial. Pressure increase causes water to enter the tube as air volume in the tube is reduced. It is sensitive, inexpensive, easy to maintain and accurate to about 33 ft of depth.

2. *Bourdon tube.* Ambient pressure is transmitted into a curved metal tube that tends to straighten as pressure increases. The change of tube curvature drives a gear system through linkage, to move the gauge indicator needle.

144

This gauge must be protected against loss of seal and thoroughly rinsed to prevent obstruction of water-entrance ports. Bourdon gauges are more expensive than capillary types, but they are accurate to about 200 ft of depth.

3. *Liquid or gas-filled.* These depth gauges rely on pressure variance upon an outer surface of the body of the gauge which is designed to be flexible. Such movement of the flexible area is then transmitted to the internal mechanism which, in turn, activates the indicator on the calibrated dial face. Although it is sealed against water, the gauge should be rinsed thoroughly in fresh water, kept free of dirt and crystallized materials, and treated as a delicate instrument. More expensive than the two gauges above, this type is accurate at all practical depths.

DEPTH GAUGE

Knife

Considered by most experienced divers to be an essential tool of diving, the knife often takes an important role in what may have been planned as a simple, basic skin or scuba dive. Encounters with kelp, grass, derelict lines and the nightmare of monofilament fish line—all of which require the services of a good blade to prevent or undo tangling—will prove the worth of a good knife.

The knife is a useful tool and should not be considered a weapon by the diver. The well-designed knife should have a reasonably sharp edge, a serrated or sawlike edge, strong blade and easy-to-hold handle. Most knife blades are made of stainless steel. When not in use the knife should be carried in a dependable sheath that may be firmly attached in an accessible location on the diver's

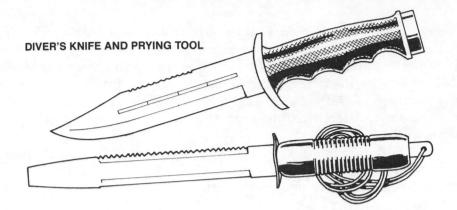

DIVER'S KNIFE AND PRYING TOOL

person, usually the leg. Though considered by many to be " just something else to snag," a lanyard from handle to sheath will prevent loss and still not seriously hamper use.

An alternative to the knife is a prying tool that has a stronger blade. Instead of the usual knife point, the end is chisel-shaped for prying or digging. It also has a sharp and a serrated edge.

Compass

The underwater magnetic compass is housed in a waterproof and pressure-resistant case that can be worn on the wrist like a watch. The strap should be long enough to go around the diver's wrist when wearing a wet suit. It is valuable when navigating both on the surface and underwater, particularly in conditions of reduced visibility. Compasses, depth gauges, and submersible tank pressure gauges are often encased in a single housing called a diver's "console."

COMPASS

All markings should be easily read and should include a fixed "lubber line" that can be aligned with the longitudinal axis of the diver's body for reference to actual direction of forward progress. Some models also have a movable face that can be rotated to indicate a specific course.

Underwater Cameras

Photography underwater requires either a camera encased in a waterproof pressure-resistant case or one specifically designed to operate efficiently underwater. Underwater cameras (self-encased) are available in a myriad of sizes for practically any use.

Unlike land photography, underwater stills and movies require that the prospective photographer be well versed in varied light, color, clarity, width and depth-of-field conditions existing in the water environment. Better than mediocre results are obtained only by study, practice, patience and consulting with experts.

Spears and Spear Guns

Before purchase or use of pole spears or spear guns, the prospective spear fisher should determine legality of their use and seek the advice of experienced area divers.

Pole spears, whether of the hand or rubber-sling thrust type, are designed for impalement of the fish at little more than arm-thrust range.

Spear guns, whether powered by elastic sling, CO_2 cartridge or explosive cartridge, are designed to propel a shaft with penetrating force. Effective underwater range varies with design and is rarely more than several times the length of the shaft.

Decompression Meter

This is considered by many divers to be an essential instrument when performing repetitive or deep dives which may require decompression stops. This instrument, when properly maintained and periodically checked, provides visual decompression information to the diver. Although eliminating much of the sometimes impractical consultation of dive tables during dive operations, it should not be used to take the place of a dive plan. Properly used, it will serve to doublecheck preconceived dive plans. New electronic "decomputers" are available that will calculate elapsed time, decompression stops, surface intervals, and no-decompression data such as residual nitrogen designators.

Miscellaneous

Many diving accessories are considered either essential or desirable. It must be remembered, however, that each one, alone or in combination with others, has its use, and that no advantage is to be gained by simply having or wearing these accessories. Knowledge of each gained through experience will dictate selection and placement for best use.

SIX

PLANNING A SCUBA DIVE

The simplicity with which scuba can be enjoyed with a minimum of essential training by no means reduces the hazards of diving. Simplicity of operation is no measure of safety. On the contrary, it tends to develop within the individual a false sense of ability that can lead to disaster. The early use of safe scuba-diving habits based on sound knowledge of the physics and physiology of diving is essential to avoid danger.

Safe scuba-diving habits are assured when sound knowledge and good judgment are used in planning a dive. Plans need not be elaborate or restrictive, but they should provide for the essential elements of diving safety. Essential elements are those that determine whether or not a scuba dive can be conducted without endangering human life. The purpose of this chapter is to present and discuss these essential elements as they affect the individual, the environment and the scuba.

The Individual

Safe-diving procedures are not new; they are established techniques based on long experience and scientific study by scientists, doctors, professional divers and in particular the United States Navy. The safety record established and maintained by our Navy in deep-and shallow-water diving is above reproach and one every scuba diver should endeavor to match.

In planning a scuba dive, thought should be given to the individual's physical capacity or fitness to perform the dive. Physical fitness should include periodic physical examinations to determine the individual's state of health and verification by a qualified medical doctor that scuba diving will not be harmful or injurious. Prior to the dive, the diver should have obtained adequate sleep and abstained from alcoholic beverages. Under no circumstances should a person dive while under the influence of alcohol, sedatives or any drug that impairs alertness. Diving with a common cold, ear fungus infection, external skin abrasions or similar handicaps should be avoided. Damage to the upper respiratory system, the middle ear or other portions of the body could cause permanent disability. Scuba divers should regularly engage in exercises demanding physical exertion and endurance, ones that provide an opportunity to increase their proficiency in the water. A partial list of recommended exercises includes distance swims with fins and mask, skin diving, water polo, cross-country running and other active athletic endeavors.

No less important than physical fitness is mental fitness. Each individual should have a sincere desire to perform a scuba dive and should have demonstrated emotional stability. The unfamiliar natural phenomena encountered in the comparatively silent world underwater, coupled with the scuba diver's own awareness of solitude, may create panic reactions. Individuals who persuade another person to perform a scuba dive against his or her will are inducing that person to risk self-destruction needlessly. Unfortunately, specific rules cannot be applied to positively determine an individual's mental fitness or emotional stability for scuba diving. Certain factors can, however, give clues to mental fitness for diving. These factors include a sincere desire to dive, no personal history of or tendency toward claustrophobia, no fear of darkness or isolation, a mind capable of formulating and implementing decisions, respect for danger and a capability for normal fear reactions without tendency to panic.

Most emergencies that arise in scuba diving can be successfully met with the proper corrective action. Physical and mental fitness offer the best assurance that an individual can get out of a hazardous situation.

The next essential elements in planning a scuba dive are the individual's knowledge of diving, aquatic ability and experience. These factors require the establishment of safe boundaries equal to the degree of knowledge, training and skill of the individual. When planning a scuba dive, the individual must carefully consider these factors and establish his or her own safe boundaries. Clubs and other organizations will find it useful to establish a classification of divers on the basis of their knowledge, aquatic ability and experience. The following is offered as a suggested rating scale:

A. The *student* diver is one who is diving for the first time or who has limited knowledge of diving, possesses only meager aquatic ability or is unfamiliar with scuba equipment. Such divers should confine their activity to swimming pools under the supervision of a competent instructor.

B. The second classification of scuba divers in general is that of *basic* diver. This diver has achieved a basic knowledge of the theory of diving, shown sufficient aquatic ability and become familiar with the operation of scuba equipment. Their experience in scuba diving is still limited, and basic scuba divers should restrict their diving to safe environmental conditions and do their open-water training under the supervision of capable, experienced scuba divers and instructors.

C. Qualification as a *senior* or *advanced* scuba diver represents outstanding knowledge of the theory of diving, aquatic ability and extensive open-water scuba diving experience. In addition, the senior or advanced diver must exercise good leadership and accept personal responsibility for the safety of divers with less knowledge, ability or experience.

The next consideration in planning a scuba dive is to evaluate those essential elements of diving safety that must be accomplished with another scuba diver. Scuba divers should never consider themselves to be completely self-sufficient, self-sustaining individuals. The elements of diving safety to be considered, evaluated and established with another individual in planning a scuba dive are: the "Buddy" System, an Underwater Communications System and the Emergency Assistance Plan.

The Buddy System

The buddy system is an absolutely necessary diving procedure that must be understood and followed before every skin or scuba dive. Simply defined, it means that no skin or scuba diver, regardless of ability or experience, should ever undertake a dive alone but must be accompanied by at least one other qualified diver who has acknowledged and accepted the responsibility for the partner's safety under any circumstances requiring mutual assistance.

1. To facilitate the most effective safety measures when utilizing the buddy system demands the utmost knowledge of each other's ability and judgment, and the strict observance of a well-defined diver-distance range. Diver-distance range is that distance separating one buddy from another during performance of a scuba dive. This range may vary, depending on visibility, depth and dive-site conditions, but should normally not exceed 10 to 12 ft, even with good visibility. Greater distance and more freedom of travel are often desirable, but the widened interval between divers reduces the chances of rendering immediate assistance in an emergency situation. Remember, the buddy system is for mutual safety and benefit. Why lessen its potential benefits? Scuba dives at night or in conditions of limited visibility should be avoided. If circumstances warrant a night scuba dive, buddies should maintain contact with each other by using a "buddy line." This technique requires two divers to employ a held line 3 to 10 ft long, depending on conditions and the direction of the dive.

DIVERS USING A BUDDY LINE

2. The mutual protection and responsibility accepted by dive buddies also require that they observe definite rules of the underwater conduct. They should know how to:

(a) Signal intended actions, such as ascent, descent and change of direction. Such signals must be previously arranged so that the intended actions may be executed simultaneously.

(b) Signal when visual contact is lost by tapping on scuba tanks with metal or rock, listening for a reply in similar fashion. Surfacing, if rapid reestablishment of visual contact is not made, should be done according to prior arrangement.

(c) Signal at the earliest possible moment any circumstance or situation that might create a hazardous or untenable condition.

(d) Provide confidence and reassurance to a buddy in a hazardous or unde-

152

sirable situation while maintaining self-control and implementing proper corrective action.

(e) Coordinate and achieve mutual agreement and understanding of the communication signals to be employed, the depth-time limitation to be observed and the underwater activities contemplated.

(f) Establish a working knowledge of each other's regular and safety equipment, including the buoyancy control device.

Underwater Communications System

Effective underwater communications are necessary for the safe and efficient conduct of any sport dive. Signals used for individual or special purposes are very diverse and to the imagination of each buddy team because they are not necessarily instrumental in assuring the safe conclusion of the dive.

The American National Standard Institute Skin and Scuba Diving Hand Signals have been selected after considerable investigation and study; they are easily transmitted, received and understood in the various conditions encountered in sport diving. The signals are hand motions instead of finger motions, to make them usable by divers both wearing and not wearing mittens. As often as possible, the signals were derived from those with similar meanings on land, to reduce the learning effort and time. Being hand signals releases them from the unreliabilities of mechanical or electronic devices, thereby making the underwater communications relatively reliable.

Signal systems using other than hand signals have not been standardized because of their extremely limited use by sport divers. WHISTLE BLAST, LIGHT FLASH, TANK TAP and HAND SQUEEZE signals are generally restricted to attracting attention and should be used by sport divers for that purpose. Once attention is gained, further exchange of information should be by hand signals. Sport divers needing LINE PULL signals for use in special circumstances may use those presented in the *U.S. Navy Diving Manual*.

NO.	SIGNAL	MEANING	COMMENT
1.	Hand raised, fingers pointed up, palm to receiver	Stop	Transmitted the same as a traffic policeman's STOP
2.	Thumb extended downward from clenched fist	Go down or Going down	
3.	Thumb extended upward from clenched fist	Go up or Going up	

NO.	SIGNAL	MEANING	COMMENT
4.	Thumb and forefinger making a circle with 3 remaining fingers extended if possible	OK! or OK?	Divers wearing mittens may not be able to distinctly extend 3 remaining fingers (see both drawings of signal)
5.	Two arms extended overhead with fingertips touching above head to make a large O shape	OK! or OK?	A diver with only one arm free may make this signal by extending that arm overhead with fingertips touching top of head to make the O shape. Signal is for long range
6.	Hand flat, fingers together, palm down, thumb sticking out, then hand rocking back and forth on axis of forearm	Something is wrong	This is the opposite of OK! The signal does not indicate an emergency
7.	Hand waving overhead (may also thrash hand on water)	Distress	Indicates immediate aid required
8.	Fist pounding on chest	Low on air	Indicates signaler's air supply is reduced to the quantity agreed upon in predive planning
9.	Hand slashing or chopping throat	Out of air	Indicates that signaler cannot breathe for some reason
10.	Fingers pointing to mouth	Let's Buddy Breathe	The regulator may be either in or out of the mouth
11.	Clenched fist on arm extended in direction of danger	Danger	

Signals employed by divers to increase the efficiency of their dives are natural signals, local signals and those created for special circumstances. Natural signals (those whose meaning is obvious in any language) include: shrugging the shoulders for "I don't know," nodding the head for "yes," shaking the head for "no," pointing to a gauge to mean "what does it read," and hugging oneself for "it's cold." Local signals (those applicable to a specific diving area) include: a cupped hand for "abalone" and thumb and first two fingers opening and closing for "moray eel." Special signals (those created for special circumstances, such as instruction) include: two index fingers alongside each other for "get with your buddy," hand flat with palm down for "level off," and pointing to the tank belt buckle for "take your tank off."

Regardless of the experience and knowledge of the diver, it is always prudent to review the standard and any other signals and their meanings prior to each dive so that no confusion results during the dive.

All signals are to be answered by the receiver repeating the signal as sent.

SKIN AND SCUBA DIVING HAND SIGNALS

Answers to signals 7, 9 and 10 should include the receiver's approaching and offering aid to the signaler. Tapping on tank with metal or rock when not otherwise communicating is a sound emergency signal that means: "I'm going to surface. Join me."

The use of hand or line signals does not allow the signaling of complicated messages or instructions. It does, however, provide a simple system that can be codified and memorized by individuals for use in a variety of circumstances. Such signals must be clearly understood and practiced by dive buddies before commencing a dive. All signals must be promptly answered or returned exactly as given. Thus, a positive means of determining that the signal has been received and correctly understood is assured. A communications system, properly used, does much to reduce the hazards of scuba diving and is of great comfort to the diver.

Emergency Assistance Plan

An emergency assistance plan should be agreed to immediately upon the selection of buddies and/or tenders and the adoption of a communications system. The selection of dive buddies and the use of communications are two basics essential to effective emergency assistance.

An effective emergency assistance plan calls for one diver, ideally the most able scuba diver accompanying the diving party, to exercise complete supervision over the dive and the divers. This "dive master" should maintain supervision from a boat or other surface position and be equipped to give emergency assistance at a moment's notice. The instructions of the dive master must be clear, concise and obeyed instantly before, during and after a scuba dive, particularly during actual emergencies. It must be clearly understood that the dive master occupies a position of authority. *In addition to other responsibilities the master should know the location and nature of all natural and manmade hazards in the vicinity of the diving site and caution all divers accordingly. The dive master should also know the name, location and telephone number of those organizations that render emergency assistance, such as police department, fire department, life-saving stations, first-aid stations, hospitals and the nearest recompression chamber.*

Someone within the scuba-diving group must be accomplished in the techniques of artifical respiration and first aid. Equipment essential to lifesaving must be at hand. Scuba-diving accidents seldom just happen; they are caused by inadequate knowledge, ability, experience, planning or preparation. Most underwater situations that are likely to cause accidents can be anticipated.

Planning can prevent an unfavorable circumstance from developing into an accident or fatality. The greatest danger of all is to be emotionally or physically unprepared, or to lack the proper equipment, to render emergency assistance when a life may be in the balance.

Underwater emergency situations are most easily avoided by close buddy support and attention. The onset of panic in a diver can often be reversed by a buddy's firm, confident grip on the arm or hand. However, close approach to a diver completely in panic may not be advisable.

Specific skills and evacuation plans are needed for the treatment of the unconscious diver. Techniques have been developed for scuba rescue and in-water mouth-to-mouth resuscitation, and these techniques should be practiced. A specific plan for evacuation of a diving casualty is part of the emergency assistance plan. One member of the diving party should accompany the injured diver to the treatment center to describe the particulars of the injury. The accompanying diver often will be knowledgeable about diving-related injuries and treatment and must make this knowledge known to attending physicians. There are many documented cases of diving casualties being treated improperly because medical personnel either were not aware of the origin of the injury or were ignorant of the right treatment.

External heart massage (cardiopulmonary resuscitation, "CPR") requires no additional equipment and can be administered immediately. Administration of oxygen for hypoxia and decompression sickness for an injured but breathing diver will significantly improve the response to your first-aid treatment.

The Scuba Dive

In planning a scuba dive, the main elements of diving safety must be carefully studied and understood. These essential elements include the reliability of the scuba, duration of the air supply and its purity, checking of the unit's proper working order, operation of the mechanical safety features, and care and storage of equipment.

One of the essential elements of the scuba itself is its reliability. Reliability means that it will work as intended with the least possibility of mechanical failure when properly maintained. Safe standards of reliability seldom, if ever, can be obtained in any homemade rig or with parts designed for other purposes.

Selection of diving equipment is mostly a matter of personal choice and of fitting the price to the pocketbook. A wide field of competition has led to production of good-quality, trouble-free, safe equipment. Well-known manufacturers offer a variety of such equipment to suit the needs and desires of divers at almost every level of experience. Evaluation and selection should be made after consulting more experienced divers, checking guarantees and, whenever possible, examining more than one brand or type. The latter can often be accomplished by renting or borrowing the chosen brand. The U. S. Navy evaluates diving equipment only for its own purposes and in no case publicly approves or disapproves commercial items. No manufacturer is authorized to use Navy Approval as an advertising claim.

If new or unfamiliar equipment is to be used, complete and thorough testing should be performed in a safe area. Before testing, manufacturer's instruction booklets on proper care, maintenance and function should be consulted to ensure that proper attention is given to any peculiarities of the specific unit.

The following predive check items should be followed with use of any of the current types of open-circuit air-breathing apparatus:

A. Be sure that the tanks contain only certified-pure breathing air. Air that contains contaminants such as carbon monoxide can cause serious trouble, even death.

B. Know the pressure in the tanks before each dive. Figure the depth-time limitation for the deepest depth intended. Whenever possible, plan each dive to avoid the need for decompression. Exceeding the depth-time limits without the right allowance for decompression is especially dangerous when necessary recompression treatment of bends is not immediately available.

Decompression diving is not recommended for the usual sport-diving situation. Repetitive dives compiled according to the Navy tables should be emphasized as the most rigorous diving activity one can be involved in unless a recompression chamber is available within 5 minutes of the dive location.

C. Immediately before entry, a diver should be sure, through personal inspection, that the main high-pressure valve is open and that the demand regulator is working properly. Any malfunction or imperfection, such as hard breathing, unusual valve changes or loose fittings, calls for suspending the dive until proper corrections have been made.

RESERVE AIR VALVE IN OFF POSITION

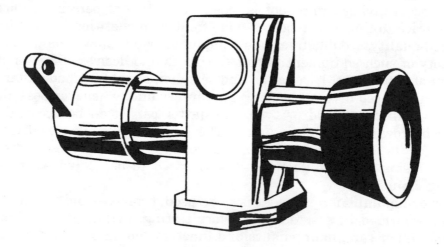

Continuous readout pressure gauges on regulators for scuba tank pressure should be standard equipment.

D. Mechanical safety features on most present-day scuba units include a reserve-air feature and quick-release harness assembly, The diver using the scuba should be doublechecked by the swim buddy on the operation of the reserve-air feature and the proper assembly of the harness quick-release feature. The actual operation of both these safety features should then be demonstrated to the dive master, who should personally check that the reserve-air supply control valve is in the OFF position. The predive check of equipment must include the condition of the inflatable vest. All valves should be checked. This includes oral inflation and, if attached, the overpressure release. The gas cartridge or air-tank mechanism and available supply should be checked. Buddies and the dive master should be thoroughly familiar with all features of the vests worn. The predive test can then be carried out by a shallow dive in the immediate vicinity of the diving site to be sure that the units are working properly before descending to the desired depth and task.

Planning a scuba dive does not end with the descent of the diver into the depths. The plan must also include proper care and storage of the equipment upon completion of the dive. Generally, carrying out a few simple tasks will ensure the readiness of equipment for the next day of diving. Upon surfacing, the diver should first close all high-pressure valves. If this is the last dive of the operation, the following steps should be accomplished in sequence:

1. Wash the scuba in fresh water, being careful to place the dust cover over the high-pressure inlet on the demand regulator.
2. Cleanse all rubber components of grease, oil or other organic solvents.
3. Drain and dry the apparatus.
4. Store the equipment in a clean, safe place where the air tanks can be protected from dropping, sharp blows and excessive heat.
5. Vest, wet suit, mask, hood, boots, gloves and metering devices should be washed, dried and stored to prevent deterioration or damage.

NAVIGATION

One fact for consideration here is another basic: *direction*. Up and down are usually not a problem. Direct passage is a different matter. There are no roads, signposts or (for lack of a better word) landmarks. The lack of these things may make unguided travel rather haphazard. Swimming in a straight line in an unmarked void is, for most, nearly impossible. If the dive plan calls for travel in a certain direction, it must include knowledgeable use of a compass. The following is basic information and must be added to by practice and further study. In planning a dive in any but the clearest water, a good compass is an essential piece of equipment. It is usually well worth the extra effort in time and energy saved to run through the directional courses planned before entering the water. This makes it easier to follow the plan once underwater and subject to limited visibility. Always knowing your bearing from the point on the surface to which you intend to return is a reassuring feeling.

Most diving compasses will have a clearly visible "lubber" line that runs parallel to the length of the body when positioned as shown. This line will indicate the direction in which the diver is swimming in relation to true north as indicated by the compass needle. By pointing the lubber line in the direction you wish to follow and maintaining the same angle between lubber line and compass needle, you can stay on the desired heading. Some compasses also have a rotating face with two index or bracket marks that can be aligned over the needle for quick reference. As long as the needle is kept between the marks, the swimmer is on the desired course when following the lubber line.

Practice in using the diving compass will make it a reliable aid to navigating, both on the surface and below. This should include 90° turns to the right and left while leaving the index marks at the original setting. Quick mental adjustment to directional changes will also greatly reduce the chance of disorientation when surfacing in a fog or other obstruction to visibility.

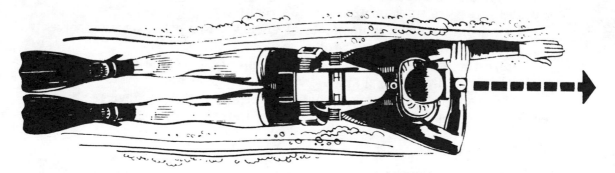

USING THE COMPASS

SEVEN

REPETITIVE DIVING

During the 12-hour period following a scuba dive, the quantity of nitrogen in the diver's body will gradually decrease to its normal level. If, within this period, a second dive is made—called a repetitive dive—the diver must consider the current residual nitrogen level within the body when planning for the dive. The procedures for conducting a repetitive dive are summarized in the figure on page 164.

Terms frequently used in discussions of the decompression tables are defined as follows:

Depth—when used to indicate the depth of a dive, means the maximum depth attained during the dive, measured in feet of seawater (fsw).

Bottom Time—the total elapsed time from the moment the diver leaves the surface in descent to the time (next whole minute) that ascent begins, measured in minutes.

Decompression Stop—specified depth at which a diver must remain for a specified length of time to eliminate inert gases from the body.

Decompression Schedule—specific decompression procedure for a given combination of depth and bottom time as listed in a decompression table; it is normally indicated as feet/minutes.

Single Dive—any dive conducted 12 or more hours after the last previous dive.

Residual Nitrogen—nitrogen gas that is still dissolved in a diver's tissues after surfacing.

Surface Interval—the time a diver has spent on the surface following a dive; beginning as soon as the diver surfaces and ending as soon as the next descent starts.

Repetitive Dive—any dive conducted within a 12-hour period following a previous dive.

Repetitive Group Designation—a letter relating directly to the amount of residual nitrogen in a diver's body for a 12-hour period following a dive.

Residual Nitrogen Time—and amount of time, in minutes, which must be added to the bottom time of a repetitive dive to compensate for the nitrogen still in solution in a diver's tissues from a previous dive.

Single Repetitive Dive—a dive for which the bottom time used to select the decompression schedule is the sum of the residual nitrogen time and the actual bottom time of the dive.

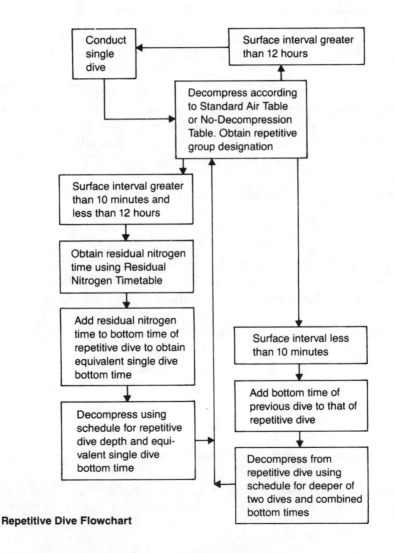

Repetitive Dive Flowchart

164

Upon completing the first dive, the diver will have a Repetitive Group Designation assigned to him or her by either the Standard Air Table or the No-Decompression Table. This designation relates directly to the residual nitrogen level upon surfacing. As nitrogen passes out of the tissues and blood, the repetitive group designation changes. The Residual Nitrogen Table permits this designation to be determined at any time during the surface interval.

Just prior to beginning the repetitive dive, the residual nitrogen time should be determined using the Residual Nitrogen Table. This time is added to the actual bottom time of the repetitive dive to give the bottom time of the equivalent single dive. Decompression from the repetitive dive is conducted using the depth and bottom time of the equivalent single dive to select the appropriate decompression schedule. Equivalent single dives which require the use of exceptional exposure decompression schedules should, whenever possible, be avoided.

To assist in determining the decompression schedule for a repetitive dive, a systematic repetitive dive worksheet, shown below, should always be used.

If still another dive is to follow the repetitive dive, the depth and bottom time of the first equivalent single dive should be inserted in part 1 of a second repetitive dive worksheet.

Repetitive Dive Worksheet

I. PREVIOUS DIVE:

_____ minutes ☐ Standard Air Table
_____ feet ☐ No-Decompression Table
_____ repetitive group designation

II. SURFACE INTERVAL:

_____ hours_____ minutes on surface
Repetitive group from I _____
New repetitive group from surface
Residual Nitrogen Timetable _____

III. RESIDUAL NITROGEN TIME:

_____ feet (depth of repetitive dive)
New repetitive group from II _____
Residual nitrogen time from
Residual Nitrogen Timetable _____

IV. EQUIVALENT SINGLE DIVE TIME:

___ minutes, residual nitrogen time from III
+___ minutes, actual bottom time of repetitive dive
=___ minutes, equivalent single dive time

V. DECOMPRESSION FOR REPETITIVE DIVE:

_____ minutes, equivalent single dive time from IV
_____ feet, depth of repetitive dive
Decompression from (check one):
☐ Standard Air Table   ☐ No-Decompression Table
☐ Surface Table Using Oxygen   ☐ Surface Table Using Air
☐ No decompression required

Decompression Stops: _____ feet_____ minutes
_____ feet_____ minutes
_____ feet_____ minutes
Schedule used _____   _____ feet_____ minutes
Repetitive group _____   _____ feet_____ minutes

NO-DECOMPRESSION LIMITS AND REPETITIVE GROUP DESIGNATION TABLE FOR NO-DECOMPRESSION AIR DIVES 7.5.2

The No-Decompression Table serves two purposes. First, it summarizes all the depth and bottom time combinations for which no decompression is required. Second, it provides the repetitive group designation for each no-decompression dive. Even though decompression is not required, an amount of nitrogen remains in the diver's tissues after every dive. If he dives again within a 12-hour period, the diver must consider this residual nitrogen when calculating decompression.

Each depth listed in the No-Decompression Table has a corresponding no-decompression limit given in minutes. This limit is the maximum bottom time that a diver may spend at that depth without requiring decompression. The columns to the right of the no-decompression limits column are used to determine the repetitive group designation which must be assigned to a diver subsequent to every dive. To find the repetitive group designation enter the table at the depth equal to or next greater than the actual depth of the dive. Follow that row to the right to the bottom time equal to or next greater than the actual bottom time of the dive. Follow that column upward to the repetitive group designation.

Depths above 35 feet do not have a specific no-decompression limit. They are, however, restricted in that they only provide repetitive group designations for bottom times up to between 5 and 6 hours. These bottom times are considered the limitations of the No-Decompression Table and no field requirement for diving should extend beyond them.

Example—

Problem—In planning a dive, the Master Diver wants to conduct a brief inspection of the work site, located 160 feet below the surface. What is the maximum bottom time which he may use without requiring decompression? What is his repetitive group designation after the dive?

Solution—The no-decompression limit corresponding to the 160-foot depth in the No-Decompression Table is 5 minutes. Therefore, the Master Diver must descend to 160 feet, make his inspection and begin his ascent within 5 minutes without having to undergo decompression.

Following the 160-foot depth row to the 5-minute column, the repetitive group designation at the top of this column is D.

NO-DECOMPRESSION LIMITS AND REPETITIVE GROUP DESIGNATION TABLE FOR NO-DECOMPRESSION AIR DIVES

Depth (feet)	No-decompression limits (min)	A	B	C	D	E	F	G	H	I	J	K	L	M	N	O
10		60	120	210	300											
15		35	70	110	160	225	350									
20		25	50	75	100	135	180	240	325							
25		20	35	55	75	100	125	160	195	245	315					
30		15	30	45	60	75	95	120	145	170	205	250	310			
35	310	5	15	25	40	50	60	80	100	120	140	160	190	220	270	310
40	200	5	15	25	30	40	50	70	80	100	110	130	150	170	200	
50	100		10	15	25	30	40	50	60	70	80	90	100			
60	60		10	15	20	25	30	40	50	55	60					
70	50		5	10	15	20	30	35	40	45	50					
80	40		5	10	15	20	25	30	35	40						
90	30		5	10	12	15	20	25	30							
100	25		5	7	10	15	20	22	25							
110	20			5	10	13	15	20								
120	15			5	10	12	15									
130	10			5	8	10										
140	10			5	7	10										
150	5			5												
160	5				5											
170	5				5											
180	5				5											
190	5				5											

Source: U.S. Navy Diving Manual

RESIDUAL NITROGEN TIMETABLE FOR REPETITIVE AIR DIVES 7.5.3

The quantity of residual nitrogen in a diver's body immediately after a dive is expressed by the repetitive group designation assigned to him by either the Standard Air Table or the No-Decompression Table. The upper portion of the Residual Nitrogen Table is composed of various intervals between 10 minutes and 12 hours, expressed in hours: minutes (2:2 1 = 2 hours 21 minutes). Each interval has two limits; a minimum time (top limit) and a maximum time (bottom limit).

Residual nitrogen times, corresponding to the depth of the repetitive dive, are given in the body of the lower portion of the table. To determine the residual nitrogen time for a repetitive dive, locate the diver's repetitive group designation from his previous dive along the diagonal line above the table. Read horizontally to the interval in which the diver's surface interval lies. The time spent on the surface must be between or equal to the limits of the selected interval.

Next, read vertically downwards to the new repetitive group designation. This designation corresponds to the present quantity of residual nitrogen in the diver's body. Continue downward in this same column to the row which represents the depth of the repetitive dive. The time given at the intersection is the residual nitrogen time, in minutes, to be applied to the repetitive dive.

If the surface interval is less than 10 minutes, the residual nitrogen time is the bottom time of the previous dive. All of the residual nitrogen will be passed out of the diver's body after 12 hours, so a dive conducted after a 12-hour surface interval is not a repetitive dive.

There is one exception to this table. In some instances, when the repetitive dive is to the same or greater depth than the previous dive, the residual nitrogen time may be longer than the actual bottom time of the previous dive. In this event, add the actual bottom time of the previous dive to the actual bottom time of the repetitive dive to obtain the equivalent single dive time.

Example—
Problem—A repetitive dive is to be made to 98 fsw for an estimated bottom time of 15 minutes. The previous dive was to a depth of 102 fsw and had a 48-minute bottom time. The diver's surface interval is 6 hours 28 minutes (6:28). What decompression schedule should be used for the repetitive dive?
Solution—Using the repetitive dive worksheet—

RESIDUAL NITROGEN TIMETABLE FOR REPETITIVE AIR DIVES

Repetitive group at the beginning of the surface interval

```
A   0:10
    12:00*

B   0:10   2:11
    2:10   12:00*

C   0:10   1:40   2:50
    1:39   2:49   12:00*

D   0:10   1:10   2:39   5:49
    1:09   2:38   5:48   12:00*

E   0:10   0:55   1:58   3:23   6:33
    0:54   1:57   3:22   6:32   12:00*

F   0:10   0:46   1:30   2:29   3:58   7:06
    0:45   1:29   2:28   3:57   7:05   12:00*

G   0:10   0:41   1:16   2:00   2:59   4:26   7:36
    0:40   1:15   1:59   2:58   4:25   7:35   12:00*

H   0:10   0:37   1:07   1:42   2:24   3:21   4:50   8:00
    0:36   1:06   1:41   2:23   3:20   4:49   7:59   12:00*

I   0:10   0:34   1:00   1:30   2:03   2:45   3:44   5:13   8:22
    0:33   0:59   1:29   2:02   2:44   3:43   5:12   8:21   12:00*

J   0:10   0:32   0:55   1:20   1:48   2:21   3:05   4:03   5:41   8:41
    0:31   0:54   1:19   1:47   2:20   3:04   4:02   5:40   8:40   12:00*

K   0:10   0:29   0:50   1:12   1:36   2:04   2:39   3:22   4:20   5:49   8:59
    0:28   0:49   1:11   1:35   2:03   2:38   3:21   4:19   5:48   8:58   12:00*

L   0:10   0:27   0:46   1:05   1:26   1:50   2:20   2:54   3:37   4:36   6:03   9:13
    0:26   0:45   1:04   1:25   1:49   2:19   2:53   3:36   4:35   6:02   9:12   12:00*

M   0:10   0:26   0:43   1:00   1:19   1:40   2:06   2:35   3:09   3:53   4:50   6:19   9:29
    0:25   0:42   0:59   1:18   1:39   2:05   2:34   3:08   3:52   4:49   6:18   9:28   12:00*

N   0:10   0:25   0:40   0:55   1:12   1:31   1:54   2:19   2:48   3:23   4:05   5:04   6:33   9:44
    0:24   0:39   0:54   1:11   1:30   1:53   2:18   2:47   3:22   4:04   5:03   6:32   9:43   12:00*

O   0:10   0:24   0:37   0:52   1:08   1:25   1:44   2:05   2:30   3:00   3:34   4:18   5:17   6:45   9:55
    0:23   0:36   0:51   1:07   1:24   1:43   2:04   2:29   2:59   3:33   4:17   5:16   6:44   9:54   12:00*

Z   0:10   0:23   0:35   0:49   1:03   1:19   1:37   1:56   2:18   2:43   3:11   3:46   4:30   5:28   6:57   10:06
    0:22   0:34   0:48   1:02   1:18   1:36   1:55   2:17   2:42   3:10   3:45   4:29   5:27   6:56   10:05   12:00*

NEW→  Z   O   N   M   L   K   J   I   H   G   F   E   D   C   B   A
GROUP DESIGNATION
```

*Dives following surface intervals of more than 12 hours are not repetitive dives. Use actual bottom times in the Standard Air Decompression Tables to compute decompression for such dives.

REPETITIVE DIVE DEPTH	Z	O	N	M	L	K	J	I	H	G	F	E	D	C	B	A
40	257	241	213	187	161	138	116	101	87	73	61	49	37	25	17	7
50	169	160	142	124	111	99	87	76	66	56	47	38	29	21	13	6
60	122	117	107	97	88	79	70	61	52	44	36	30	24	17	11	5
70	100	96	87	80	72	64	57	50	43	37	31	26	20	15	9	4
80	84	80	73	68	61	54	48	43	38	32	28	23	18	13	8	4
90	73	70	64	58	53	47	43	38	33	29	24	20	16	11	7	3
100	64	62	57	52	48	43	38	34	30	26	22	18	14	10	7	3
110	57	55	51	47	42	38	34	31	27	24	20	16	13	10	6	3
120	52	50	46	43	39	35	32	28	25	21	18	15	12	9	6	3
130	46	44	40	38	35	31	28	25	22	19	16	13	11	8	6	3
140	42	40	38	35	32	29	26	23	20	18	15	12	10	7	5	2
150	40	38	35	32	30	27	24	22	19	17	14	12	9	7	5	2
160	37	36	33	31	28	26	23	20	18	16	13	11	9	6	4	2
170	35	34	31	29	26	24	22	19	17	15	13	10	8	6	4	2
180	32	31	29	27	25	22	20	18	16	14	12	10	8	6	4	2
190	31	30	28	26	24	21	19	17	15	13	11	10	8	6	4	2

RESIDUAL NITROGEN TIMES (MINUTES)

Change 2   *Source:* U.S. Navy Diving Manual

169

Repetitive Dive Worksheet

I. PREVIOUS DIVE:

_48_ minutes   ☑ Standard Air Table
_102_ feet   ☐ No-Decompression Table
_M_ repetitive group designation

II. SURFACE INTERVAL:

_6_ hours _28_ minutes on surface
Repetitive group from I _M_
New repetitive group from surface
Residual Nitrogen Timetable _B_

III. RESIDUAL NITROGEN TIME:

_98_ feet (depth of repetitive dive)
New repetitive group from II _B_
Residual nitrogen time from
Residual Nitrogen Timetable _7_

IV. EQUIVALENT SINGLE DIVE TIME:

_7_ minutes, residual nitrogen time from III
+_15_ minutes, actual bottom time of repetitive dive
=_22_ minutes, equivalent single dive time

V. DECOMPRESSION FOR REPETITIVE DIVE:

_22_ minutes, equivalent single dive time from IV
_98_ feet, depth of repetitive dive
Decompression from (check one):
☐ Standard Air Table ☐ No-Decompression Table
☐ Surface Table Using Oxygen ☐ Surface Table Using Air
☑ No decompression required

Decompression Stops: _____ feet _____ minutes
                            _____ feet _____ minutes
                            _____ feet _____ minutes
Schedule used _____   _____ feet _____ minutes
Repetitive group _____   _____ feet _____ minutes

Change 1

SUMMARY

Remember, it is not recommended that sport divers make dives of sufficient duration or depth to require staged decompression according to the U. S. Navy Standard Decompression Tables. The reasons behind this recommendation have been clearly stated earlier in this book. At the same time, many sport divers may often find themselves in situations where they have an opportunity to make more than one dive in a 12-hour period at depths in excess of 30 or 40 ft. On these occasions, intelligent use of the tables described in this chapter will enable sport divers to enjoy their underwater activities without the danger of decompression sickness or the need for staged decompression.

EIGHT

SCUBA LIFESAVING

Prevention of accidents by careful planning, preparation, and always diving with a competent buddy is as important as knowing what to do in an emergency. Whether diving in a group or as a single pair, staying close to your buddy at all times will greatly reduce the chance of an accident.

Rescue problems involving divers often differ from those involving swimmers. Much of diving is done in areas normally not used for recreational swimming. Many of these areas, far from organized lifeguard or other protection, involve rocks, reefs, marine animals or plants, unusual currents and strong surges, and are remote from easily accessible routes.

For these reasons, a scuba diver's effectiveness in open water will be much greater if he or she has mastered some fundamental techniques for assisting a buddy or another diver who is experiencing difficulty.

SIGNS OF DISTRESS

Quick detection of the early signs of distress in a fellow diver can often prevent more serious problems from developing and can save a life without the need for a dramatic rescue effort. Sensitivity to the following signs of diver's stress in your companions—or, for that matter, in yourself—is a critical component of scuba lifesaving:

1. A sick or injured diver
2. A poorly or inappropriately equipped diver
3. A diver who is making mistakes before he or she ever gets into the water or immediately upon entering the water

Photos appearing on pages 172, 174, 177 178-179 courtesy of the National YMCA Scuba Program.

HIGH TREADING: A SIGN OF A DIVER IN TROUBLE

4. A diver who exhibits tension by a high-pitched voice, nervous laughter or other verbal signs
5. A diver who has unusual difficulty with his or her equipment or who otherwise unnecessarily hesitates before entering the water
6. A diver who exhibits improper techniques in entering the water and carrying out the rest of the dive plan
7. A diver who exhibits high treading upon entering the water, excitedly treading water with the upper body exposed above the surface
8. A diver who removes mask, regulator or other equipment after he or she has entered the water
9. A diver who clings to anchor lines ladders or other surface-related objects after he or she has entered the water
10. A diver with poor buoyancy control
11. A diver who experiences extreme difficulty in pressure equalization
12. A diver who swims erratically underwater in terms of speed and direction, or who tends to swim away from his or her buddy
13. A diver who ascends or descends unexpectedly or in the wrong manner

In addition to obvious signs of distress, such as struggling or unconsciousness, the 13 unlucky signs listed above are tipoffs of possible trouble to come. Their early detection can eliminate the need to put the following lifesaving skills into practice.

MISSING DIVER

An emergency situation may exist if a diver has not been seen or if exhaust bubbles have not been noted for a period of time longer than normal. A lookout (dive master) should be stationed to maintain constant check of every diver's location. If the mandatory "buddy system" has been maintained, the absence of the diver should be quickly noted. Suggested action is as follows:

A. Immediately determine where the diver was last seen.

B. Move to that area and look for bubbles.

C. A bottom search team should immediately cover the area. Use the appropriate search pattern. Take into consideration existing currents that might alter the assumed location of the missing diver. Work downstream from the area in which the diver was last seen.

D. Check the possibility that the diver has left the area (gone ashore) without notifying the group.

E. If available, send for additional help to aid in the search.

STRUGGLING SURFACE DIVER

Although skin diving and scuba diving are considered underwater sports, the most common form of distress you are likely to encounter is struggling on the surface. The signs are as follows:

1. Low in water, head thrown back
2. Mouthpiece and/or mask off or removed
3. Considerable arm movement
4. Inefficient, bicycling kick
5. Noncommunicative and nonresponsive
6. Grasping at any surface object, including another diver

The key to stabilizing such a surface victim is to use his or her own equipment or else provide buoyancy. Self-rescue should be encouraged while maintaining a safe distance, and a struggling diver should be approached only as a last resort. The basic steps in stabilizing a struggling scuba diver on the surface are as follows:

1. Assess the situation carefully in terms of the nature of the problem and available alternatives for assistance.
2. Encourage the struggling diver to stabilize himself or herself using his or her own equipment while you maintain a safe distance.
3. If contact is necessary, approach the victim under the water, reaching up toward his or her weight belt hook release and BC emergency inflator.

4. Attack both the weight belt release and the BC inflator simultaneously, using the most convenient target of opportunity.
5. In dropping the victim's weight belt, make sure it is clear of the victim's body, and yours, before releasing.
6. Make sure the individual's BC is fully inflated before surfacing from beneath the distressed diver. Employ his or her auto-inflator if the CO_2 system is inadequate or inaccessible.
7. Surface outside the victim's reach or directly behind the victim.

The above procedure or any other designed to assist the diver struggling on the surface should be thoroughly practiced under an instructor's guidance with the help of a third "safety diver" before attempting to apply it in an actual situation.

SUBMERGED UNCONSCIOUS DIVER

Any diver found unconscious underwater is in mortal danger and should be brought immediately to the surface using great care. This care should be directed not only at saving the life of the distressed diver but also toward maintaining the safety of the rescuer. The basic principles for such a rescue are as follows:

1. Maintain the diver's airway even if he or she has stopped breathing or appears to have exhausted his or her air supply. Hold the regulator in place in the victim's mouth, or replace it if it has been lost: *Never purge the regulator into the diver's airway when replacing it.*
2. Get between the diver and the bottom before beginning your ascent, rather than just reaching down toward the victim.
3. Remember, your buoyancy will increase as you ascend. Using the surface CO_2 system to inflate a BC at depth can be very dangerous. Tempered use of the auto-inflator is advised if necessary to initiate ascent. Use the victim's buoyancy if possible. Be prepared to vent a BC during ascent to control your rate.
4. Make strong use of your own legs to establish an ascent rate. Push off from the bottom if necessary, and establish a broad water kick as soon as you leave the bottom. Remember, your fins can be used to break an ascent as you approach the surface and your buoyancy increases.
5. *Do not forget to breathe normally yourself during this recovery procedure.* You must avoid any tendency to hold your own breath as you concentrate on the victim.
   This procedure, like the previous one, should be practiced under heavy supervision before trying it in an open-water situation. It should be practiced only in shallow depth, and the acting victim should retain his or her regula-

tor in the mouth and breathe normally throughout the practice procedure. Additional air should not be added to the BC during practice of this procedure.

TOWS AND EXTRICATION

A tired or injured diver who is conscious but not actively struggling on the surface and who is buoyant enough to secure his or her airway may be towed by his or her tank valve or BC collar or may be pushed through the water by having the victim lie on his or her back and place the fins on the shoulders of the assisting diver.

Interestingly enough, it is not unusual for a diver's anxiety to increase during the tow. For this reason, the towing diver should be alert to reassure and/ or control the distressed diver during a surface tow. Also, divers who are under tow should be closely watched to ensure an open airway and so that they do not slip into unconsciousness without the knowledge of the rescuer.

In almost all cases, a distressed diver's scuba equipment must be removed before extricating him or her from the water. Any tow is also greatly expidited by

FOOT PUSH: TOW FOR THE CONSCIOUS VICTIM

GEAR DITCHING

removal of the distressed diver's weight belt and scuba equipment. Three factors are important in jettisoning a distressed diver's gear. First, the assisting diver must be familiar with all equipment releases and their operation. Obviously, this familiarization is the best acquired before a dive, when no one really anticipates an emergency. If this has not been done, or if he distressed diver does not happen to be your buddy with whom you conducted a predive check, then you must take a few seconds to assess the diver's equipment before attempting to jettison it. A second important factor is to pull all of the gear clear before handing it to another diver or dropping it in open water. Forgetting just one equipment attachment and then dropping the gear can seriously complicate the rescue procedure. The third important factor in jettisoning gear is not to allow this procedure to distract assisting divers from maintaining an adequate airway for the distressed diver. Remember, maintaining a diver's airway takes precedence over any tow or extrication in a rescue procedure.

A special consideration in ditching a diver's scuba gear occurs when the diver is wearing a buoyancy compensator permanently attached to the scuba tank backpack. In some cases, the pack is designed so that the tank can be easily removed from it while the pack itself remains strapped to the body. The feasibility of this must be quickly determined by assisting divers in an emergency situation. When this alternative does not appear to be feasible, the entire unit, including the BC, usually can be safely removed from a diver who is wearing a wet-suit jacket providing positive buoyancy once other equipment is jettisoned. Usually, assisting divers can make intelligent decisions on such matters, as long as they are aware of all the factors involved.

Other tows available to assisting divers include a head carry and a modified version of the traditional cross-chest carry, in which the rescuer can actually use the distressed diver's equipment for support by reaching across his or her inflated BC.

A "do-si-do" tow, similar to the move used by square dancers, is effective in maintaining visual contact with the distressed diver and is the tow most commonly used in performing the deep-water rescue breathing described in the next chapter of this book.

The following considerations for extrication of a distressed diver from the water are taken from the manual *Scuba Life Saving and Accident Management*, published by the National YMCA Underwater Activities Program.

MODIFIED CROSS-CHEST TOW

EGRESS

Removing a victim from the water may be the most difficult part of a rescue. Part of the pre-dive assessment should include consideration of how a rescuer could get a bulky, unconscious victim back through heavy surf, coral formations, mud, or onto a pier, dock, or boat. All the while the victim may need resuscitating. Before attempting to take any victim from the water, check for removal of his weight belt, which should have been previously dropped along with his tank. Both can be removed by assistants, if available, during the tow or by yourself, if you can do so. The rescuer's encumbering gear should also be removed. Rescuer(s) must remove their fins (or have an assistant remove them) before attempting to walk with the victim. If you are giving the victim artificial respiration, check his carotid artery for a pulse as soon as you can do so effectively (in shallow water, or at the side of a boat or pier, for instance). If none is present, get the victim onto a hard flat surface, land or boat, as soon as possible. Manual chest compressions must be given along with ventilations by one or two persons trained in Cardio-Pulmonary Resuscitation (CPR); chest compressions cannot be done in the water. There is a technique for giving CPR on a rescue board or paddle board, but it is difficult and should not be attempted by the untrained. An unconscious victim's head and chest should be tilted slightly down as he is removed from the water if you can do so without wasting time. This will allow water to drain from his airways.

When placing a victim on a sloping deck or ground, his head should be protected from injury and placed lower than his feet.

In cases where a back or neck fracture is suspected, care should be taken to avoid any twisting, bending, flexing or extending of the back or neck. The victim should be fastened securely with many ties or straps to a back board before being removed from the water. This is extremely difficult to accomplish in deep water.

Use the motion of the water to float the victim to a high spot onto a boat ramp, rocks or shore. Time your efforts with the waves or swell.

Assistants should be enlisted to help as soon as they are available. Call for them early. The rescuer(s) doing the towing may be too exhausted to climb aboard without help or may even sink silently while the victim is being handled.

Both victims' and rescuers' buddies should be accounted for to prevent a multiple tragedy.

Preparation For Egress May Be Complicated

Small Boats

Even the most agile uninjured swimmer will frequently have great difficulty climbing back into a small boat. If you are alone and can't get back in by yourself, you certainly won't be able to get your incapacitated buddy aboard!

The best equipped dive boats will have stern platform at or slightly below water level allowing relatively easy access for a fully equipped diver. Some also have a ladder to climb onto the platform and/or onto the boat. In calm waters, this is the ideal situation. The rescuer can swim the victim up to the platform, cross the victim's arms on it and hold them there with one hand as he climbs aboard. One of the standard lifesaving pool lifts can get the victim aboard.

Rough water creates problems. The boat and platform will rock back and forth and up and down. An incautious diver can be swept under and knocked unconscious or injured by the oscillations of the platform. A stern or safety line with floats provides a hand-hold and will keep the divers from being swept away; the line should already be attached before the dive began. You can use assistants. Call for help. If none is available, keep the victim between you and the platform and try to use any surge to wash him aboard. Once on, hold him tightly to avoid being swept off and try to get on with the next surge yourself.

If your small boat has no platform or ladder and no help is available, a line should have been strung into the water over the side from near the bow to the stern prior to the dive. (If this was not done, you may be able to rig some anchor line this way.) This can then be used as a step for re-entry of a small boat. If the victim is unable to hang on, he may have to be secured by his hands with another line to keep his face out of the water while you climb in. You can then unfasten his hands and try to pull him in, using one of the pool type lifts.

Many people have been injured trying to climb into an outboard motor boat by stepping on the cavitation plate of the motor; this is a tempting but dangerous spot to climb, especially in a heavy sea. Propellor blades and metal protuberances can cause bad cuts or lacerations. The dive boat should have a ladder.

If the victim is able to climb into a small ladderless boat with help, the rescuer may be able to give him a boost by letting him step on his shoulders while the rescuer is under water holding onto the gunwale or transom with his hands.

If assistants are available on board they may be able to reach over the gunwale or stern, grab the victim' s arms—a rescuer on each of the victim's arms if necessary—and haul him aboard. They may need to haul the rescuer in the same way.

Larger Boats, Piers and Cliffs

If the boat's gunwale is too high to reach over, a rope with a bowline knot tied in it may be used. The line is thrown over the side and slipped under the victim's arm with the knot at the middle of his back. A thick heavy line will be strong enough to hold the victim without bruising him. One or more lighter lines can be attached to this loop if extra assistants are available. In this way, the victim' s weight is divided among many, easing the load.

Lifting an incapacitated victim into a boat or onto any high dock presents a serious problem to the rescuer. Even when a platform or ladder are present, this is a very difficult chore for one, but even two or three people, will have difficulty when the gunwale or transom have to be surmounted. A similar problem exists where an egress is necessary up a vertical facing such as a wall, cliff, bank, or dock. The following description applies to all of these situations, although a lift onto a boat is used as an example.

A technique has been devised using only a sturdy piece of line, called the "rope lift." This lift utilizes the principle of mechanical advantage and can be used by one or more rescuers. The weight of the victim is effectively reduced by one-half. The rescuer should choose the largest diameter rope conveniently available to avoid chafing the victim, but almost any rope will do, even a section of anchor line. If there is adequate slack, it is not necessary to disconnect the line from any attachments. A rope that sinks will work better.

An easier way to lift an incapacitated person is to roll him up in a net. If one end of the net is secured and a 200 lb. victim is rolled aboard by pulling on the other end, the rescuer will be pulling only 100 lbs. If there are two people pulling, each one will have only about 50 lbs. to lift.

The person who attempts to effect a scuba rescue in or through surf (waves breaking on a beach, either sand or rocks or coral) will encounter a set of problems unlike any other environment. Mistakes by the rescuer could prove fatal, not only to the victim but to the rescuer as well.

As the rescuer approaches the surf zone from open water, he must begin to pay constant attention to approaching waves. A rescuer and victim unexpectedly assaulted by a breaking wave can be separated with the victim thus lost. Being thrown about against the bottom and each other can cause injury to both. It is much safer to exit the surf more slowly between waves than hurry into a hazardous situation.

Because of the energy of breaking waves, it's likely that the unprepared rescuer will lose his victim in surf if he is not using a tow that assures him full control. A back tow ("spread eagle") grasping the victim' s vest, a cross chest tow, or a "do-si-do" will prove most effective. Large waves generally will come in "sets" or groups of 3 to 6 waves about 10 to 15 seconds apart with 2 to 3 minutes of smaller waves between sets. The wise rescuer will attempt to exit the surf zone during this "lull" between sets of larger waves, waiting beyond the surf zone if necessary for the lull to occur.

If the victim is very apprehensive or panicky, it may be necessary to pause seaward of the surf zone in order to calm him prior to attempting egress. *Never* attempt to tow a panicky victim through surf to shore. Verbal explanation of the rescuer's actions may help in easing the victim's anxiety.

If, after starting towards shore with the victim, it appears to the rescuer that they may be caught by large breaking waves, he should consider moving seaward again and waiting out the set as preferable to being thrown about by the surf.

In all cases, the rescuer must be aware that the mask will likely be displaced and could become a problem. Thus it probably should be removed prior to egress through the surf zone. Likewise, the tank could be turned into a dangerous object by a breaking wave and should be removed from both victim and rescuer before entering the surf zone, if possible.

The rescuer should tow the victim from the back towards shore so as to have greater control and continued observation of the surf. As a broken wave approaches, the rescuer should turn the victim toward shore, hold him firmly, cover the mouth and nose if unconscious and let the wave strike him from behind. Surf is often acccompanied by rip currents and the rescuer must be cognizant of these so as to avoid being swept seaward against his will.

Multiple rescuers are desirable in surf situations and should be utilized beyond the surf zone if at all possible. This is particularly true where the victim is unconscious or disabled and must be carried from the water. If two rescuers are present, the victim should be transported with one on either side, towing by the arms into chest deep water. The victim can then be dragged by the arms up on shore.

If three rescuers are available, the third can use the "foot push" until all can stand, at which point buoyancy should be used to get the victim's knees over the third rescuer's shoulders while the first two utilize the "do-si-do" tow in tandem.

If the rescue is being accomplished around rocks the rescuer should let the victim take the brunt of any collisions to avoid creating a two-victim, no-rescuer situation.

Once having passed through this surf zone, exit from the water may still prove difficult. Utilization of bystanders could be helpful. If all else fails, the victim can be stripped of any remaining gear and rolled up any incline out of the water.

When exiting from deep water onto an adjacent rock or reef, the rescuer should tow the victim as close to the rocks as possible, then attempt to "ride" a swell up onto the rock with the buoyant victim turned sideways and held in front of the prone rescuer. After getting up above the rocks, the receding wave will drop the two onto the rocks where the rescuer can get his hands and knees braced while preventing the victim from rolling off. The rescuer must brace on the rocks as soon as he makes contact, and hold on until the water from the swell which deposited him there has receded. He can then attempt to roll the victim higher on the rocks in this interval before the next swell. As the next swell sweeps over the rocks the rescuer should attempt to use this energy to move the victim higher. As the new swell recedes, the rescuer will need to brace, as before, to prevent being swept off. Additional assistance can be very helpful in removing the victim from the rocks.

GENERAL CONSIDERATIONS

Scuba rescue and accident management can be quite complex. Indeed, most training agencies offer specialty certifications in this one particular area of expertise. The information on the preceding pages is presented primarily to enable the basic open-water diver to provide assistance to himself or herself and to others in a few basic emergency situations. Serious skin divers and scuba divers are advised to include training in this important field as part of their continuing underwater education.

NINE

DIVING FIRST AID

Most diving accidents can be prevented, but even the best-trained diver on the best-run dive may get into real trouble when least expecting it. It is not enough to know how to "do it right" in the first place. You also have to know what to do if things go wrong. Whether a mishap on a dive turns into a full-blown tragedy can depend entirely on you or your buddy. There will seldom be a doctor on the scene to handle a medical emergency, and there may not be a hospital within miles; so you are on your own. If you have had good first-aid training and carry with you to every dive site a plan for how to obtain emergency assistance as quickly as possible, doing the right thing will be almost automatic.

As in the case of diver rescue, complete training and certification programs are available in first aid in general and in diving first aid in particular. The purpose of the information on the following pages is to provide basic open-water divers with sufficient guidelines to enable them to deal intelligently with problems that could occur for those who do not use adequate care in approaching the underwater environment. Again, continuing education in this area is encouraged.

Remember, the best way to handle an accident is to keep it from happening. Accident prevention starts with being sure you are fit for diving and does not stop until you are back on shore after a safe dive made possible by your training in handling yourself underwater and knowing how to plan dives and stay out of trouble. One definition of first aid is "keeping an accident from becoming a tragedy." This chapter should serve as a guide to what divers should know about first aid, a review of the essentials and a place to look up certain facts (such as care of injuries from marine animals) that can be very important but hard to remember.

187

GENERAL PRINCIPLES

Very few serious accidents can be handled entirely without professional medical assistance. However, the fact that such assistance is not immediately at hand need not result in loss of life. A few fairly simple first-aid procedures can almost always handle the situation in the meantime. Calmly applying proper first aid on the spot is far better than madly rushing the victim to the nearest doctor or hospital. This does not mean that there should be any needless delay in getting professional help. In treating the victim of any accident, the first step is to *size up the situation* rapidly but accurately. This will tell you what to do first, and doing the right thing first can be a matter of life or death. Splinting a broken bone is useless if the victim dies within minutes because his or her breathing has stopped, and artificial respiration won't help a victim who is rapidly bleeding to death. If you have someone to help you, the really important things can be done almost simultaneously provided you know what needs to be done. Ask yourself these questions:

1. *Is the victim breathing?* If not, artificial respiration takes precedence over absolutely everything except the need to control massive bleeding—— which you are not likely to miss.
2. *Is the victim bleeding?* Rapid loss of blood can cause death in a few minutes, so it clearly must be controlled at once. Even less obvious bleeding can cause shock or death in a relatively short time, so it must be discovered and stopped.
3. *Is the victim in shock?* Shock can and does follow almost any type of injury and can cause death even though the initial injury was unlikely to do so.

If none of these problems demanding immediate attention is found, then proceed to examine the victim as thoroughly as possible so as to find *all* the injuries that he or she may have sustained. Be extremely gentle and do not move the victim any more than absolutely necessary in the process of examination or when loosening clothing. Be particularly careful to avoid unnecessary moving of the head and neck. If the neck happens to be broken, such movement can cause death or permanent paralysis. If a broken bone is found or suspected, immobilize the part before moving the victim.

In general, the victim should be kept lying flat with head level with the body—at least until you are sure of the full extent of the injuries. Unless circumstance demands prompt removal to a safer place, do not move the victim unless you are sure it is safe to do so or until he or she can be moved properly by means of a stretcher or suitable substitute.

Remember that *your first duty is not to do harm*. It is better to do nothing than to do something that makes matters worse. Send for medical help immediately if you can. Never delay getting help while you do things like nonessential bandaging. It is always possible that some condition you may have overlooked, such as internal bleeding or a head injury, demands medical attention urgently.

DEALING WITH ASPHYXIA (STOPPAGE OF BREATHING)

In diving accidents, there are many causes for the stopping of breathing. Whatever the cause, when breathing has stopped, the victim must be supplied with air by some method. Many methods of artificial respiration (causing an alternate increase and decrease in chest expansion) have been devised and practiced since man recognized the need for such action. Most have succeeded in moving little or no air, although they have on occasion been used successfully.

Very careful and exhaustive research has shown that the oldest method of all—inflating the victim by mouth—can be by far the most effective, with no gadgets whatever, provided that the head and neck are placed in the proper position. This method (now called Rescue Breathing) of "mouth-to-mouth or mouth-to-nose" artificial respiration utilizes the rescuer's exhaled air. The exhaled air has more than enough oxygen to supply the needs of the victim. The rescuer knows positively at every instant whether air is going in and out adequately, so that if obstruction occurs he or she will know it at once and take action. A child can successfully ventilate even a large adult, and the method can be used anywhere (even in the water) and under conditions where other methods would be difficult, damaging or impossible.

The sole objection to Rescue Breathing stems from squeamishness, bashfulness, prejudice and fear of acquiring an infection. Only fear of an infection is an obstacle that intelligent people should be willing to admit, and the actual danger of contracting a serious disease is extremely slight. It should not deter you from using the method on a fellow diver or on anyone in apparent asphyxia distress. When properly done, the method does not involve inhaling the victim's breath. The chances that the victim has a communicable disease or, if so, that the rescuer could contract it, are remote.

The following concise description of the method was combined from the American Red Cross First *Aid Text* and the American Heart Association *Cardio-Pulmonary Discussion Guide*. See pages 191-192 for the numbered sequence.

1. If possible, place the victim on a firm, flat surface (do not put anything under the shoulders or let the head hang over an edge), preferably with the lower extremities higher than the head. Remember that the head and neck position in relation to the body is essential and can be achieved properly under any conditions, even when both victim and operator are in the water. Turn the head to one side and clear the mouth of any regurgitated food or

foreign material. This may be accomplished by opening the mouth with one hand and inserting one or two fingers to sweep material from the mouth (1).

2. Tilt the victim's head backward as far as possible to provide an open airway. This may be accomplished by lifting the neck close to the head with one hand and pushing the forehead with the palm of the other until the neck is extended and the airway straightened. This action serves to "jut" the jaw forward (2).

The palm so placed on the forehead puts the thumb and forefinger in position to pinch-seal the nose. Alternate straightening and opening of the airway can be achieved by pulling or pushing the lower jaw into a jutting position (3,4).

Opening the airway may promote voluntary breathing. Watch for rise and fall of the chest, listen for sounds of exhalation, or feel the exhaled air against your cheek or ear. If no respiration is detected, start breathing for the victim as follows.

3. With the head tilted back, jaw forward as described and illustrated (5), pinch the nostrils closed, or close the nostrils with your cheek. Take a deep breath, open your mouth wide and place it tightly over the victim's mouth and blow (6, 7). Look to see that the chest rises. Following the rise of the chest, remove your mouth, maintain the "jutted"-jaw and extended-neck condition, and observe the fall of the chest. This is the exhalation phase caused by natural relaxation of extended chest muscles. If the expansion and contraction of the chest occurred, repeat the process at a rate of once every 5 seconds (12 times per minute) for adults. Infants and small children will require that the inflation or expansion phase be restricted in volume but increased in rate up to 20 times per minute. If a baby or small child is being resuscitated, the neck and jaw position straightening the airway must be maintained. The nose and mouth can be covered by your mouth or the nose sealed by your cheek. Inflation is controlled relative to the size of the victim. A slight puff may be all that is necessary to obtain inflation.

If inflation does not occur, or is inadequate and difficult to attain, the jaw and neck position should be rechecked and the mouth examined for any obstruction without delay. Having corrected position and cleared the mouth, renew the effort to inflate the lungs.

If regurgitation of water or stomach contents occurs, the head should be turned to the side to permit drainage so as to prevent forced aspiration of foreign material into the airway. If, after checking the jaw and neck position and clearing the mouth, obstruction is still present, the victim should be rolled to the side and a sharp blow or blows delivered between the shoulder blades (8). During the foregoing operations, care should be taken to maintain

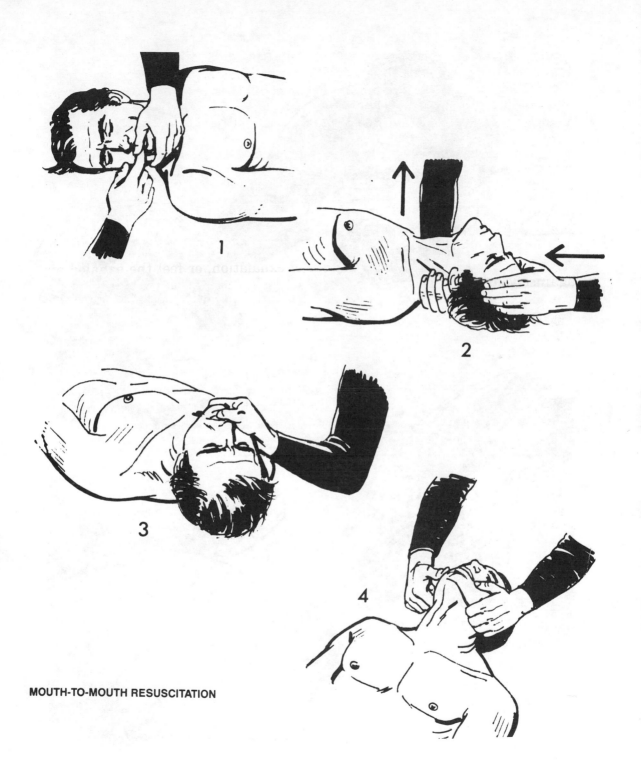

MOUTH-TO-MOUTH RESUSCITATION

5

6

7

8

192

the open airway. Even with the victim turned on the side, the resuscitator can effectively function from behind by leaning over the victim.

4. If conditions exist that do not permit the preceding mouth-to-mouth procedure, mouth-to-nose resuscitation may be accomplished. The jaw may be jutted forward by placing fingers under the chin and lifting the jaw upward and forward. The thumb and forefinger may be used to seal the mouth. This jutting of the jaw may be assisted by the other hand lifting at the angle of the jaw as shown. The mouth covers the nose and nostrils and the inflation is performed at the same rate as in the mouth-to-mouth. Remember to keep the jutted-jaw, open-airway position throughout the process of inhalation and exhalation.

Every diver should be familiar with Rescue Breathing and should, when possible, practice applying it under a number of circumstances. The rescue of an unconscious nonbreathing diver or swimmer may be made at quite a distance from shore. Resuscitation efforts should be started as soon as the victim has been brought to the surface. Weight belt or belts should be dropped, if necessary, and the vest of the victim and/or the resuscitator should be inflated to promote positive buoyancy. The resuscitator, supported by the inflated vests, should experience little difficulty in attaining the required head and neck position and performing mouth-to-mouth or mouth-to-nose resuscitation. Experimentation will disclose that the procedure may be performed while progress is made toward shore or base. Similar efforts may be performed using an inner tube, surfboard, or the side or stern of a small craft as a supporting medium. Regardless of the flotation used, you must remember that the mouth must be cleared and the aforementioned open-airway position maintained.

The key to effective deep-water rescue breathing is keeping as much of your body, as well as the victim's, in the water as possible. This can be accomplished by turning the victim's head to the side to gain access to the airway while the rescuer remains low in the water.

While mouth-to-mouth rescue breathing in deep water is fast and requires no equipment, the rescuer may tire quickly and could introduce water into the victim's lungs in rough conditions. An alternative is mouth-to-snorkel rescue breathing. Start with the chin pull, holding the victim's head against your chest with one hand and a snorkel, acquired from your gear or the victim's, in the other. Clear the water from the snorkel by letting it run out, and keep it clear by bending the tube end up or by holding it in your teeth. Place the snorkel flange over the victim' s mouth, and seal the victim's nose with the thumb and forefinger of the same hand. Then place the tube end of the snorkel in your mouth and blow. After filling the victim's lungs, remove the tube end from your mouth and allow the victim's air to escape through the tube.

Courtesy National YMCA Program

THE HEIMLICH MANEUVER

An obstruction of a diver's airway can occur for many reason's including regurgitation of food resulting from nausea.

An effective method of dislodging food from the windpipe is known as the Heimlich maneuver, named for the physician who developed it.

Standing (or kneeling if the victim is seated) behind the choking victim, whose head, upper torso and arms are permitted to lean forward, the rescuer puts both arms around the victim's waist below the rib cage. With one fist grasped in the other hand, the rescuer presses the fist *upward* quickly *into* the victim's abdomen with the hands only. This forces the lungs to expel air that dislodges the food mass blocking the windpipe. Do not squeeze the victim with the arms.

The same result is had with the victim lying face up on the ground and the rescuer kneeling astride the lower part of the body. With the heel of one hand placed on top of the other, the rescuer presses quickly into the abdomen below the rib cage.

In either position, upright or supine, the victim must have his or her mouth cleared of food with the rescuer's fingers to keep from reswallowing it. Do not give up if success is not immediate in expelling the obstruction. Keep up the quick, sharp pressure thrusts until the victim is able to breathe.

HEIMLICH MANEUVER—UPRIGHT POSITION

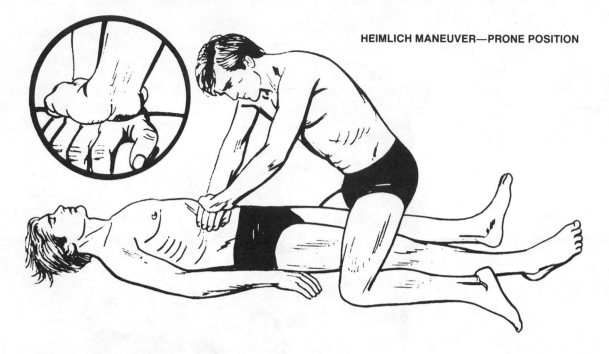

Should a choking diver be without the assistance of a buddy, punching the upper abdomen with the fists, or pressing it against some firm edge, allows self administration of the Heimlich maneuver.

Remember, to avoid cracking the ribs of the victim, or causing other injuries, the rescuer must press *inward* and *upward* with the *hands*—do not squeeze with the arms.

DEALING WITH CARDIAC ARREST (HEART FAILURE)

Heart stoppage can be caused by a number of things, such as drowning, complications of pulmonary barotrauma, physiological stress and so on. A person in cardiac arrest will turn blue and will have no pulse. The condition will not change with the administration of mouth-to-mouth resuscitation, since oxygenated blood from the lungs will not be circulated to the tissues. A victim of cardiac arrest requires cardiopulmonary resuscitation (CPR) immediately.

The victim should be flat on the ground. The rescuer kneels beside the victim and gives the victim four rapid mouth-to-mouth breaths, then locates the lower tip of the breastbone with the finger. Place the heel of the right hand above the finger, then place the left hand over the right. With a brisk but firm downward pressure, depress the bottom third of the breastbone about an inch and a half. Let your body weight do the job rather than trying to muscle it. Relax, remove the pressure and repeat in intervals of once a second. Press, release, press, release.

The downward pressure compresses the heart, forcing the blood out into the system, and the reaction and release bring the blood back into the heart. This combination substitutes for the actual heartbeat.

Mouth-to-mouth respiration must be administered about every 15 strokes of CPR. Two full breaths should be forced into the victim's lungs, then resume the CPR. If there is other help available, let the second person administer the mouth-to-mouth artificial respiration at the rate of once every five CPR strokes. This will allow the normal rate of breathing of 12 times per minute.

Carry out the proceedure until the victim's pulse is renewed and breathing is resumed. Color will improve with this restoration of vital signs.

There is the possibility that under some circumstances bodily injury can result from CPR. The haste, enthusiasm or lack of training of the rescuer may cause too strong a pressure, resulting in cracked ribs or a broken breastbone. Training in CPR is necessary and may be obtained through the Red Cross First

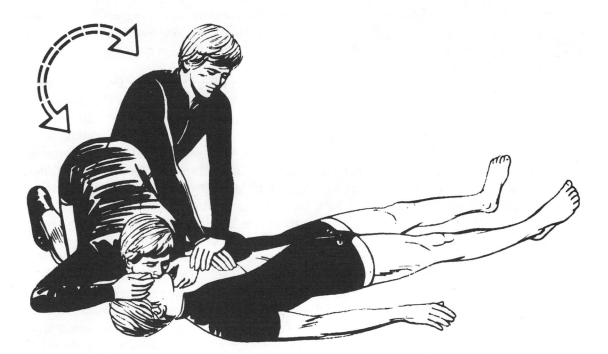

CARDIOPULMONARY RESUSCITATION (CPR)

Aid training program, or the local Heart Association may run CPR training programs. In any event, administer CPR if the heart has stopped, for the person will surely die without this help.

Performance of CPR in deep water is extremely difficult and requires many hours of training and the use of specially modified scuba equipment. Also, detection of a pulse and other signs related to cardiac arrest is almost impossible to do with a diver in open water. When cardiac arrest is suspected in a diving injury, the victim should be removed from the water to the nearest firm surface as quickly as possible for the initiation of CPR.

CONTROL OF BLEEDING

Nothing is more urgent than stopping rapid loss of blood, and only artificial respiration is more important than control of even moderate bleeding. Four different methods of control can be employed, either singly or in combination, using materials at hand:

1. *Direct pressure on the wound* either by hand or dressing (sterile or clean cloth in several folds) bandaged in place. It is desirable to use sterile dressings on any wound to reduce the danger of infection. However, serious loss of blood caused by waiting for or transporting to such a dressing may prove far more dangerous than an infection. Bandages should be applied firmly but not tightly enough to hamper circulation.

2. *Hand or finger pressure on the artery* supplying the area of the wound will slow or stop most bleeding from the extremities until a dressing and bandage are applied. The pressure points located on the inner side of the arm, which cause the brachial artery to be compressed against the arm bone, and pressure points on either side of the groin, which cause the femoral artery to be compressed against the front of the pelvis, are most easily found and most widely used. Others are described in older manuals but have little value, or are difficult to find and hold for any length of time.

3. *Elevation of the affected part* will serve to slow serious bleeding at its onset and during subsequent transport to a doctor or hospital.

4. *The tourniquet is the last resort.* Remember that when a tourniquet is incorrectly placed, venous bleeding is increased and arterial bleeding is unaffected. When a tourniquet is placed correctly several inches above the wound, the blood supply to the area below the constricting band is completely shut off, and the tissues will die from loss of oxygen and food unless surgical attention is obtained within a short time. Contrary to past technique, the *tourniquet should not be loosened* except by the doctor. If, as a last

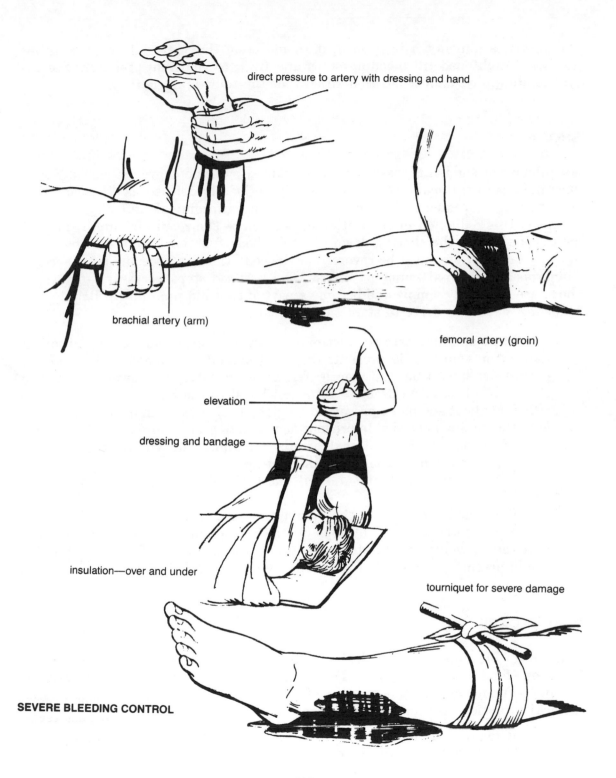

direct pressure to artery with dressing and hand

brachial artery (arm)

femoral artery (groin)

elevation

dressing and bandage

insulation—over and under

tourniquet for severe damage

SEVERE BLEEDING CONTROL

resort, a tourniquet is applied, it should be of flat material about 2 inches wide, tightened till bleeding stops and fixed to continue pressure. The attending physician must be notified that the tourniquet is in place.

SHOCK

All injuries or sudden illnesses are accompanied by some degree of shock. Reference here is to *traumatic shock*, which may be briefly defined as "the condition resulting from reduced blood circulation." The anatomical and physiological causes of this reduction in circulation are complex. The resultant diminishing of circulation causes the slowing down of all the body functions. This slowing down of the vital functions must be reversed or the condition may become more serious than was the original injury or illness. The first-aid steps necessary to reverse shock are relatively simple and become a part of first-aid procedures. Briefly, the following steps will serve to start the reversal:

1. Place and maintain the victim in a prone, quiet, comfortable position. If nausea or vomiting is present, the head should be turned to the side to permit drainage from the mouth. Whenever possible, the lower extremities should be elevated to promote return of blood to the heart.
2. Body heat should be preserved by placing insulating material under and over the victim as needed to prevent heat loss to ground and air. If the victim or the surface is wet and cold, insulation under the victim is of greater importance than insulation over the victim.
3. Perform necessary first aid with as little disturbance of the victim as possible.
4. When and if conscious, the victim may complain of thirst. Fluid intake should be restricted to small sips of water. Abdominal injury or conditions that may involve immediate surgery and the presence of extreme nausea would preclude giving any fluids to the victim. Alcohol should not be given.

WOUND CARE

Aside from bleeding control, which has been discussed, here are a few general directions for the care of wounds. Following them will greatly reduce the chance of infection and add to the comfort of the victim, as well as make the later medical attention less complicated.

1. Whenever giving first-aid care to any opening in the skin, the first-aid person should have clean hands.

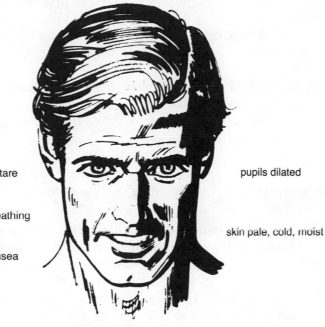

vacant stare

pupils dilated

shallow, irregular breathing

skin pale, cold, moist

nausea

SHOCK SIGNS AND SYMPTOMS

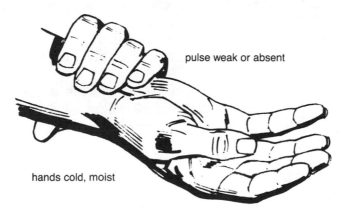

pulse weak or absent

hands cold, moist

2. Soap and clean water (preferably boiled) may be used to cleanse the area of the wound. Care must be exercised to prevent dirt or foreign material from entering.

3. If the wound will receive further care by a physician, it is best that no antiseptic be applied. Consult your doctor concerning antiseptics to be placed in first-aid kits.

4. Cover the wound with a sterile dressing and bandage in place snugly but not so tightly that circulation is impaired.

5. Even in minor wounds, if any sign of infection appears (redness, swelling, pus), bring it to the attention of a physician.

TETANUS PREVENTION

Tetanus (lockjaw) is a common disease caused by germs found in soil, dirt, mud and elsewhere. These germs enter the body through a break in the skin. Minor wounds, particularly punctures, can be dangerous if sustained where contamination is at all likely; this makes it mandatory that the victim be protected against the disease. This is particularly true of divers injured in mud or dirty water. There are two methods of protection: use of *tetanus antitoxin*, which requires several injections at the time of injury and may cause troublesome reactions; and the use of *tetanus toxoid*, which seldom causes any difficulty. Tetanus toxoid is given as a routine immunization, and most people have had it either as children or as members of the armed forces. If the individual has received a "booster" *within three years*, all that needs to be given at the time of injury is a small additional dose. Unfortunately, few adults keep their boosters up to date and, if injured, must receive the antitoxin instead. A sensible diver will get the protection of tetanus toxoid immunization and will apply for the additional dose if injured on land or in the water.

Since much diving water is contaminated to some degree, divers are also exposed to all waterborne diseases. It therefore makes good "safe diving sense" to see your doctor to be sure that all your immunization shots are up to date.

DEALING WITH FRACTURES

First aid for fractured bones consists mainly of careful handling (or no handling unless necessary) so as not to increase the injury. If the victim must be moved or transported other than in an ambulance under expert supervision, the fracture should be immobilized. Using whatever *suitable* materials are at hand (appropriate length, weight and strength) for splints, apply these in such a manner as to keep the broken bone ends from moving and at the same time prevent movement of the adjacent joints. Careful transportation and treatment for shock are essential.

DEALING WITH BURNS

First aid for burns is dependent on the degree and the amount of area involved. Burns are classified as:

First Degree—reddening of the skin;
Second Degree—blisters;
Third Degree—charring or deep destruction of tissues.

Pain of burns involving less than 20 percent of the body surface may be greatly reduced by immersion in clean, cold water (preferably ice). If immersion of the area is not practical, ice-cold wet applications may be used. Immersion or packs should continue until pain is eliminated.

Regular burn care should follow ice-water immersion. The area should be covered with a sterile pad bandaged firmly in place and of sufficient thickness to exclude air.

A small first- or second-degree burn may be cared for by the application of a medically approved preparation and a sterile dressing.

The commonest type of burn suffered by divers is sunburn. Long exposure, both in and out of water, has taken all the pleasure out of many a well-planned and well-executed diving trip. Gradual tanning may be accomplished by an initial short exposure, which is increased daily until the desired protection pigment layer has been built up. Shielding the skin with light clothing or applying tanning lotions or creams will prevent painful or even serious burns.

Shock care is imperative when large areas of any degree are involved, and shock is generally a threat even where relatively small areas have suffered third-degree burns. Since infection and other complications may be involved, the attention of a physician should be sought.

DEALING WITH HYPOTHERMIA

Hypothermia, common among divers, is a condition in which the "core" temperature of the deep tissue of the body drops below the normal range of about 99°F. Below that temperature, if exposed for an excessive period, the body will respond in the form of uncontrollable shivering, loss of the sense of touch and muscle control, diminished judgment and ability to reason clearly and, eventually, blacking out and death. A diver suffering from hypothermia should be rewarmed as promptly as possible. This means that his or her normal core temperature should be completely restored, not just superficially, but to the point of sweating, before diving is resumed.

Rewarming can be accomplished by taking a hot bath, which is preferable to a shower. Only the trunk of the body should be covered with the warm water, however, to prevent a potentially fatal "after-drop" of the body's core temperature from sudden vasodilation of the extremities. The diver should then dress in warm, dry clothing to contain body heat. It could take hours to restore the lost heat. Drinking alcohol during this period is not advisable because it accelerates the loss of body heat in cold surroundings. Hot, nourishing liquids, such as soup, are useful once the victim of hypothermia is fully alert.

Wet suits are now by far the most common form of protective clothing, but they lose insulating value at depth because of compression of the air cells in the foam material. In some commercial diving situations, warm water is pumped through the diver's suit. For deep work and extreme cold, newer types of dry suit are in demand.

DEALING WITH PRESSURE-RELATED ILLNESS OR INJURY

As you learned earlier, increased partial pressures of individual gases can sometimes create problems for the scuba diver. These can include carbon dioxide or carbon monoxide poisoning and nitrogen narcosis. First aid for conditions brought about by lack or excess of breathing components, unless complicated by stoppage of respiration and circulation, usually consists of surfacing and getting rest and fresh air. Carbon dioxide excess and, in particular, carbon monoxide excess can be effectively dealt with by administering pure oxygen.

First-aid measures for squeezes during descent are usually limited to making the victim comfortable and advising that further diving activities be suspended. Mask and suit squeeze areas respond to cold wet packs initially and later to warm wet packs.

As indicated earlier, pulmonary barotrauma and its resulting complications, as well as decompression sickness, present similar symptoms. They also respond to similar first-aid and treatment procedures. Victims of suspected pulmonary barotrauma or decompression sickness should receive first aid until they can be seen by a physician. Those suspected of having incurred a pulmonary barotrauma should be placed in a Trendelenberg position, with the legs elevated at an angle as steep as 45 degrees and the body turned slightly to the left side. The administration of oxygen in using the Trendelenberg position of ten can have dramatic effects on the symptoms of pulmonary barotrauma and decompression sickness. However, those even slightly suspected of having acquired either of these diving ailments should be examined by a specialist in hyperbaric medicine at the earliest opportunity.

Air embolism and decompression sickness usually require immediate recompression if permanent injury or even death is to be averted. Diving first aid should be directed at obtaining treatment as soon as possible.

The Diving Accident Network (DAN) can be contacted to expedite this treatment. Their phone number is (919) 684-8111.

If the victim is unconscious or unable to communicate, the first-aid person must make every attempt to learn the history of the dive and the events leading to the collapse so that they may be passed on as accurately as possible to the recompression facility. The signs, symptoms, time elapsed from onset and first-aid measures instituted must be forwarded with the victim.

The depth and bottom time of dive or dives, the conditions under which the ascent was made (breathing normally or not breathing), scheduled decompression not taken—all are facts to be determined and forwarded with the victim to the recompression facilities. Lay diagnosis is an educated guess of condition guided by events and evaluation of observed signs. Making such a diagnosis or evaluation of condition is a desirable procedure for facilitating treatment and report making, but must not delay transportation to a recompression chamber or to first-aid care. If air embolism or decompression sickness is a possibility, time is an all-important factor. The victim must be transported as soon as possible to recompression and adequate medical attention. Knowledge of the agency to contact for such transportation and the location of the nearest hyperbaric facility capable of handling the probable condition is necessary to every planned dive.

Even casual examination of treatment tables indicates that much more is involved than simply taking the diver to increased pressure until he or she feels better and then bringing him or her up. Doing that will generally make matters worse. The offending bubble or bubbles must not only be compressed to a size that no longer causes symptoms, but also be induced to go back into solution. As in the case of treating gas embolism (above), the possibility of providing adequate treatment in the water can virtually be ruled out. Knowing the location of the nearest recompression chamber, knowing how to reach it quickly and having lines of communication for advice are almost as important in decompression sickness as in gas embolism.

HEATSTROKE

Symptoms are hot, dry, flushed skin, very rapid pulse, high body temperature and sudden collapse.

Heatstroke is the result of prolonged overheating, which results in a critical rise in body temperature and body water depletion. It can be avoided by wearing protective clothing and limiting physical exertion. This is a serious medical emergency. Body temperature must be lowered promptly to prevent possible brain damage and even death.

The major factor in treating heatstroke is to cool the body to a safe level as quickly as possible by removing from exposure to sun or other heat source. Bathe entire body with cool water or, if possible, immerse entirely, being sure to keep victim's nose and mouth above water. Give fluids to drink, preferably a weak solution (1 teaspoon of salt in 1 quart water) of salt water. Summon a doctor, or transport victim to medical attention upon recovery.

HEAT EXHAUSTION

Symptoms are nausea, vomiting, rapid pulse, fainting, cold clammy skin, dizziness, headache, continued sweating and difficulty in breathing.

Heat exhaustion is a result of exposure to heat during strenuous labor. If victim is wearing an exposure suit, remove and keep body from becoming chilled. Lay on back in cool, shady place, head lower than body. Administer a weak solution (1 teaspoon salt in 1 quart water) of salt water. Recovery should be fairly prompt, but headache and weakness may linger.

SEASICKNESS (MOTION SICKNESS)

Symptoms are the usual nausea, dizziness, thick dry tongue, sickly green, pallid complexion and vomiting.

This is one of the most common hazards of diving from small craft or surface platforms. Vomiting when submerged can cause strangulation and death. The use of certain commercially produced motion-sickness remedies may alleviate the complaint, but they may also contain antihistamines that will create a dangerous condition of drowsiness or carelessness. Diving when seasick should be discontinued and not resumed until the diver feels up to it.

EAR INFECTION

Symptoms are itching or pain in the ear, crusting or scabbing of the ear canal, and excretion of fluid from the canal, accompanied by fungus growth and flaking at ear opening, redness or swelling around ear.

Divers are subject to various forms of ear infection or fungus, especially when operating in tropical or other warm waters. High humidity and repeated immersion can accelerate the condition. The best treatment is prevention. Ears should be kept clean and dry. The use of cotton swabs is not recommended because they tend to irritate the ear canal and could puncture the drum. Numerous medications are available but it is advisable to consult a doctor for treatment if an infection is contracted.

SEA URCHIN SPINES

The sea urchin, like motion sickness, is one of the most common hazards to the diver. Its many spines are very brittle and will break off at the slightest touch. If the spines perforate the skin, they will immediately cause sharp, burning pain accompanied by redness and swelling of the area affected.

Remove exposed spines with tweezers. Those that are broken off at the skin surface are almost impossible to extract, and probing with a needle will only break them into smaller pieces. Generally the spines will be dissolved in about a week. Others may fester and may be squeezed out to where they can be removed with tweezers. Commercial ointments that will speed the dissolving process are available, but it is advisable to see a doctor if the wounds seem to require further treatment.

FIRST-AID KIT

The first-aid kit should be a sound, well-made box of durable, moisture-proof construction. Appropriate first-aid materials should be part of any dive preparation. The following articles should be included:

Box of adhesive compresses (assorted sizes).
Package of 3 in. × 3 in. sterile gauze pads packed individually.
2-in. roller bandages.
Large gauze dressings 12 in. × 12 in., sterile.
Two or three triangular bandages.
Pair of scissors.
Pair of tweezers.
Dowel ½ in. 6 in. tourniquets.
Plastic box of baking soda.
Box of aspirin (5-gr. tablets).
Antihistamine tablets and ointment. (These should be available without prescription.)
Meat tenderizer with papaya extract dissolved in water for local application is helpful in reducing the effects of jellyfish and Portuguese man-of-war stings.
Package of Band-Aids.
Bottle of iodine or mercurochrome, or tincture of Zephiran (benzalkonium chloride), a good marine antiseptic.

Roll of adhesive tape.
Pack of single-edge razor blades.
Clean needle.
Chapstick.
Small bottle of fresh water.
Motion-sickness pills.
Thermometer.

DIVER FIRST-AID COMMANDMENTS

1. First-aid training helps avoid panic.
2. Think and identify the problem and first aid required.
3. Act calmly, quickly and effectively.
4. Note the circumstances for the doctor's use.
5. Know your sources of help in advance.
6. In advance, list closest recompression chambers by address and telephone number.
7. Carry a first-aid kit in your diving gear and this book as a handy reference.
8. Drill and review first aid with your dive buddies.
9. Log and report all accidents.
10. Know your subject—*First Aid*.

INJURIES FROM CONTACT WITH MARINE LIFE

The following information is a general coverage for first aid that may be administered by the diver with subsequent attention by a physician:

Marine-Life Injuries—Cause and Treatment

Cause	Prevention	Symptoms	First Aid
Marine Plants	Avoid fast, entangling movements.		Move straight up to surface. Look for clear spot. Drop straight down and swim to clear area. Repeat till clear of plant bed.
Coral	Wear shoes, gloves, protective clothing around coral. Avoid contact; be especially careful of surge effects towards coral heads.	Cuts, abrasions, welts, pain and itching. Severe reactions are not usual.	Rinse area with baking-soda solution, weak ammonia or plain water. Apply cortisone or antihistamine ointment. Antihistamine may be given by mouth to reduce initial pain and reaction. When initial pain subsides, cleanse the area with soap and wa-

Cause	Prevention	Symptoms	First Aid
			ter, apply an antiseptic, and cover with sterile dressings Severe cases or those not responding readily should be referred to a physician.
Sea Urchin	Avoid contact. Spines will penetrate most forms of protective covering.	Often immediate and intense burning sensation followed by, redness, swelling and aching. Weakness, loss of body sensations, facial swelling and irregular pulse may be noted. Severe cases involving paralysis, respiratory distress and even death have been noted.	Remove as many spines as possible with forceps (tweezers, pliers). Cleanse the area and cushion with large, loose dressings. If signs of infection appear, seek medical attention promptly.
Cone Shells	Avoid contact with soft parts of the animal.	Puncture wound. Reduction of blood supply (cyanosis). Stinging, burning sensation at first. Numbness, abnormal sensation begins at wound and spreads rapidly. In severe cases: paralysis, respiratory distress, coma, heart failure.	No specific care. Remove from water immediately. Keep lying down. Get medical attention as soon as possible. See section on first aid for venomous fish sting (general).
Jelly Fish (Coelenterates) Sea Nettles, Portuguese Man-of-War, Sea Wasp	Be alert—avoid contact. Wear protective clothing when present, also on night dives. Avoid whole or partial "dead" parts either in or out of water.	Variable, according to species. Vary from mild stinging to intense burning, throbbing or shooting pain; may be accompanied by unconsciousness, reddened skin, welts, blisters, swelling, skin hemorrhage. In some cases, shock, cramps, loss of tactile senses, vomiting, paralysis, respiratory difficulty and convulsions, and death. The Sea Wasp has caused death within several minutes.	Obtain buddy assistance and leave water. Remove tentacles and as much of stinging material as possible, with cloth, seaweed or sand. Avoid spreading. Apply weak ammonia solution or saturated solution of baking soda in water or fresh clean water. Do not apply alcohol. Apply cortisone or antihistamine ointment. Anesthetic ointment to relieve pain. Obtain medical attention as soon as possible in severe cases. If the Portuguese Man of-War or Sea Wasp is the cause, medical help is essential.
Octopus	Avoid tentacles. Porous clothing will hinder action of cups. To prevent bite, avoid mouth area at tentacle origin.	Beak bites produce stinging, swelling, redness and heat. Bleeding out of proportion to size of wound.	Apply cold compresses. Keep lying down, feet elevated. Get medical attention as soon as possible if bitten.

Cause	Prevention	Symptoms	First Aid
Sting Rays	Avoid stepping on in shallow water. Shuffle fins to scare away. Avoid contact with barb at base of tail.	Pain within minutes. Fainting and weakness. Pain increases and may affect entire limb within 30 minutes. Pain maximum in 90 minutes. Wound may be of puncture or laceration type.	No specific care other than bleeding control if profuse. Remove from water immediately. Wash with sterile saline solution or cold, clean water. Remove remaining portions of barb sheath. Soak in plain hot water for 30 minutes. Hot compresses may be used if soak is not practical. Get medical attention promptly if wound is in chest or abdomen or if symptoms do not subside with heat application.
Venomous Fish: Catfish, Weeverfish, Scorpion Fish, Rabbit Fish, Ratfish, Toadfish, Zebra Fish, Surgeonfish, Stonefish	When diving in unfamiliar areas, consult local divers or appropriate information source regarding existing harmful marine life native to the area.	Variable with type and contact. Usually of puncture type but may be lacerations. Poison introduced by spines causes redness, swelling, pain, general malaise, muscle spasm, respiratory distress with convulsions, and death in severe cases.	Three objectives of care are to: (1) alleviate pain, (2) combat effects of venom, (3) prevent secondary infection. Remove from water immediately. Irrigate with clean, cold water. Make small incision across the wound, apply suction. Soak in water as hot as can be tolerated (without scalding) for 30 to 60 minutes. Epsom salts added to water may be beneficial. Further cleansing should be done after soaking. Obtain medical aid as soon as possible.
Bite Wounds: Shark, Barracuda, Moray Eel, others	Avoid attracting the predators. Swim quietly while surveying the underwater area. Avoid wearing shiny equipment or sun reflecting on face plate when predators are near. The best prevention is to get out of the water when possibly harmful fish are present.	Serious lacerations from curved bite of Shark, straight bite of Barracuda and jagged combination of puncture and laceration by Moray Eel usually cause severe bleeding, loss of tissue and extreme shock.	Control serious bleeding by whatever method or methods are possible, immediately. Remove from water immediately. Treat shock and get medical (surgical) aid as soon as possible. Remember, loss of blood can be deadly in a short time, and only immediate control can prevent death.

Cause	Prevention	Symptoms	First Aid
Sea Snakes	Avoid handling or contact with netted specimens. Their reported docile nature may be overrated.	Little local sign at bite area. Toxic signs appear within 20 minutes after bite. Malaise, anxiety, euphoria, muscle spasm, respiratory distress, convulsions, unconsciousness, all signs of shock. Mortality rate, 25 percent.	Leave water immediately. Place restricting band above the bite so as to slow the venous flow to the heart. *This is not a tourniquet.* Loosen every 30 minutes. Keep victim at complete rest. Get medical aid quickly. If possible, identify the snake (IT MAY NOT BE A POISONOUS TYPE).
Inedible poisonous marine animals (too numerous and varied to list)	Consult local divers, fishermen, state or federal bulletins if planning to dive, spear fish in unfamiliar area. Seafood edible in one area may be poisonous in another.	Variable. Usually start with tingling about lips and tongue, spreading to extremities. Nausea, vomiting, diarrhea and thirst are common. Muscular incoordination, numbness, paralysis and convulsions are not uncommon. Symptoms may occur any time within 30 hours after eating the fish.	Empty the stomach as soon as possible. Large amounts of water (5 or 6 glasses), warm and with salt added, should be swallowed. A touch of the finger on the palate will then usually bring up the stomach contents. More water will aid in cleansing the intestinal tract. If rash or welts appear, and the victim is able, cool showers may give some relief. If poisoning is due to eating clams or mussels, baking soda added to the water is beneficial. Obtain the services of a doctor. Save a small quantity of the fish for analysis and possible aid to medication in severe cases.

TEN

CONTINUING EDUCATION

Observation of recreational diving over the past quarter-century has clearly shown that experience and continuing education contribute significantly not only to the diver's enjoyment of the sport but also to the safety with which the sport is practiced. The accessibility of both experience and education to the recreational diver is increasing daily. Although diving remains a "frontier" sport, this frontier is broadening every day as additional diving environments are identified, new resorts and charter operations are opened, and travel opportunities expand. Diver education is also expanding to keep pace with available opportunities. Serious recreational divers will want to take advantage of available continuing education to maintain their skills and knowledge and to extend their ability to safely explore the underwater world that is now open to them.

Continuing education generally takes three forms: progressive education, specialty training and leadership development. Progressive education first brings the student diver through basic training and then into open-water qualification, often through a single introductory course. The certified diver may then proceed through intermediate and advanced levels, each involving more open-water experience. For most certification organizations, Master Diver represents the top of the progressive ladder. Divers who reach this level of progressive education have experienced a wide range of diving environments and activities. They are often required to acquire certain specialty ratings and perhaps some form of leadership certification to reach this high level of recognized diving proficiency.

A plethora of specialty training opportunities is now available to the recreational diver. The prerequisites for specialty training vary with the specialty involved. Some specialty courses may be entered through the basic diver level; others require a higher level on the progressive education ladder and/or some other specialty preparations. Although each certification agency offers its own menu of specialty training opportunities, most offer training in the following areas:

1. Boat diving
2. Cave and cavern diving *(which should never be attempted without extensive specialized training)*
3. Coral reef appreciation and ecology
4. Deep diving
5. Diving emergency medicine, including diving first aid
6. Ice diving *(which also requires special training before it is practiced by a diver with any level of experience)*
7. Night diving
8. Rescue diving
9. Search and recovery diving
10. Underwater archeologhy
11. Underwater hunting
12. Underwater photography
13. Wreck diving

New specialty areas continue to be developed as diver interest and capability expand. You will probably want to take advantage of the formal education opportunities that are now available for safe and meaningful introduction to the various specialty areas of diving.

Finally, many recreational divers will wish to share the exciting experience of their sport with others. The third form of continuing education in diving offers an opportunity to do this through teaching. Most underwater certification agencies offer Teaching Assistant ratings for those who wish to explore teaching at the most basic level under continuous supervision. Assistant Instructor ratings require additional training, and full Instructor status is available to the experienced diver who has the interest and ability to pursue the art and science of underwater education. Most certification agencies also have Dive Master ratings available for those who wish to supervise underwater activities without necessarily becoming involved in teaching.

As you can see, the recreational diver who pursues the opportunities of continuing education can expand not only his or her own expertise but also the horizons of others who have an interest in the sport. *The New Science of Skin and Scuba Diving* makes these horizons virtually unlimited.

Underwater photography and wreck diving are only two of the many specialty fields that can be pursued in continuing underwater education.

215

APPENDIXES

A. Council for National Cooperation in Aquatics

CNCA is an umbrella organization for over 30 national agencies and organizations that have a strong interest and involvement in aquatics. Since 1951, this council of cooperating organizations has had as its goal ". . . to enhance the field of aquatics . . .." One of the council's basic objectives is to bring together national agencies with a common interest in aquatic safety and education, for productive interaction. There have been many results of this cooperation: the development of the classic training text *New Science of Skin and Scuba Diving*; publication of a concerted inter-agency stance on aquatic programs for preschoolers; CNCA chairmanship of the inter-agency Z86 Committee, devising national safety standards for sport scuba diving; formation of the broadly based National Advisory Committee on Aquatic Exercise; etc. These and other such combined efforts have impacted on aquatics to a great degree because they WERE combined efforts : national organizations working cooperatively for the enhancement of aquatics.

CNCA is also a professional association for individuals. The only professional association that covers the broad spectrum of aquatics, CNCA is committed to activities, publications and programs that will provide opportunities for professional growth and development to practitioners in *all* aquatic activities. Advantages to continuing personal membership include discounts on the many publications of CNCA, discounts on conference fees, the quarterly National Aquatics Journal, and several other fine member benefits.

CNCA conferences provide opportunity for individuals to meet and hear national leaders, to exchange ideas with others involved in similar activities, and to become informed on research and educational information critical to their personal professional development, and to their safe enjoyment of aquatic sports. CNCA conferences provide opportunity for individuals to share their knowledge with colleagues and professionals in related fields. Sustained by over 30 national aquatic-related organizations, CNCA conducts the only national aquatic conferences sponsored by so broad a group. The opportunity for agency interaction at this level and to this degree is unique to CNCA.

National conferences offer sessions in the broad spectrum of aquatic interests, and speakers present current research and excellent information. The conferences are always a valuable professional development experience for participants. CNCA conferences are, indeed, THE MOST SIGNIFICANT GATHERING OF AQUATIC PROFESSIONALS IN THE U.S.A.

For membership and conference information, contact:

CNCA
901 W. New York St.
Indianapolis, Indiana 46223

THE COUNCIL FOR NATIONAL COOPERATION IN AQUATICS

STRIVING FOR EXCELLENCE   COMMITTED TO THE PROFESSIONAL

MEMBER ORGANIZATIONS

Amateur Athletic Union of the U.S.
American Academy of Pediatrics
American Alliance for Health, Physical Education, Recreation and Dance
American Camping Association
American Red Cross
American Public Health Association
American Swimming Coaches Association
Boy Scouts of America
Boy's Clubs of America
Girl Scouts of the U.S.A.
International Academy of Aquatic Art
International Association of Dive Rescue Specialists
International Swimming Hall of Fame
Joseph P. Kennedy, Jr. Foundation
National Association of Intercollegiate Athletics
National Association of Underwater Instructors
National Board of the Young Women's Christian Association
National Collegiate Athletic Association
National Forum for Advancement of Aquatics
National Employee Services and Recreation Association
National Jewish Welfare Board
National Junior College Athletic Association
National Recreation and Park Association
National Safety Council
National Swim and Recreation Association
National Water Safety Congress
President's Council on Physical Fitness and Sports
Professional Association of Diving Instructors
Royal Life Saving Society Canada
The Athletic Institute
Underwater Society of America
United States Lifesaving Association
United States Office of Education
United States Professional Diving Coaches Association
United States Synchronized Swimming

B. United States Navy Air Decompression Tables*

When air is breathed under pressure, as discussed in Chapter Four, the inert nitrogen diffuses into the various tissues of the body. Nitrogen uptake by the body continues, at different rates for the various tissues, as long as the partial pressure of the inspired nitrogen is higher than the partial pressure of the gas absorbed in the tissues. Consequently, the amount of nitrogen absorbed increases with the partial pressure of the inspired nitrogen (depth) and the duration of the exposure (time).

When the diver begins to ascend, the process is reversed as the nitrogen partial pressure in the tissues exceeds that in the circulatory and respiratory systems. The pressure gradient from the tissues to the blood and lungs must be carefully controlled to prevent too rapid a diffusion of nitrogen. If the pressure gradient is uncontrolled, bubbles of nitrogen gas can form in tissues and blood, resulting in decompression sickness.

To prevent the development of decompression sickness, special decompression tables have been established. These tables take into consideration the amount of nitrogen absorbed by the body at various depths for given time periods. They also consider allowable pressure gradients that can exist without excessive bubble formation and the different gas elimination rates associated with various body tissues.

Stage decompression, requiring stops of specific durations at given depths, is used for air diving because of its operational simplicity. It will be found that the decompression tables require longer stops at more frequent intervals as the surface is approached due to the higher gas expansion ratios occurring at shallow depths.

Selection of Decompression Schedule

The decompression schedules of all the tables are given in 10- or 20-ft depth increments and, usually, 10-minute bottom time increments. Depth and bottom time combinations from actual dives, however, rarely exactly match one of the decompression schedules listed in the table being used. As assurance that the selected decompression schedule is always conservative—(A) always select the schedule depth to be equal to or the next depth greater than the actual depth to which the dive was conducted, and (B) always select the schedule bottom time to be equal to or the next longer bottom time than the actual bottom time of the dive.

If the Standard Air Decompression Table, for example, was being used to select the correct schedule for a dive to 97 ft for 31 minutes, decompression would be carried out in accordance with the 100/40 schedule.

NEVER ATTEMPT TO INTERPOLATE BETWEEN DECOMPRESSION SCHEDULES

If the diver was exceptionally cold during the dive, or if the work load was relatively strenuous, the next longer decompression schedule than the one normally followed should be selected. For example, the normal schedule for a dive to 90 ft for 34 minutes would be the 90/40 schedule. If the diver were exceptionally cold or fatigued, the 90/50 schedule ahould be followed.

Rules During Ascent

After the correct decompression schedule has been selected, it is imperative that it be exactly followed. Without exception, decompression must be completed according to the selected schedule unless the directions to alter the schedule are given by a diving medical officer.

The decompression stop times, as specified in each decompression schedule, begin as soon as the diver reaches the stop depth. Upon completion of the specified stop time, the diver ascends to the next stop, or to the surface, at the proper ascent rate. DO NOT INCLUDE ASCENT TIME AS PART OF STOP TIME.

Omitted Decompression

Certain emergencies may interrupt or prevent specified decompression. Blow-up, exhausted air supply, bodily injury and the like constitute such emergencies. If the diver shows any symptoms of decompression sickness or gas embolism, immediate treatment using the appropriate oxygen or air recompression treatment table is essential. Even if the diver shows no symptoms of ill effects, omitted decompression must be made up in some manner to avert later difficulty.

Repetitive Dives

During the 12-hour period after an air dive, the quantity of residual nitrogen in a diver's body will gradually reduce to its normal level. If, within this period, the diver is to make a second dive—called a repetitive dive—he or she must consider the current residual nitrogen level when planning for the dive. The procedures for conducting a repetitive dive are summarized on page 164.

AIR DECOMPRESSION TABLES

U.S. Navy Standard Air Decompression Table

The USN decompression tables are the result of years of scientific study, calculation, animal and human experimentation, and extensive field experience. They represent the best overall information available, but as depth and time increases, they tend to be less accurate and require careful application. Lacking the presence of a trained Diving Medical Officer or someone otherwise qualified, the tables must be rigidly followed to ensure maximum diving safety. Variations in decompression procedures are permissible only with the guidance of a qualified diving medical officer in emergency situations.

These limits are not to be exceeded without the approval of the Diving Officer in charge of the operation, and then, only after careful consideration of the potential consequences involved.

If the bottom time of a dive is less than the first bottom time listed for its depth, decompression is not required. The diver may ascend directly to the surface at a rate of 60 ft per minute. The repetitive group designation for no-decompression dives is given in the No-Decompression Table.

Example—

Problem—Diver Bowman has just completed a salvage dive to a depth of 143 feet for 37 minutes. He was not exceptionally cold or fatigued during the dive. What is his decompression schedule and his repetitive group designation at the end of the decompression?

Solution—Select the equal or next deeper and the equal or next longer decompression schedule. This would be the 150/40 schedule.

ACTION	TIME	TOTAL ELAPSED ASCENT TIME
	(min:sec)	(min:sec)
Ascend to 30 feet at 60 fpm	1:53	1:53
Remain at 30 feet	5:00	6:53
Ascend to 20 feet	0:10	7:03
Remain at 20 feet	19:00	26:03
Ascend to 10 feet	0:10	26:13
Remain at 10 feet	33:00	59:13
Ascend to surface	0:10	59:23
Repetitive Group Designation	"N"	

Source: U.S. Navy Diving Manual

222

U.S. Navy Standard Air Decompression Table

Depth (feet)	Bottom time (min)	Time to first stop (min:sec)	Decompression stops (feet) 50	40	30	20	10	Total ascent (min:sec)	Repetitive group
40	200						0	0:40	*
	210	0:30					2	2:40	N
	230	0:30					7	7:40	N
	250	0:30					11	11:40	O
	270	0:30					15	15:40	O
	300	0:30					19	19:40	Z
50	100						0	0:50	*
	110	0:40					3	3:50	L
	120	0:40					5	5:50	M
	140	0:40					10	10:50	M
	160	0:40					21	21:50	N
	180	0:40					29	29:50	O
	200	0:40					35	35:50	O
	220	0:40					40	40:50	Z
	240	0:40					47	47:50	Z
60	60						0	1:00	*
	70	0:50					2	3:00	K
	80	0:50					7	8:00	L
	100	0:50					14	15:00	M
	120	0:50					26	27:00	N
	140	0:50					39	40:00	O
	160	0:50					48	49:00	Z
	180	0:50					56	57:00	Z
	200	0:40				1	69	71:00	Z
70	50						0	1:10	*
	60	1:00					8	9:10	K
	70	1:00					14	15:10	L
	80	1:00					18	19:10	M
	90	1:00					23	24:10	N
	100	1:00					33	34:10	N
	110	0:50				2	41	44:10	O
	120	0:50				4	47	52:10	O
	130	0:50				6	52	59:10	O
	140	0:50				8	56	65:10	Z
	150	0:50				9	61	71:10	Z
	160	0:50				13	72	86:10	Z
	170	0:50				19	79	99:10	Z

*See No-Decompression Table for repetitive groups.

U.S. Navy Standard Air Decompression Table

Depth (feet)	Bottom time (min)	Time to first stop (min:sec)	Decompression stops (feet) 50	40	30	20	10	Total ascent (min:sec)	Repetitive group
80	40						0	1:20	*
	50	1:10					10	11:20	K
	60	1:10					17	18:20	L
	70	1:10					23	24:20	M
	80	1:00				2	31	34:20	N
	90	1:00				7	39	47:20	N
	100	1:00				11	46	58:20	O
	110	1:00				13	53	67:20	O
	120	1:00				17	56	74:20	Z
	130	1:00				19	63	83:20	Z
	140	1:00				26	69	96:20	Z
	150	1:00				32	77	110:20	Z
90	30						0	1:30	*
	40	1:20					7	8:30	J
	50	1:20					18	19:30	L
	60	1:20					25	26:30	M
	70	1:10				7	30	38:30	N
	80	1:10				13	40	54:30	N
	90	1:10				18	48	67:30	O
	100	1:10				21	54	76:30	Z
	110	1:10				24	61	86:30	Z
	120	1:10				32	68	101:30	Z
	130	1:00			5	36	74	116:30	Z
100	25						0	1:40	*
	30	1:30					3	4:40	I
	40	1:30					15	16:40	K
	50	1:20				2	24	27:40	L
	60	1:20				9	28	38:40	N
	70	1:20				17	39	57:40	O
	80	1:20				23	48	72:40	O
	90	1:10			3	23	57	84:40	Z
	100	1:10			7	23	66	97:40	Z
	110	1:10			10	34	72	117:40	Z
	120	1:10			12	41	78	132:40	Z
110	20						0	1:50	*
	25	1:40					3	4:50	H
	30	1:40					7	8:50	J
	40	1:30				2	21	24:50	L
	50	1:30				8	26	35:50	M
	60	1:30				18	36	55:50	N
	70	1:20			1	23	48	73:50	O
	80	1:20			7	23	57	88:50	Z
	90	1:20			12	30	64	107:50	Z
	100	1:20			15	37	72	125:50	Z

*See No-Decompression Table for repetitive groups.

Source: U.S. Navy Diving Manual

U.S. Navy Standard Air Decompression Table

Depth (feet)	Bottom time (min)	Time to first stop (min:sec)	Decompression stops (feet)							Total ascent (min:sec)	Repetitive group
			70	60	50	40	30	20	10		
120	15								0	2:00	*
	20	1:50							2	4:00	H
	25	1:50							6	8:00	I
	30	1:50							14	16:00	J
	40	1:40						5	25	32:00	L
	50	1:40						15	31	48:00	N
	60	1:30					2	22	45	71:00	O
	70	1:30					9	23	55	89:00	O
	80	1:30					15	27	63	107:00	Z
	90	1:30					19	37	74	132:00	Z
	100	1:30					23	45	80	150:00	Z
130	10								0	2:10	*
	15	2:00							1	3:10	F
	20	2:00							4	6:10	H
	25	2:00							10	12:10	J
	30	1:50					3		18	23:10	M
	40	1:50						10	25	37:10	N
	50	1:40					3	21	37	63:10	O
	60	1:40					9	23	52	86:10	Z
	70	1:40					16	24	61	103:10	Z
	80	1:30				3	19	35	72	131:10	Z
	90	1:30				8	19	45	80	154:10	Z

Depth (feet)	Bottom time (min)	Time to first stop (min:sec)	Decompression stops (feet)									Total ascent (min:sec)	Repetitive group
			90	80	70	60	50	40	30	20	10		
140	10										0	2:20	*
	15	2:10									2	4:20	G
	20	2:10									6	8:20	I
	25	2:00								2	14	18:20	J
	30	2:00								5	21	28:20	K
	40	1:50							2	16	26	46:20	N
	50	1:50							6	24	44	76:20	O
	60	1:50							16	23	56	97:20	Z
	70	1:40						4	19	32	68	125:20	Z
	80	1:40						10	23	41	79	155:20	Z

*See No-Decompression Table for repetitive groups.

U.S. Navy Standard Air Decompression Table

Depth (feet)	Bottom time (min)	Time to first stop (min:sec)	Decompression stops (feet)									Total ascent (min:sec)	Repetitive group
			90	80	70	60	50	40	30	20	10		
150	5										0	2:30	C
	10	2:20									1	3:30	E
	15	2:20									3	5:30	G
	20	2:10								2	7	11:30	H
	25	2:10								4	17	23:30	K
	30	2:10								8	24	34:30	L
	40	2:00							5	19	33	59:30	N
	50	2:00							12	23	51	88:30	O
	60	1:50						3	19	26	62	112:30	Z
	70	1:50						11	19	39	75	146:30	Z
	80	1:40					1	17	19	50	84	173:30	Z
160	5										0	2:40	D
	10	2:30									1	3:40	F
	15	2:20								1	4	7:40	H
	20	2:20								3	11	16:40	J
	25	2:20								7	20	29:40	K
	30	2:10							2	11	25	40:40	M
	40	2:10							7	23	39	71:40	N
	50	2:00						2	16	23	55	98:40	Z
	60	2:00						9	19	33	69	132:40	Z

Depth (feet)	Bottom time (min)	Time to first stop (min:sec)	Decompression stops (feet)											Total ascent (min:sec)	Repetitive group
			110	100	90	80	70	60	50	40	30	20	10		
170	5												0	2:50	D
	10	2:40											2	4:50	F
	15	2:30										2	5	9:50	H
	20	2:30										4	15	21:50	J
	25	2:20									2	7	23	34:50	L
	30	2:20									4	13	26	45:50	M
	40	2:10								1	10	23	45	81:50	O
	50	2:10								5	18	23	61	109:50	Z
	60	2:00							2	15	22	37	74	152:50	Z
180	5												0	3:00	D
	10	2:50											3	6:00	F
	15	2:40										3	6	12:00	I
	20	2:30									1	5	17	26:00	K
	25	2:30									3	10	24	40:00	L
	30	2:30									6	17	27	53:00	N
	40	2:20								3	14	23	50	93:00	O
	50	2:10							2	9	19	30	65	128:00	Z
	60	2:10							5	16	19	44	81	168:00	Z

Change 2 *Source:* U.S. Navy Diving Manual

U. S. Navy Standard Air Decompression Table

Depth (feet)	Bottom time (min)	Time to first stop (min:sec)	Decompression stops (feet)											Total ascent (min:sec)	Repeti- tive group
			110	100	90	80	70	60	50	40	30	20	10		
190	5												0	3:10	D
	10	2:50										1	3	7:10	G
	15	2:50										4	7	14:10	I
	20	2:40									2	6	20	31:10	K
	25	2:40									5	11	25	44:10	M
	30	2:30								1	8	19	32	63:10	N
	40	2:30								8	14	23	55	103:10	O

Change 2

C. United States Navy Recompression Treatment Tables

RULES FOR RECOMPRESSION TREATMENT FOR PROFESSIONAL USE ONLY

Always

1. Follow the Treatment Tables accurately.
2. Have qualified tender in chamber at all times during recompression.
3. Maintain the normal descent and ascent rates.
4. Examine patient thoroughly at depth of relief or treatment depth.
5. Treat an unconscious patient for gas embolism or serious decompression sickness unless the possibility of such a condition can be ruled out without question.
6. Use air tables only if oxygen is unavailable.
7. Be alert for oxygen poisoning if oxygen is used.
8. In the event of oxygen convulsion, remove the oxygen mask and keep the patient from harming himself.
9. Maintain oxygen usage within the time and depth limitations.
10. Check patient's condition before and after coming to each stop and during long stops.
11. Observe patient for at least 6 hours after treatment for recurrence of symptoms.
12. Maintain accurate timekeeping and recording.
13. Maintain a well-stocked medical kit at hand.

Never

1. Permit any shortening or other alteration to the tables except under the direction of a trained Diving Medical Officer.
2. Let patient sleep between depth changes or for more than one hour at any one stop.
3. Wait for a bag resuscitator. Use mouth-to-mouth immediately if breathing ceases.
4. Break rhythm during resuscitation.
5. Permit the use of oxygen below 60 feet.
6. Fail to report symptoms early (diver).
7. Fail to treat doubtful cases.
8. Allow personnel in the chamber to assume any cramped position which may interfere with complete blood circulation.

Note: The utilization of a He-O_2 breathing medium is an option to be considered at the discretion of the cognizant medical officer as determined by the circumstances of the individual case.

Recompression Chamber

Recompression chambers are not used only for the treatment of decompression sickness and surface decompression, but also for administering pressure and oxygen tolerance tests for divers and prospective divers. In other than diving applications, suitable chambers may be found being used for medical treatment (both routine and emergency), in research laboratories and in military and commercial aviation schools and operating facilities.

Page 268 lists those places, both military and civilian, where a chamber may possibly be located. This list may prove useful while planning for an operation, since the diving team must always know the location and type of the nearest chamber before the operation begins. When diving at depths of 170 feet or greater, a chamber must be available at the dive site.

Source: U.S. Navy Diving Manual
Change 2

Diagnosis of Decompression Sickness and Gas Embolism

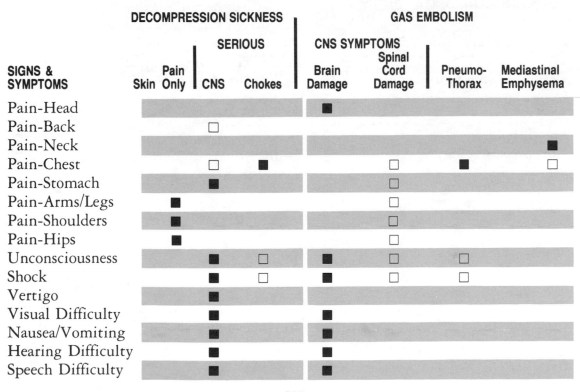

SIGNS & SYMPTOMS	DECOMPRESSION SICKNESS				GAS EMBOLISM			
			SERIOUS		CNS SYMPTOMS			
	Skin	Pain Only	CNS	Chokes	Brain Damage	Spinal Cord Damage	Pneumo-Thorax	Mediastinal Emphysema
Pain-Head					■			
Pain-Back			□					
Pain-Neck								■
Pain-Chest			□	■	□		■	□
Pain-Stomach			■		□			
Pain-Arms/Legs	■				□			
Pain-Shoulders	■				□			
Pain-Hips	■				□			
Unconsciousness			■	□	■	□	□	
Shock			■	□	■	□	□	
Vertigo			■					
Visual Difficulty			■		■			
Nausea/Vomiting			■		■			
Hearing Difficulty			■		■			
Speech Difficulty			■		■			

| SIGNS & SYMPTOMS | DECOMPRESSION SICKNESS | | | | GAS EMBOLISM | | | |
| | | | SERIOUS | | CNS SYMPTOMS | | | |
	Skin	Pain Only	CNS	Chokes	Brain Damage	Spinal Cord Damage	Pneumo-Thorax	Mediastinal Emphysema
Balance Lack			■		■			
Numbness	□		■		■	□		□
Weakness		□	■		■	□		
Strange Sensations	□		■		■	□		
Swollen Neck								■
Short of Breath			□	□	□	□	□	□
Cyanosis				□	□	□	□	□
Skin Changes	■							

■ Probable
□ Possible Cause

CONFIRMING INFORMATION

Diving History

	Yes	No
Decompression Obligation?	□	□
Decompression Adequate?	□	□
Blow-up?	□	□
Breath-hold?	□	□
Non-pressure Cause?	□	□
Previous Exposure?	□	□

Patient Examination	Yes	No
Does diver feel well?	□	□
Does diver look and act normal?	□	□
Does diver have normal strength?	□	□
Are diver's sensations normal?	□	□
Are diver's eyes normal?	□	□
Are diver's reflexes normal?	□	□
Is diver's pulse rate normal?	□	□
Is diver's gait normal?	□	□
Is diver's hearing normal?	□	□
Is diver's coordination normal?	□	□
Is diver's balance normal?	□	□
Does the diver feel nauseated?	□	□

DIVING EMERGENCIES

Change 2

DECOMPRESSION SICKNESS TREATMENT   GAS EMBOLISM TREATMENT

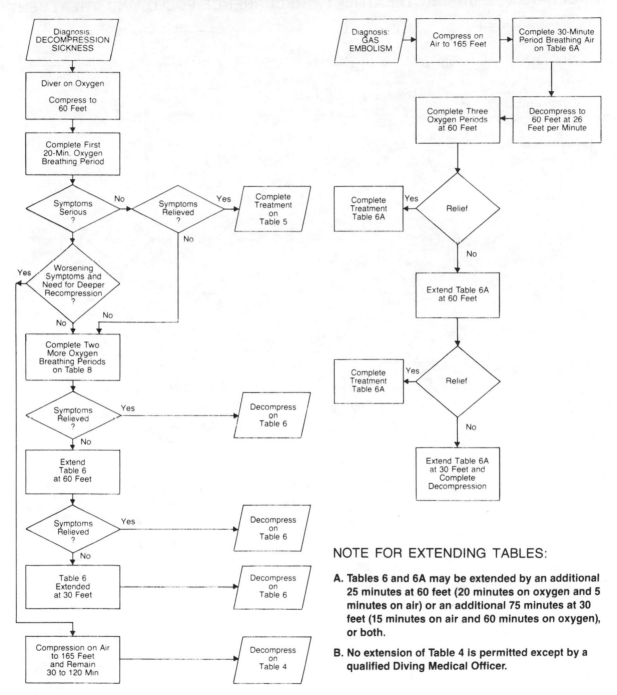

Decompression Sickness Treatment and Gas Embolism Charts.

Change 2   *Source:* U.S. Navy Diving Manual

231

RECURRENCE DURING TREATMENT   RECURRENCE FOLLOWING TREATMENT

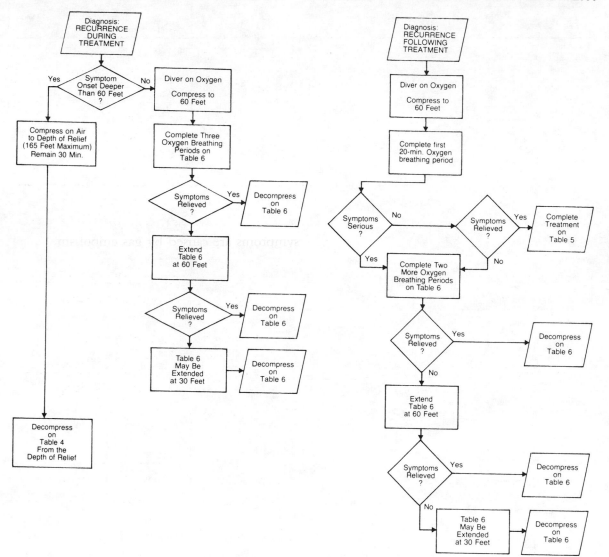

Recurrence During Treatment and Recurrence Following Treatment Charts.

Change 2

LIST OF U.S. NAVY RECOMPRESSION TREATMENT TABLES*

TABLE	USE
5 — Oxygen Treatment of Pain-only Decompression Sickness	Treatment of pain-only decompression sickness when symptoms are relieved within 10 minutes at 60 feet.
6 — Oxygen Treatment of Serious Decompression Sickness	Treatment of serious decompression sickness or pain-only decompression sickness when symptoms are not relieved within 10 minutes at 60 feet.
6A — Air and Oxygen Treatment of Gas Embolism	Treatment of gas embolism. Use also when unable to determine whether symptoms are caused by gas embolism or severe decompression sickness.
1A — Air Treatment of Pain-only Decompression Sickness— 100-foot Treatment	Treatment of pain-only decompression sickness when oxygen unavailable and pain is relieved at a depth less than 66 feet.
2A — Air Treatment of Pain-only Decompression Sickness— 165-foot Treatment	Treatment of pain-only decompression sickness when oxygen unavailable and pain is relieved at a depth greater than 66 feet.
3 — Air Treatment of Serious Decompression Sickness or Gas Embolism	Treatment of serious symptoms or gas embolism when oxygen unavailable and symptoms are relieved within 30 minutes at 165 feet.
4 — Air Treatment of Serious Decompression Sickness or Gas Embolism	Treatment of worsening symptoms during the first 20-minute oxygen breathing period at 60 feet on Table 6, or when symptoms are not relieved within 30 minutes at 165 feet using air treatment Table 3.

*Change 2 presents oxygen treatment tables before air treatment tables because the oxygen breathing method is preferred. Use of Decompression Table 5A, Minimal Decompression, Oxygen Breathing Method for Treatment of Decompression Sickness and Gas Embolism, has been discontinued.   Change 2

Table 5—Oxygen Treatment of Pain-only Decompression Sickness

1. Treatment of pain-only decompression sickness when symptoms are relieved within 10 minutes at 60 feet.
2. Descent rate—25 ft/min.
3. Ascent rate—1 ft/min. Do not compensate for slower ascent rates. Compensate for faster rates by halting the ascent.
4. Time at 60 feet begins on arrival at 60 feet.
5. If oxygen breathing must be interrupted, allow 15 minutes after the reaction has entirely subsided and resume schedule at point of interruption.
6. If oxygen breathing must be interrupted at 60 feet, switch to TABLE 6 upon arrival at the 30 foot stop.
7. Tender breathes air throughout. If treatment is a repetitive dive for the tender or tables are lengthened, tender should breathe oxygen during the last 30 minutes of ascent to the surface.

Depth (feet)	Time (minutes)	Breathing Media	Total Elapsed Time (hrs:min)
60	20	Oxygen	0:20
60	5	Air	0:25
60	20	Oxygen	0:45
60 to 30	30	Oxygen	1:15
30	5	Air	1:20
30	20	Oxygen	1:40
30	5	Air	1:45
30 to 0	30	Oxygen	2:15

TABLE 5 DEPTH/TIME PROFILE

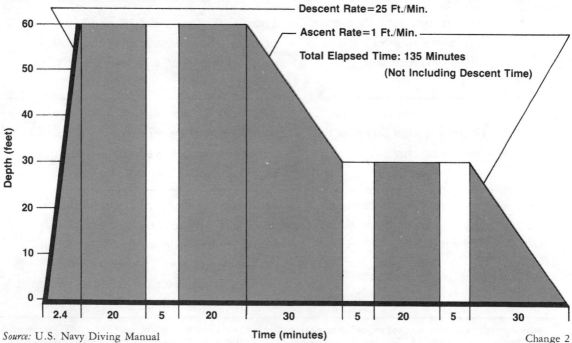

Descent Rate=25 Ft./Min.

Ascent Rate=1 Ft./Min.

Total Elapsed Time: 135 Minutes
(Not Including Descent Time)

Source: U.S. Navy Diving Manual

Change 2

Table 6—Oxygen Treatment of Serious Decompression Sickness

1. Treatment of serious or pain-only decompression sickness when symptoms are not relieved within 10 minutes at 60 feet.
2. Descent rate—25 ft/min.
3. Ascent rate—1 ft/min. Do not compensate for slower ascent rates. Compensate for faster rates by halting the ascent.
4. Time at 60 feet—begins on arrival at 60 feet.
5. If oxygen breathing must be interrupted, allow 15 minutes after the reaction has entirely subsided and resume schedule at point of interruption.
6. Tender breathes air throughout. If treatment is a repetitive dive for the tender or tables are lengthened, tender should breathe oxygen during the last 30 minutes of ascent to the surface.
7. Table 6 can be lengthened by an additional 25 minutes at 60 feet (20 minutes on oxygen and 5 minutes on air) or an additional 75 minutes at 30 feet (15 minutes on air and 60 minutes on oxygen), or both.

Depth (feet)	Time (minutes)	Breathing Media	Total Elapsed Time (hrs:min)
60	20	Oxygen	0:20
60	5	Air	0:25
60	20	Oxygen	0:45
60	5	Air	0:50
60	20	Oxygen	1:10
60	5	Air	1:15
60 to 30	30	Oxygen	1:45
30	15	Air	2:00
30	60	Oxygen	3:00
30	15	Air	3:15
30	60	Oxygen	4:15
30 to 0	30	Oxygen	4:45

TABLE 6 DEPTH/TIME PROFILE

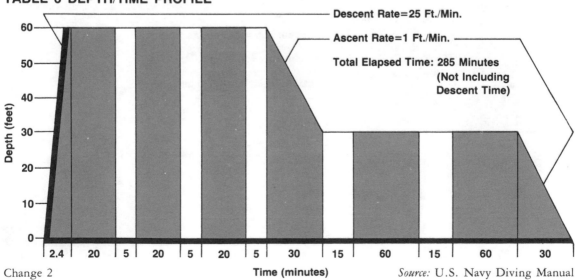

Descent Rate=25 Ft./Min.

Ascent Rate=1 Ft./Min.

Total Elapsed Time: 285 Minutes (Not Including Descent Time)

Change 2

Source: U.S. Navy Diving Manual

235

Table 6A—Air and Oxygen Treatment of Gas Embolism

1. Treatment of gas embolism. Use also when unable to determine whether symptoms are caused by gas embolism or severe decompression sickness.
2. Descent rate—as fast as possible.
3. Ascent rate—1 ft/min. Do not compensate for slower ascent rates. Compensate for faster ascent rates by halting the ascent.
4. Time at 165 feet—includes time from the surface.
5. If oxygen breathing must be interrupted, allow 15 minutes after the reaction has entirely subsided and resume schedule at point of interruption.
6. Tender breathes air throughout. If treatment is a repetitive dive for the tender or tables are lengthened, tender should breathe oxygen during the last 30 minutes of ascent to the surface.
7. Table 6A can be lengthened by an additional 25 minutes at 60 feet (20 minutes on oxygen and 5 minutes on air) or an additional 75 minutes at 30 feet (15 minutes on air and 60 minutes on oxygen), or both.

Depth (feet)	Time (minutes)	Breathing Media	Total Elapsed Time (hrs:min)
165	30	Air	0:30
165 to 60	4	Air	0:34
60	20	Oxygen	0:54
60	5	Air	0:59
60	20	Oxygen	1:19
60	5	Air	1:29
60	20	Oxygen	1:44
60	5	Air	1:49
60 to 30	30	Oxygen	2:19
30	15	Air	2:34
30	60	Oxygen	3:34
30	15	Air	3:49
30	60	Oxygen	4:49
30 to 0	30	Oxygen	5:19

TABLE 6A DEPTH/TIME PROFILE

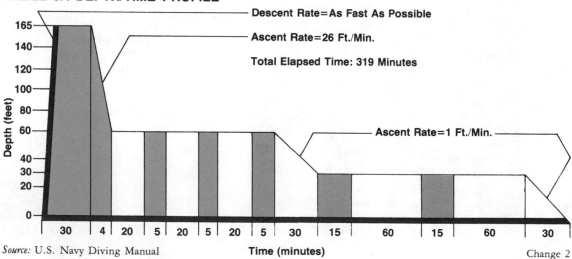

Descent Rate=As Fast As Possible

Ascent Rate=26 Ft./Min.

Total Elapsed Time: 319 Minutes

Ascent Rate=1 Ft./Min.

Depth (feet): 165, 140, 120, 100, 80, 60, 40, 30, 20, 0

Time (minutes): 30 | 4 | 20 | 5 | 20 | 5 | 20 | 5 | 30 | 15 | 60 | 15 | 60 | 30

Source: U.S. Navy Diving Manual

Change 2

236

Table 1A—Air Treatment of Pain-only Decompression Sickness—100-Foot Treatment

1. Treatment of pain-only decompression sickness when oxygen unavailable and pain is relieved at a depth less than 66 feet.
2. Descent rate—25 ft/min.
3. Ascent rate—1 minute between stops.
4. Time at 100 feet—includes time from the surface.
5. If the piping configuration of the chamber does not allow it to return to atmospheric pressure from the 10-foot stop in the one minute specified, disregard the additional time required.

Depth (feet)	Time (minutes)	Breathing Media	Total Elapsed Time (hrs:min)
100	30	Air	0:30
80	12	Air	0:43
60	30	Air	1:14
50	30	Air	1:45
40	30	Air	2:16
30	60	Air	3:17
20	60	Air	4:18
10	120	Air	6:19
0	1	Air	6:20

TABLE 1A DEPTH/TIME PROFILE

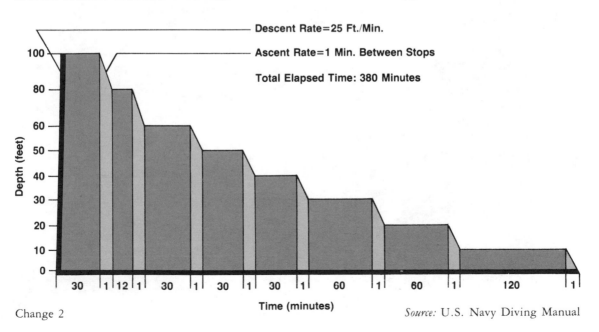

Descent Rate=25 Ft./Min.

Ascent Rate=1 Min. Between Stops

Total Elapsed Time: 380 Minutes

Change 2

Source: U.S. Navy Diving Manual

Table 2A—Air Treatment of Pain-only Decompression Sickness—165-Foot Treatment

1. Treatment of pain-only decompression sickness when oxygen unavailable and pain is relieved at a depth greater than 66 feet.
2. Descent rate—25 ft/min.
3. Ascent rate—1 minute between stops.
4. Time at 165 feet—includes time from the surface.

Deleted by Change 2

Depth (feet)	Time (minutes)	Breathing Media	Total Elapsed Time (hrs:min)
165	30	Air	0:30
140	12	Air	0:43
120	12	Air	0:56
100	12	Air	1:09
80	12	Air	1:22
60	30	Air	1:53
50	30	Air	2:24
40	30	Air	2:55
30	120	Air	4:56
20	120	Air	6:57
10	240	Air	10:58
0	1	Air	10:59

TABLE 2A DEPTH/TIME PROFILE

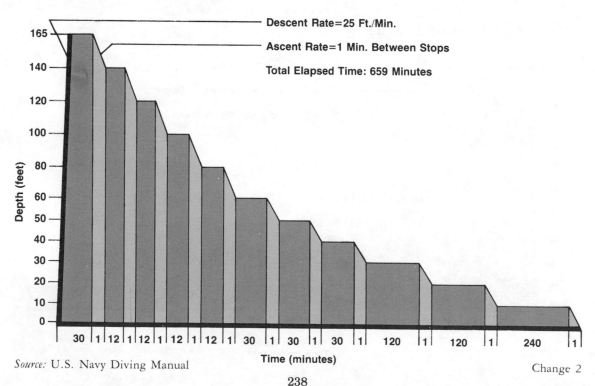

Descent Rate=25 Ft./Min.

Ascent Rate=1 Min. Between Stops

Total Elapsed Time: 659 Minutes

Source: U.S. Navy Diving Manual

Change 2

238

Table 3—Air Treatment of Serious Decompression Sickness or Gas Embolism

1. Treatment of serious symptoms or gas embolism when oxygen unavailable and symptoms are relieved within 30 minutes at 165 feet.
2. Descent rate—as rapidly as possible.
3. Ascent rate—1 minute between stops.
4. Time at 165 feet—includes time from the surface.

Deleted by Change 2

Depth (feet)	Time	Breathing Media	Total Elapsed Time (hrs:min)
165	30 min.	Air	0:30
140	12 min.	Air	0:43
120	12 min.	Air	0:56
100	12 min.	Air	1:09
80	12 min.	Air	1:22
60	30 min.	Air	1:53
50	30 min.	Air	2:24
40	30 min.	Air	2:55
30	12 hr.	Air	14:56
20	2 hr.	Air	16:57
10	2 hr.	Air	18:58
0	1 min.	Air	18:59

TABLE 3 DEPTH/TIME PROFILE

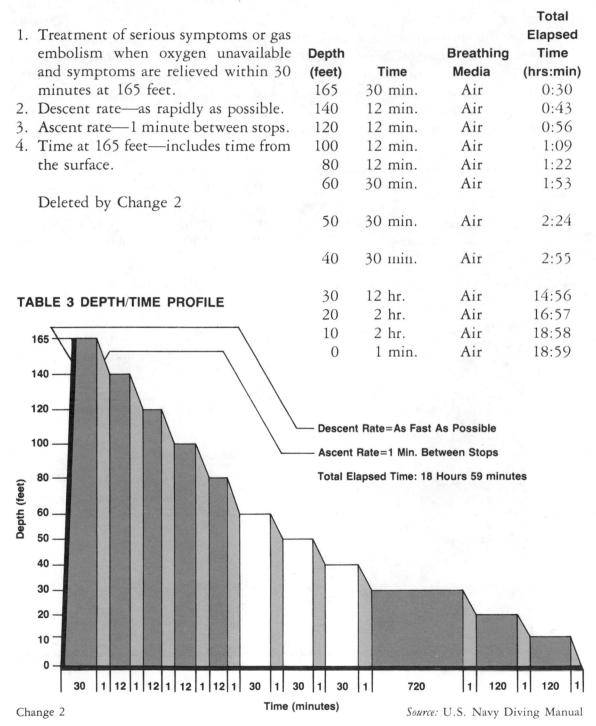

Descent Rate=As Fast As Possible

Ascent Rate=1 Min. Between Stops

Total Elapsed Time: 18 Hours 59 minutes

Time (minutes)

Change 2

Source: U.S. Navy Diving Manual

Table 4—Air Treatment of Serious Decompression Sickness or Gas Embolism

1. Treatment of worsening symptoms during the first 20-minute oxygen breathing period at 60 feet on Table 6, or when symptoms are not relieved within 30 minutes at 165 feet using air treatment Table 3.
2. Descent rate—as rapidly as possible.
3. Ascent rate—1 minute between stops.
4. Time 165 feet—includes time from the surface.

Deleted by Change 2

Depth (feet)	Time	Breathing Media	Total Elapsed Time (hrs:min)
165	½ to 2 hr.	Air	2:00
140	½ hr.	Air	2:31
120	½ hr.	Air	3:02
100	½ hr.	Air	3:33
80	½ hr.	Air	4:04
60	6 hr.	Air	10:05
50	6 hr.	Air	16:06
40	6 hr.	Air	22:07
30	11 hr.	Air	33:08
30	1 hr.	Oxygen (or air)	34:08
20	1 hr.	Air	35:09
20	1 hr.	Oxygen (or air)	36:09
10	1 hr.	Air	37:10
10	1 hr.	Oxygen (or air)	38:10
0	1 min.	Oxygen	38:11

TABLE 4 DEPTH/TIME PROFILE

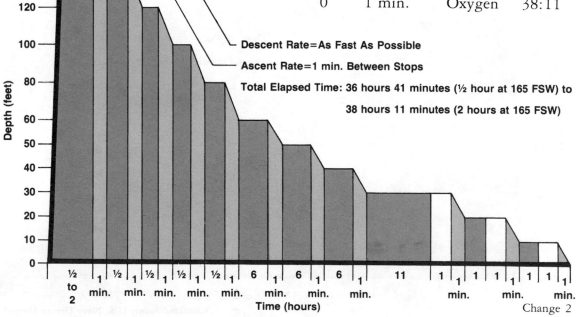

Descent Rate=As Fast As Possible

Ascent Rate=1 min. Between Stops

Total Elapsed Time: 36 hours 41 minutes (½ hour at 165 FSW) to 38 hours 11 minutes (2 hours at 165 FSW)

Change 2

POSSIBLE LOCATIONS OF SUITABLE RECOMPRESSION CHAMBERS

Tenders
Salvage vessels
Submarine rescue vessels
Fleet tugs (some)
Naval shipyards
Major naval bases
Naval air stations
Submarine bases
Diving schools
EOD Units
UDT Units
Research laboratories
Test ranges

Harbor clearance units
Torpedo stations
Air Force hospitals
Army Corps of Engineers
  facilities
FAA facilities
VA hospitals
Civilian research
  laboratories
Universities
Commercial diving firms
  and schools

The type, size and utility of recompression chambers found at such diverse locations will, or course, vary widely. As long as the chamber is large enough to hold the patient and keep him under reasonable pressure, its use should not be ruled out.

Although constructed in accordance with the appropriate Military Specification, all chambers rated at the same pressure do not have the same physical dimensions with the exception of the aluminum chambers. Steel chambers are usually custom-made for the facility in which they are to be installed. Consequently, internal volumes of steel chambers are not standard and must be calculated for each chamber. The following equations can be used to approximate the internal volume of any U.S. Navy chamber.

$$V = \text{chamber volume, cubic feet} = 0.00046 \, D^2L$$

$$V_1 = \text{inner lock volume, cubic feet} = 0.70 \, V_e$$

$$V_0 = \text{outer lock volume, cubic feet} = 0.30 \, V_e$$

where,

D = inside diameter of shell, inches
L = overall length of chamber, inches.

Change 2 *Source:* U.S. Navy Diving Manual

D.—Underwater Accident Report

UNDERWATER ACCIDENT REPORT

Forward report to:

NATIONAL UNDERWATER ACCIDENT DATA CENTER

P.O. Box 68 — Kingston, R. I. 02881

VICTIM INFORMATION

Name of Victim: ....
Last   First   Middle

Address: ....

.... State ....

Victim's Sex ..... Age ..... Hgt. ...... Wgt. ......

Marital Status: M .... S .... D .... W ... UNK ...

Occupation ....

Employer ....

LOCATION OF ACCIDENT

Location of Accident ....
(use landmarks,
distance from ....
prominent terrain
features. Attach ....
Chart or Map
if available) .... State ....

CIRCLE LOCATION
(By Code Number)
1. Ocean, Bay, Sea   4. River
2. Minor Lake, Pond, Slough 5. Major Lake, Pond
3. Quarry, Pit, Open Mine   6. Swimming Pool
3A. Cave   7. Great Lakes

TIME AND PLACE OF ACCIDENT

Date and Time of Accident ....
Day Mo. Yr. Use 24-Hr. Clock

Date and Time of Death ....

Date and Time of Recovery ....

Death Occurred in Water? ....
(Yes or No)

Autopsy Performed: ....
(Yes or No)

Cause of Death: ....

Medical Examiner ....
Name

....

....
Address   Phone

CODE FOR NON-FATAL INCIDENT
Circle one only (A, B, C, or D) which best
describes seriousness of incident. Important:
Report all "incidents", however minor. Describe in detail on page 4. Include equipment factors.

A. Incapacitating injury rendering person
   unable to perform normal activities as
   walking or diving or to leave scene without assistance.
B. Nonincapacitating evident injury as loss
   of blood, abrasions, lump on head, etc.

C. Possible injury indicated by complaining
   of pain, blackout, limping, nausea, etc.
D. Incident with no apparent injury, (near
   miss, etc.)

DESCRIPTION OF DIVES AND ACTIVITIES

Description of all dives within previous 12 hours
including accident dive.

Depth	Time Down	Surface Interval
....	....	....
....	....	....
....	....	....
....	....	....
....	....	....

Type of Diving: (Explain if Necessary)

Scuba ...... Skin ...... Other ..... Unknown .....

Others in accident ....
(Yes or No)

Separate report filed ....
(Yes or No)

At time of incident,
Activities engaged in:

Recreational .....
Commercial .....
Under instruction .....
Instructing .....
Cave diving .....
Spear fishing .....
Photography .....
Night diving .....

At time of incident,
Buddy record:

Diving alone .....
Diving with buddy .....
Buddy distance
Diving with more
than one .....
Distance to next
nearest diver .....

Vessels involved ....
(Yes or No)

U.S. Coast Guard aid sought ....
(Yes or No)

(Give Details in "Description of Accident",
Name, Captain, Address, Phone, etc.)

WITNESSES

Name	Address	Phone	Function/Role
....	....	....	....
....	....	....	....
....	....	....	....
....	....	....	....

Reported by:

Name ....

Address ....

City .... Phone ....

Other Contacts:

Name ....

Address ....

City .... Phone ....

ENVIRONMENTAL CONDITIONS

Sea: Calm .... Moderate .... Rough ....   Weather: Clear .. Cloudy .. Fog .. Snow .. Rain ..

Current: Slight .. Moderate .. Strong .. Direction ...   Thunderstorm .. Tornado, Hurricane .. Other ..

Wave Height: ... Water Depth: ... Type Bottom: ...   Wind Force .. Direction ....

Water Temperature: (°F) ....   Air Temperature: (°F) .. ....

VISIBLE INJURIES

Illustrate all visible injuries (cuts, abrasions, fractures, etc.)

....

....

....

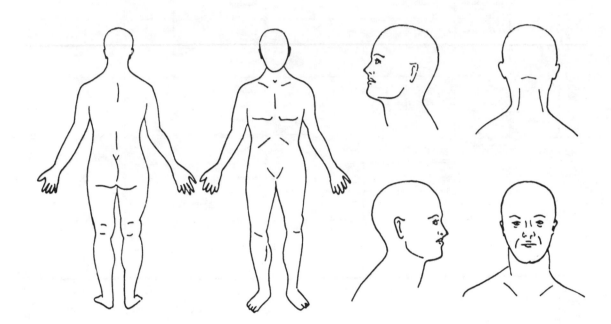

EXPERIENCE DATA

Swimming Experience: Years ......   *Courses and Agency*

Skindiving Experience: Years ......   (1) .... Certification Date ....

Scuba Experience: Years ......   (2) .... -DO- ......

    (3) .... -DO- ......

HUMAN FACTORS

Hours of sleep in past 24 hours ....

Time of last meal .... What and how much? ....

Time of last alcoholic drink .... What and how much? ....

Any known physical ailments, disability or impairment? ....

....

243

EQUIPMENT DATA

NOTE: *Equipment Brand, Type and Serial Number data need be included only if malfunction or failure was contributory to the incident.*

Equipment Data Date and Time of Inspection	Brand, Type	Present Before Diving (Yes or No)	Present at Time of Recovery (Yes or No)	Condition	Equipment	Brand, Type, Serial No.	Present Before Diving (Yes or No)	Present at Time of Recovery (Yes or No)	Condition
Diving Suit					Knife (Posit.)				
Hood					Ab Iron				
Boots or Socks					Flashlight				
Gloves or Mits					Depth Gauge				
Mask					Spear Gun				
Snorkel					Compass				
Fins					Regulator				
Weight Belt (lbs.)					Tank				
Buckle					Reserve				
Flotation Device					Watch				
Other Equipment									

Flotation Device: Used .... (Yes or No)

Tested after event? .... (Yes or No)

Regulator Tested? .... (Yes or No)

Results ....

Tank: Air Left .... MFG. .... Date .... (PSIG)

Last Hydro-Test Date ....

Last Visual Inspection Date ....

Internal Condition: Clean ....

    Slight Corrosion ....

    Extensive Corrosion ....

By: ....
        NAME   ADDRESS   PHONE

Special Comments on Equipment ....

Equipment Inspected by: ....
        NAME   ADDRESS   PHONE

Equipment: Released to/or Held by: ....
        NAME   ADDRESS   PHONE

DETAILED DESCRIPTION OF ACCIDENT

Describe in detail how the accident happened, including what the person was doing, any specific marine life or objects and the action or movement which led to the event. Include details of first aid or resuscitation efforts. Describe any "Decompression" and/or "Recompression-Treatment" in description of accident.

....
....
....
....
....
....
....
....
....
....
....
....
....
....
....
....
....
....
....
....
....
....

American National Standard Z-86.2 "Underwater Accident
Report Form" approved by ANSI, September 27, 1973.

E. Air Purity Requirements for Underwater Breathing*

1. The subsequent paragraphs briefly describe the minimum specification requirements for air to be used for sport-diving activities. This includes atmospheric air as well as air synthesized by blending oxygen and nitrogen in the proper proportions.

A detailed description of the several grades of air available will be found in CGA Pamphlet G-7.1 which can be ordered from the Compressed Gas Association, Inc., 500 Fifth Avenue, New York, New York 10036. This pamphlet covers specification requirements for all types and grades of air which are commercially available and for which an end usage has been established through combined industrial experience. It does not attempt to recommend or establish end-usage designations for specific types or grades of air, since such decisions must be made by the user. Consideration of this information has caused the Z-86 Committee of American National Standards Institute (ANSI) to designate Grade E as the minimum quality of air to be used for sport-diving activities.

A companion Pamphlet G-7, which can be ordered from the same source, discusses precautions that should be taken when air is used for breathing purposes.

2. Limiting characteristics in Grade E breathing air:

a. Oxygen percentage by volume—19 to 23 (balance predominantly nitrogen).

b. The water content of compressed air required may vary with the intended use from *saturated* to *very dry*. If a specific water limit is required, it should be specified as a limiting dewpoint or concentration in parts per million by volume. Dewpoint is normally expressed in temperature °F at 1 atmosphere absolute pressure. A conversion table equating °C and parts per million by volume is shown below:

Dew Point °F	Dew Point °C	PPM (V/V)	MG/LIT
—110	—78.9	0.58	0.00045
—105	—76.1	0.94	0.00070
—100	—73.3	1.5	0.0011
—95	—70.5	2.3	0.0017
—90	—67.8	3.2	0.0024
—85	—65.0	5.0	0.0037
—80	—62.2	7.1	0.0055
—75	—59.4	10.6	0.0079
—70	—56.7	16.1	0.012

*Promulgated by Z-86 Committee.

Dew Point °F	Dew Point °C	PPM (V/V)	MG/LIT
—65	—53.9	24.2	0.018
—60	—51.1	30.9	0.023
—55	—48.3	43.0	0.032
—50	—45.6	60.5	0.045
—45	—42.8	87.3	0.065
—40	—40.0	121	0.09
—35	—37.2	161	0.12
—30	—34.4	229	0.17
—25	—31.6	382	0.21
—20	—28.9	403	0.30
—15	—26.1	538	0.40
—10	—23.3	685	0.51
—5	—20.5	900	0.67
—0	—17.8	1,180	0.88

Moisture Conversion Data (all referred to 70°F and 14.7 psig):
c. Condensed hydrocarbons—5 parts per million by volume.
d. Carbon monoxide—10 parts per million by volume.
e. Carbon dioxide—500 parts per million by volume.
f. Odor is difficult to measure. Breathing air should be free of any pronounced odor.

3. There are several adequate analytical techniques used to determine the content of each constituent of air. These procedures are described in CGA Pamphlet G-7.1 referred to earlier.

A relatively inexpensive way to check the carbon monoxide and carbon dioxide content is with an apparatus employing a comparison tube filled with a color reactive tube. (Two manufacturers of this type of equipment are the Mine Safety Appliances Co. of Pittsburgh, Pa. and Unico Environmental Instruments, Inc. of Fall River, Mass. Undoubtedly there are other manufacturers of whom we are not aware.)

F. American National Standard Minimum Course Content for Safe Scuba Diving Instruction*

1. SCOPE AND PURPOSE

This standard provides minimum course content requirements for safe scuba (self-contained underwater breathing apparatus) instructions in sport diving. The requirements set forth herein should, under no conditions, be considered as standards for optimum training in the use of scuba. Instructional programs which extend beyond these requirements should, in fact, be encouraged.

The requirements of this standard are meant to be comprehensive but general in nature. That is, the standard presents all the subject areas essential for minimum scuba training in sport diving, but it does not give a detailed listing of the skills and information encompassed by each area. For example, these minimum specifications require that a basic skin and scuba course should cover the physical description, operating principles, use, and maintenance of at least fifteen equipment items. These items are simply listed in the standard; it is assumed that detailed course outlines which meet this standard would include specific techniques for the use and maintenance of each item.

Although the information categories outlined herein are given in what may appear to be a logical sequence, the outline should not be reviewed as a lesson plan. That is, the order in which the information is presented in this standard, while important, should not necessarily define the sequence of a class lesson plan. Similarly, the requirements presented in this document do not indicate the emphasis which should be placed upon a particular subject area, or the manner in which these subjects

*This standard is one of a series of American National Standards on underwater safety. American National Standards Committee Z-86 was initiated on July 13, 1961, under the secretariat of the Compressed Gas Association. On March 25, 1968, the Council for National Cooperation in Aquatics became secretariat of the Z-86 project.

The Z-86.3 Subcommittee on Safe Diving Instruction consists of representatives from each of the major organizations involved in sport diver instruction on a national basis, as well as other individuals with personal expertise in the field. Representatives of localized instructor groups with notable reputations and interest are also consulted. Work sessions were held at regularly scheduled meetings of the Z-86 Standards Committee, at special meetings of the subcommittee, and in connection with a variety of national conventions and conferences which brought together a large number of persons concerned with sport diver instruction. The chairman of the subcommittee also corresponded and met individually with those in a position to contribute to the standard. Late in September of 1971, a major draft review and work session was held with the top management of the four major national instructor organizations. Specific questions raised at that meeting were resolved on an individual basis during the next few months. Early in 1972 the standard was submitted to the Standard Institute for approval. It was approved as an American National Standard on August 31, 1972.

are to be taught. Course outlines, lesson plans, and other training aids prepared by nationally recognized organizations responsible for sport diver training should be used as guidelines for the sequencing and emphasis of course content requirements presented in this standard. Decisions as to sequencing and emphasis should be left to the discretion of the certified instructor and should be made within the context of environmental factors, student characteristics, and other relevant considerations.

For the purposes of this standard, basic scuba (open-circuit air) instruction is defined as that traditionally required for certification by a nationally recognized training organization. This certification, in turn, generally entitles a card holder to procure air, equipment, and other services at diving shops throughout the country. It is assumed that such individuals have received training in the fundamentals of the sport adequate to permit them to engage safely in open-water diving with experienced companions.

2. ELIGIBILITY FOR CERTIFICATION

2.1 Prerequisites. In order to be certified as a Basic Scuba Diver, an individual shall meet the following minimum prerequisites:

2.1.1 Age. The individual shall be at least 15 years of age; there is no upper age limit.

2.1.2 Physical Condition and Watermanship. The individual shall be able to swim 200 yards continuously without fins in less than 6 minutes, and shall be able to stay afloat or tread water for 10 minutes without accessories.

2.2 Recommendations. In addition to the prerequisites for a basic scuba diving course given in *2.1,* it is also recommended that applicants for training have successfully completed a junior or senior lifesaving course, or otherwise demonstrated the ability and discipline to complete a formal aquatic course involving both classroom and water activities.

It is also strongly recommended that the candidate for training be certified as medically fit for diving by a licensed physician who has been appraised of the physical and medical stresses associated with this sport.

3. MINIMUM COURSE CONTENT

3.1 Prerequisite and Introductory Information. To the greatest extent possible the following information should be made available to students prior to the first class meeting, and then reiterated at that time:

    I. Course prerequisites (see *2.1*)
    II. Scope of course
       A. Content
       B. Limitations of eventual qualification
    III. Equipment requirements
    IV. Safety regulations and other course procedures

3.2 Equipment. Students to be certified should demonstrate a basic understanding of the physical description, operating principles, maintenance, and competent use of the items listed in *3.2.* The subcategories of information which should be taught about the face mask are presented as an example of recommended course detail in covering physical description, maintenance, and competent use of each equipment item.

   I. Face mask
     A. Physical description
       1. Lens
       2. Skirt
       3. Band
       4. Strap
       5. Anchor
       6. Equalizer
       7. Purge
       8. Shape
       9. Contour
     B. Maintenance
       1. Inspection
       2. Cleaning
       3. Storage
     C. Use
       1. Donning
       2. Sealing
       3. Pressure equalization
       4. Clearing
       5. Defogging
  II. Fins
 III. Snorkel
 IV. Inflatable flotation vests
  V. Exposure suits
 VI. Weights and belt
VII. Float and flag
VIII. Knife
 IX. Scuba
     A. Tanks
     B. Valves
       1. Spring-loaded reserve
       2. Other
     C. Demand regulators
     D. Submersible pressure gage
     E. Backpacks and quick-release harness
  X. Other accessory items. Students to be certified should demonstrate general familiarity with:
     A. Compass

B. Depth gauge
C. Spear gun
D. Decompression meter

3.3 Physics of Diving. Students to be certified should demonstrate a basic understanding of the physical principles of matter and their application to diving activities and hazards.
- I. Acoustics
- II. Vision
- III. Buoyancy
- IV. Gas laws—air consumption
- V. Heat loss

3.4 Medical Problems Related to Diving. Students to be certified should demonstrate a basic understanding of the cause, symptoms, first aid and treatment, and prevention of the medical problems listed in *3.4.* Discussion of cause, symptoms, first aid and treatment, and prevention should cover those issues described in nationally recognized textbooks.

- I. Direct effects of pressure (mechanical)
  - A. Descent
    1. Ears
    2. Sinuses
    3. Mask
    4. Lungs
    5. Suit
    6. Teeth
    7. Stomach and intestines
  - B. Ascent
    1. Gas expansion (ears, sinuses, lungs, stomach and intestines)
    2. Lung overexpansion (air embolism and related accidents, including mediastinal emphysema, pneumothorax, and subcutaneous emphysema)
- II. Indirect effects of pressure (physiological)
  - A. Decompression sickness
  - B. Nitrogen narcosis
  - C. Carbon dioxide toxicity
    1. Breath-holding
    2. Scuba diving
  - D. Oxygen toxicity
  - E. Anoxia—breath-holding
  - F. Carbon monoxide toxicity

- III. Other hazards
  - A. Fatigue and exhaustion
  - B. Exposure

C. Drowning
D. Cramps
E. Injuries due to marine life
1. Bites
2. Poisonous seafoods, stings, and punctures
3. Venom
4. Mechanical injuries (abrasions, etc.)
F. Voluntary hyperventilation and shallow-water blackout
G. Involuntary hyperventilation

3.5 Scuba Water Skills. Students to be certified should demonstrate the ability to competently perform the following skills:
I. Entry
II. Descent and ascent, including pressure equalization
III. Underwater swimming
IV. Mask-clearing
V. Mouthpiece-clearing—snorkel and regulator
VI. Buddy system, including buddy breathing
VII. Underwater and surface vest and buoyancy control
VIII. Underwater problem-solving
IX. Full-gear surface-snorkel swimming
X. Weight-belt ditching
XI. Gear removal and replacement in water
XII. Emergency ascent

3.6 Use of Diving Tables. Students to be certified should demonstrate the ability to determine no-decompression limits and general familiarity with tables used to solve problems regarding:

I. Decompression
II. Repetitive dives

3.7 Diving Environment. Students to be certified should demonstrate knowledge of local and general conditions and their best possible effect on the diver with regard to the following:
I. Water
A. Temperature
B. Clarity
C. Movements (surface action, currents, tides, etc.)
D. Density
II. Topography
A. Bottoms
B. Shorelines
III. Marine and Aquatic Life

A. Animal

B. Plant

3.8 General Information and Procedures. Students to be certified should demonstrate a working knowledge of the following:

    I. Dive planning
   II. Use of equipment accessories
  III. Communications, both underwater and on the surface
  IV. Surface survival techniques
   V. Skin and scuba rescue techniques
  VI. Diving-related first aid
 VII. Safe shore and boat diving procedures

3.9 Open-Water Training. Students to be certified must demonstrate the ability to comfortably adapt to the diving environment in scuba gear. Skills to be demonstrated should include items I through IX of 3.5, except buddy breathing.

GLOSSARY

GLOSSARY OF SKIN AND SCUBA DIVING TERMS

ABSOLUTE PRESSURE—total pressure from all sources such as atmosphere and water. Usually referred to in absolute atmospheres (ATA).

ABSORBENT—a substance capable of taking something into itself.

ABYSSAL DEPTH—any vast depth. Prior to the invention of the bathysphere and other modern depth-probers, this designation was given to most depths over 300 fathoms.

ADRIFT—loose from mooring or not held fast.

AIR EMBOLISM—obstruction of blood vessels by gas bubbles. In diving, the term is generally applied to obstruction of a vessel or vessels supplying the brain.

ALVEOLAR EXCHANGE—transportation of oxygen to the blood and removal of carbon dioxide in the alveoli of the lungs.

AMBIENT PRESSURE—surrounding pressure. The total air or water pressure surrounding a diver. Below the surface, it is the total of the pressure exerted by the water itself *plus* the atmosphere pressure acting on the water. Also known as *absolute pressure*.

APPARATUS—an assembly of materials or parts designed to perform a specific operation. For example, open-circuit scuba.

ARTIFICIAL RESPIRATION—any means by which an alternating increase and decrease in chest volume is created, while maintaining an open airway in mouth and nose passages. Mouth-to-mouth or mouth-to-nose resuscitation is now accepted as the best method.

BACKWASH—often called *undertow* or *runout*. Water piled on shore by breaking waves sets up an outward current.

BAR—an offshore bank or shoal forming a ridge above the bottom.

BAROTRAUMA—injury due to effects of pressure.

BENDS—*see* Decompression Sickness.

BLUFF BANK—a bank, usually located on the convex side of a river's curve, which is subject to vertical plunges due to underwater erosion. Hazardous to divers and surface craft.

BORE—a single high wave moving upstream at the mouth of a river. Caused by incoming tide opposing river current. Knowing tide tables will prevent divers from being caught by this phenomenon. Also called *eagre*.

BOYLE'S LAW—the pressure of a given quantity of gas whose temperature remains unchanged varies inversely as its volume.

BREAKERS—waves broken by shore, ledge or bar.

BREAKWATER—a structure built to break the force of waves.

BREATHING AIR—commercially prepared or machine-compressed air which is free of contaminants that would be injurious to a diver operating under pressure.

BREATHING DEVICE—an apparatus that enables divers to breathe underwater.

BUDDY BREATHING—the sharing of the same tank by two or more divers. An emergency technique used when one person's air supply is exhausted.

BUG—short for "lobster."

BUOYANCY—(1) the upward force exerted upon an immersed or floating body by a fluid; (2) neutral, positive and negative. *Neutral* allows the diver to remain at a depth without effort. *Positive* will cause the diver to rise toward the surface and requires effort to remain at depth. *Negative* results in the diver's sinking toward the bottom.

BUOYANCY CONTROL DEVICE; "BCD"—an essential basic item of sport-diving equipment. An inflatable bladder, usually worn like a vest, to provide buoyancy on or below the surface.

CALM—a wind of less than 1 knot, or about 1 mile per hour.

CHANNEL—the deeper part of a river, harbor or strait.

COASTAL CURRENTS—movements of water that generally parallel the shoreline. Such currents may be caused by tide or wind.

COMPRESSED-AIR DEMAND-TYPE UNITS—a breathing device using compressed air that is delivered to the diver through a regulator, as he demands it by inhalation.

CREST—maximum height of a wave.

CURRENT—a horizontal movement of water. Currents can be classified as tidal and nontidal. Tidal currents are caused by forces of the sun and moon and are manifested in the general rise and fall occurring at regular intervals and accompanied by movement in bodies of water. Nontidal currents include the permanent currents in the general circulatory systems of the sea as well as temporary currents arising from weather conditions.

CYCLODIAL WAVES—inshore waves that are short and choppy and forceful when produced by strong winds.

CYLINDER—in diving terminology, a compressed breathing gas container. (*See* Tank.)

DALTON'S LAW—the partial pressure of a given quantity of gas is the pressure it would exert if it alone occupied the same volume. Also, the total pressure of a mixture of gases is the sum of the partial pressures of the components of the mixture.

DARK WATER—water visibility reduced to a minimum by material in suspension or by lack of natural light.

DEBRIS—results of destruction or discard, wreckage, junk.

DECOMPRESSION—to release from pressure or compression. In diving, the term is often applied to the process of following a specific decompression table or procedure during ascent.

DECOMPRESSION SICKNESS—illness or injury resulting from formation of gas bubbles in the blood or tissues during or following ascent or decompression. In this case, the bubbles arise from gas that was dissolved in blood or tissues under increased pressure.

DENSITY—the weight (mass) of anything per unit of volume.

DIAPHRAGM—a dividing membrane or thin partition. The thin muscle separating the chest cavity from the abdominal cavity. The rubber (or other material) separating the demand chamber in a regulator from the surrounding water.

DISLOCATION WAVES—inaccurately called "tidal waves." Caused by underwater landslide, earthquake or volcanic eruption. Also called *seismic waves.*

EAGRE—*see* Bore.

EBB CURRENT—(1) the movement of tidal current away from shore or down a tidal stream; (2) a tide that is flowing out or causing a lower water level.

EDDY—a circular movement of water, in a comparatively limited area, formed on the side of a main current. May be created at a point where the mainstream passes a projection or meets an opposite current.

EEL GRASS—long, thin, green strands growing along the coast in rocky areas.

EPICENTER—the term used in oceanography, wave mechanics and other appropriate fields to denote the focal point of great waves.

ESTUARY—where tide meets river current. A narrow arm of the sea meeting the mouth of a river.

EXHALE—to breathe out.

EXPIRATION—the act of breathing out or emitting air from the lungs.

FAHRENHEIT—a thermometric temperature scale at which, under standard and atmospheric pressure, water boils at 212° above the zero of the scale and freezes at 32°.

FETCH—"length of fetch" is the extent of water over which a wind blows and develops waves. The greater the length of fetch, the greater the possibility of large waves developing.

FINS—any device attached to the feet to increase area.

FLOOD TIDE—the incoming tide at its greatest height.

FLOTATION GEAR—any device employed to support the diver or to provide additional emergency buoyancy.

FLOTSAM—wreckage of a ship or its cargo found floating on the sea.

FUNGUS—a group of simple plants that contain no chlorophyll and must therefore feed on living or dead plants or animals. The parasitic fungi are dangerous to man.

GAUGE PRESSURE—indicates the difference between absolute pressure and a specific pressure being measured. The zero reading on the average gauge indicates atmospheric pressure.

GROUND SWELL—large, usually smooth-swelling waves.

GUST—a sudden brief outburst of wind.

HEMORRHAGE—any discharge of blood from blood vessels.

HENRY'S LAW—at a constant temperature, the amount of a gas which dissolves in a liquid, with which it is in contact, is proportional to the partial pressure of that gas.

HIGH WATER—the maximum height reached by a rising tide. The height may be due to periodic tidal forces alone or be augmented by weather conditions.

HURRICANE—originates over water (as do typhoons) and consists of wind rotating counterclockwise at a tremendous velocity from 75 to 100 mph. Develops in a low-pressure center and is usually accompanied by abnormally high tides. May often travel 60 mph. Diameter may range between 150 and 300 miles. Such a storm will ruin safe diving in areas covered for many days, as well as change shoreline and bottom contours.

HYPOTHERMIA—subnormal chilling of the body.

INHALATION—the process of permitting air to enter the lungs.

INLET—a narrow strip of water running inland or between two islands.

INSPIRATION—the act of breathing in.

JETTY—a structure, as a pier, extended into a sea, lake or river to influence the current or tide in order to protect a harbor.

KELP—various large brown seaweeds.

KNOT—velocity unit of 1 nautical mile (6080.20 ft) per hour. Equivalent to 1.689 ft per sec. To convert ft per sec into knots, multiply by 0.592.

LAND BREEZE—a breeze from the direction of the land.

LANDWARD—in the direction of or being toward the land.

LEE—a sheltered place or side; that side of a ship that is farthest from the point from which the wind blows.

LEEWARD—pertaining to, or in direction of, the lee side. Opposed to *windward*.

LEEWARD TIDE—a tide running in the same direction in which the wind blows.

LEEWAY—drifting to the leeward caused by wind or tide.

LIGHT BREEZE—a wind of 4 to 6 knots.

LIMITING ORIFICE—a hole or opening, usually of calculated size, through which the passage of a liquid or gas may be restricted within specified limits, as determined by pressure drop across the opening to control the rate of flow.

LONGSHORE CURRENTS—movement of water close to and parallel to the shoreline.

LOW WATER—the minimum level reached by a falling tide. The height may be solely the result of periodic tidal forces or further affected by weather conditions.

MARTINI'S LAW—a humorous "gas law" invented to help explain *nitrogen narcosis*. The "law" states that the mental effect of each 50 ft of descent, breathing air, is approximately equivalent to that of one (American-style) dry martini.

MASK—a skirted glass window constructed to provide air space between eyes and water and to permit both eyes to see in the same plane. The regular mask covers eyes and nose only.

MODERATE BREEZE—a wind of 11 to 16 knots (13 to 18 mph).

MODERATE GALE—a wind of 28 to 33 knots (32 to 38 mph).

NARCOSIS—a reversible condition characterized by stupor or insensibility. In diving, narcosis generally refers to a state of altered mental function, ranging from mild impairment of judgment or euphoria (false sense of well-being) to complete loss of consciousness.

NAUSEA—any sickness of the stomach creating a desire to vomit.

NAUTICAL MILE—also known as a "geographical mile." A unit of distance designed to equal approximately 1 minute of arc of latitude; 6080.20 ft. It is approximately 1.15 times as long as the statute mile of 5280 ft.

NEAP TIDE—a "nipped tide" or "scanty" tide which occurs near the first and third quarters of the moon; it is low because of the sun and moon pulling at right angles to each other.

NONTIDAL CURRENT—current that is due to causes other than tidal forces. Classed as nontidals are the Gulf Stream, the Japan current, Labrador, and equatorial currents which are part of general ocean circulation. Also classed in this category are river discharges and temporary currents set up by winds.

NURSING—*see* Buddy Breathing.

PARTIAL PRESSURE—the pressure exerted by a (specified) component in a mixture of gases; the concentration of oxygen in air is 20.94 percent. If the ambient pressure is 1.0 atmosphere absolute, the partial pressure of oxygen in dry air is 0.2094 atm.

PHYSICS OF DIVING—the application of physical laws and principles to man's activities underwater.

PHYSIOLOGY OF DIVING—the organic process and phenomena dealing with life and functions of organs of human beings while in water environment.

QUICKSAND—sand that is partly held in suspension by water. Varying in depth, it easily yields to pressure of person or object. Resembles ordinary sand or mud and occurs on flat shores and along rivers having shifting currents.

RECOMPRESSION—returning a diver to increased pressure for treatment of decompression sickness (e.g.) or air embolism (e.g.). This is properly accomplished in a recompression chamber in accordance with specific rules and tables.

REEF—a ridge or chain of rocks, sand or coral occurring in or causing shallow areas.

REGULATOR—an automatic device for maintaining or adjusting the flow of air equal to the ambient pressure of the water.

RESIDUAL VOLUME—that volume of air which remains in the lungs after the most forceful exhalation.

RESPIRATORY MINUTE VOLUME—the amount of air inhaled and exhaled per minute to maintain proper body function. This is variable, depending on exertion and the individual.

RIP CURRENT—a strong current of limited area flowing outward from the shore. It may be visible as a band of agitated water with the regular wave pattern altered. This type of current is caused by the escape of water piled between shore and bar or reef by wave action. The rush of escaping water is accentuated by its flow through a gap in the bar or reef. Such currents are dangerous to the uninitiated and are the cause of many drownings at ocean beaches. However, when located by divers (skin and scuba) they are often used to facilitate entry to areas beyond the bar or reef.

RUBBER (OR DIVING) SUIT—partial or complete covering for the diver, primarily to insulate and preserve body heat. Classified as *wet* and *dry*.

RUPTURE—breaking apart, bursting, as an eardrum under equalized pressure.

SAFETY HITCH OR BUCKLE—any fastening device that may be operated to release with one hand, easily and quickly—a must.

SANDBAR—a body of sand built up by action of waves or currents.

SCUBA—*self-c*ontained *u*nderwater *b*reathing *a*pparatus. Any free unit containing necessary elements to support life under water.

SEA ANCHOR—a drag thrown overside to keep a craft headed into the wind.

SEA BOTTOM SLIDE—a landslide under water usually causing a tsunami, or dislocation wave.

SEA BREEZE—a breeze blowing over land from the sea.

SEAWARD—away from land toward the open sea.

SEAWAY—one of the sea traffic lanes or routes; a vessel's headway; an area where a moderate or rough sea is running.

SEAWORTHY—fit for aquatic hazards; able to withstand usual sea conditions.

SHOAL—a place where a sea, river, etc. is shallow because of bank or bar.

SINUS SQUEEZE—damage of tissue lining of air sinuses in the head due to failure of pressure in sinus to equalize with ambient pressure.

SKIN DIVING—diving without the use of scuba.

SLACK WATER—the state of a tidal current when its velocity is near zero, especially the moment when a reversing current changes direction and its velocity is zero. Occurs at high and low tide.

SNORKEL—a J-shaped tube, the short end of which is held in the mouth, the long end protruding above the surface, permitting breathing without raising the nose out of the water when swimming face down on the surface.

SPEAR GUN—any device that propels a spear from a gunlike frame. Usually rubber, spring or gas powered.

SPECIFIC GRAVITY—the ratio of the density of a substance to water.

SPINDRIFT—sea spray sometimes called spoondrift; the spray and water driven from the tops of waves by wind.

SPORT DIVER—one who dives with or without scuba for noncommercial purposes or love of the medium.

SPRING TIDES—the highest and the lowest course of tides occurring every new and full moon.

SPUME—frothy matter, foam or scum usually collected at water line.

SQUALL—a gust of wind generally accompanied by rain or snow with nimbus clouds. Intense and of short duration.

STANDARD ATMOSPHERIC PRESSURE—the unit of pressure used in underwater activities and called 1 atmosphere.

STORM—winds of 56 to 65 knots (64 to 75 mph). Between gale and hurricane.

STRONG BREEZE—a wind of 22 to 27 knots (25 to 31 mph).

STRONG GALE—a wind of 41 to 47 knots (47 to 54 mph).

SUIT—*see* Rubber Suit.

SURF—waves breaking upon a shore.

SURGE—a great rolling swell of water, a violent rising and falling.

SWELL—a large and more-or-less smooth wave.

SYMPTOMS—perceptible changes in body state or function that may be indicative of disease or injury. Strictly, the word applies to changes perceptible to the individual himself, but it is often used to include *signs,* which are abnormalities that can be detected by an observer or examiner. Making this distinction is often useful.

TANK—hollow metal vessel, or cylinder, used to contain compressed air or other gas. An integral part of self-contained underwater breathing apparatus. Also called *bottle*.

THERMOCLINE—a temperature gradient. Especially one making a sharp change. A layer of water in a thermally stratified body of water separating an upper warmer, lighter, oxygen-rich zone from a lower colder, heavier, oxygen-poor zone.

TIDAL VOLUME—the volume of air passing in and out of the lungs with each natural inspiration and expiration.

TIDE—the periodic rise and fall of water level due to the gravitational attraction of the moon and sun acting on the earth's rotating surface.

TIDE RIP—wave and eddies in shoal water caused by tide running off rough bottom.

TIDE WAVE—a long-period wave that has its origin in the tide-producing force and which displays itself in the rising and falling of the tide.

TOXIC—poisonous.

TROUGH—the hollow or low area between crests of waves.

UNDERTOW—current beneath surface that sweeps seaward or along a beach when waves are breaking on shore. (*See* Backwash.)

VALVE—a device that starts, stops or regulates the flow of gas or air in diving equipment.

VITAL CAPACITY—the maximum volume of air that can be expired after a maximum inspiration.

VOLUME—space measured by cubic units.

WAVE HEIGHT—the vertical distance from preceding trough to crest.

WHOLE GALE—wind of 48 to 55 knots (55 to 63 mph).

WINDWARD—the point or side from which the wind blows; toward the wind; in the direction from which the wind blows. Opposed to *leeward*.

YOKE—a device for attaching regulators to tanks so as to make a leakproof seal. No more than finger pressure should be used to attach.

INDEX

U.S. Navy, 84, 149, 157
U.S. Navy Diving Manual, 85–88, 90, 153
U.S. Navy Sealab, 91–92
U.S. Navy Standard Decompression Tables,
167–171

V
Valsalva maneuver, 32
Valve, tank, 52, 53
Vasoconstrictors, 33
Venomous fish, 210
Vertical drop dive, 27, 28
Vertigo, alternobaric, 33
Vest, skin-diving, 18
Visibility, underwater, 121–123
Voluntary hyperventilation, 38
Vomiting, 206

W
Watch, 144

Water, temperature of, 114–116
Waves, 116, 117–118
Weather, 113–114
Weeverfish, 210
Weight belt, 38–39, 70, 97–100, 102
Wet suit, 18, 19, 36, 59–61, 67, 205
Whale shark, 127, 139
Whales, 141
Whistle blast signal, 153
White tip shark, 128, 138–139
Women, special problems of, 95–96
Worm, tube, 134
Wound care, 200–202, 210
Wreck diving, 215

X
Xenon, 95

ACKNOWLEDGMENTS

The editors gratefully acknowledge the cooperation of those who provided photographs for this book.

For those appearing on 126-130, David Doubilet, renowned underwater photographer, took the photographs of the lobster, octopus, scorpion fish, barracuda, moray eel, sting ray and fire coral. Jeff Rotman took the photographs of the sea anemone, sea urchin, spider crab, eel grass and diver in kelp. Richard Ellis, recognized as the country's foremost painter of marine history, has graciously permitted the use of a number of his paintings of sharks.

Dick Geyer took the photographs of scuba diving equipment appearing throughout the book.

Tom Berkey provided the photographs for chapter openings.

A special acknowledgement goes to photographer Dale McDonald, who, with the capable assistance of model Janet Thompson, provided most of the new illustrations for this sixth edition.